Fishing
Alaska

Evan and Margaret Swensen

FALCON®

GUILFORD, CONNECTICUT
AN IMPRINT OF THE GLOBE PEQUOT PRESS

A FALCON GUIDE®

All text, maps and photos by the author except as noted.

Cover photo: Barry and Cathy Beck.

Library of Congress Cataloging-in-Publication Data

Swensen, Evan, 1935-
    [Angler's guide to Alaska]
    Fishing Alaska : formerly The angler's guide to Alaska / Evan and Margaret Swensen.
        p. cm.
    Originally published : 1992.
    ISBN 1-56044-523-8 (pbk.)
    1. Fishing—Alaska—Guidebooks. 2. Fishes—Alaska. 3. Alaska—Guidebooks. I. Swensen, Margaret, 1936- . II. Title.
SH467.S94 1997
799.1'2'09798—dc20   96-46144
                                                                       CIP

Manufactured in the United States of America
First edition/Seventh printing

Outdoor recreational activities are by their very nature potentially hazardous. All participants in such activities must assume the responsibility for their own actions and safety. The information contained in this guidebook cannot replace sound judgment and good decision–making skills, which help reduce risk exposure, nor does the scope of this book allow for disclosure of all the potential hazards and risks involved in such activities.

Learn as much as possible about the outdoor recreational activities you participate in, prepare for the unexpected, and be cautious. The reward will be a safer and more enjoyable experience.

♻ Text pages printed on recycled paper.

ACKNOWLEDGMENTS

This book began when I was a young boy. After my dad's death, my mom told tales in her kitchen of Dad's fishing, hunting, and other outdoor adventures, which inspired me to follow him. She allowed me to use the kitchen counter to box up nightcrawlers and make bread-dough bait. She praised me when I brought home a trout for dinner and cooked the fish and even helped eat it.

Thirty-seven years ago my then new bride, Margaret, and I spent our honeymoon fishing backcountry water in Yellowstone Park. She continued to support my fishing pursuits since. Mothering nine children has kept her off the stream on occasion, but she always cooked the catch and listened to fish tales brought home by excited youngsters. Margaret also did the research, made the maps, edited and proofed the text, and kept this book in balance.

The list of contributors to *Fishing Alaska* would fill many pages, as each person who touched my outdoor life, from store clerk to guide, has influenced what these pages contain. The main credit goes to these two women. I thank God that my hobby and vocation allowed me to fish Alaska for the last thirty-seven years. But more than all other people and places, I'm most grateful for these two women who really made this book possible.

CONTENTS

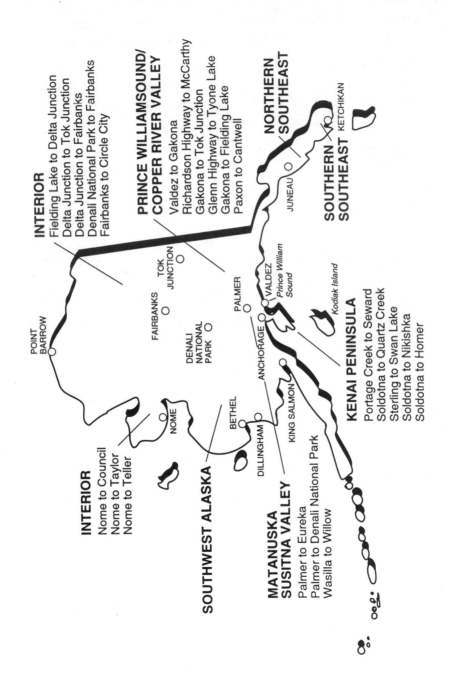

INTERIOR
Fielding Lake to Delta Junction
Delta Junction to Tok Junction
Delta Junction to Fairbanks
Denali National Park to Fairbanks
Fairbanks to Circle City

**PRINCE WILLIAMSOUND/
COPPER RIVER VALLEY**
Valdez to Gakona
Richardson Highway to McCarthy
Gakona to Tok Junction
Glenn Highway to Tyone Lake
Gakona to Fielding Lake
Paxon to Cantwell

**NORTHERN
SOUTHEAST**

**SOUTHERN
SOUTHEAST**
KETCHIKAN

JUNEAU

POINT
BARROW

FAIRBANKS

TOK
JUNCTION

VALDEZ
*Prince William
Sound*

PALMER

DENALI
NATIONAL
PARK

ANCHORAGE

Kodiak Island

NOME

BETHEL

DILLINGHAM

KING SALMON

INTERIOR
Nome to Council
Nome to Taylor
Nome to Teller

SOUTHWEST ALASKA

**MATANUSKA
SUSITNA VALLEY**
Palmer to Eureka
Palmer to Denali National Park
Wasilla to Willow

KENAI PENINSULA
Portage Creek to Seward
Soldotna to Quartz Creek
Sterling to Swan Lake
Soldotna to Nikishka
Soldotna to Homer

MAP LEGEND

Primary Routes

Secondary Roads

Unpaved Roads

Canoe Trail

River, Creek

Lake

Glacier

Waterfall

Mountain Peak

Fishing Site

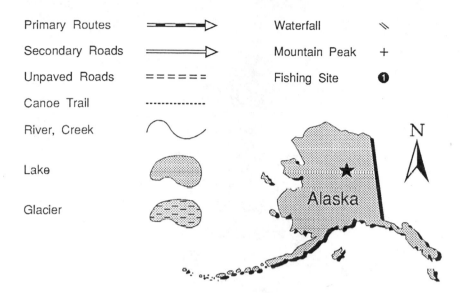

Anglers from around the world dream of fishing Alaska's pristine waters.

INTRODUCTION

Getting Ready for Alaska

Most people who eventually fish Alaska begin their trip by gathering information and putting it in their "Go to Alaska file." They obtain pamphlets from the State and brochures from lodges, guides, outfitters, and flying service companies. They write letters to friends, relatives, and business associates who live in the Great Land, and talk to anglers who've been here. They keep saving and continue planning, but soon discover the full Alaska experience also includes getting ready.

Fishing Alaska will inform and entertain and probably become part of your "Go to Alaska file." You may not get on an airplane or drive the Alaska Highway for many years, but we know *Fishing Alaska* will become part of your trip to the Last Frontier.

Fishing Alaska is not another book on how to catch fish, nor is it a complete treatment on every fishing hole in the state. The main focus is to help the first-time visitor who'll be traveling by car, camper, or motor home. Many of the best spots are not mentioned, leaving them for your discovery. Our favorite secret stream, for instance, has not been included.

Catching fish in Alaska is more a matter of timing than skill; more being in the right spot at the right time, then using the correct bait or appropriate technique. If Alaska is in your fishing future, *Fishing Alaska* will provide information you need to know so you can be on the stream when the fish are there.

"You should have been here last week!" has true meaning in Alaska. If you're ahead or behind the run, you won't connect with your trophy. One day can make a difference, and sometimes even one tide change means the difference between an empty creel and a full freezer.

We've witnessed inexperienced and uninformed anglers fishing in a known hot spot, throw the correct lure and use proper technique for several discouraging hours. Books, magazines, and other fishermen's testimony tell the tale of great catches in the angler's chosen water, but their hooks come up empty. They leave the water in frustration, depressed with their inability to duplicate what they know others have done. Then the tide changes, fish move in, smart anglers arrive, and for an hour the fishing matches Alaska's reputation. The tide peaks, fish move on, the hole cools, and the unfortunate, uninformed, upon hearing of great fishing, return, only to be further discouraged.

Fishing Alaska can make your Alaska fishing excursion a "You should have been here yesterday!" trip. Alaska's fishing is spectacular. There is no place on earth like it, but you must match your timing with the run. By following this book's fish availability charts and calendars and using just plain common sense and accepted fishing methods, you'll be the one telling the "You should have been here yesterday!" tales.

Not everyone who reads and studies this book will come to Alaska right away, but with each bit of information received and reviewed, you will enjoy

Some anglers take their dog along for good luck

a little more of the Alaska experience, even if only vicariously for the present. For some, this is their first Alaska file information. For others, it's the final filing before making reservations. For the majority, it is another part of their Alaska experience placed somewhere between first dreaming and actually coming. Trusting that *Fishing Alaska* will be a part of your Alaska lifetime adventure, we hope you're the one saying, "You should have been here yesterday!"

What's It Really Like Anyway

Sportfishing is Alaska's number one sport and outdoor recreation activity. More people participate in fishing than all other Alaska leisure activities combined. Alaskans spend their vacations, holidays, days off, and time before and after work in pursuit of fish. A large percentage of visitors to the Great Land spend their time with rod in hand, and millions yet to visit dream of fishing Alaska.

Alaska is a land of unlimited fishing opportunities, but it's almost impossible for someone to get their arms around the entire Alaska angling possibilities in one lifetime. For over three-and-a-half decades, we have fished the state, both for pleasure and as my vocation, and we have only approached the potential. So it is with *Fishing Alaska*. It's only a primer, not an attempt to cover all the options.

Most of Alaska is huge and remote, and when it comes to sportfishing, this

A nice start to a full stringer of Dolly Varden.

relates to expensive. However, fishing the Great Land need not be a budget-breaker. Roadside angling can be productive and enjoyable, with the only expense being the price of a few gallons of gasoline. Many of my most memorable times have been within casting distance of the highway. In Alaska, *when* is more important than *where*.

Different than most other states where fishermen are required to go to the fish, Alaska is unique: the fish come to the angler. Each season five different species of Pacific salmon migrate to their natal streams, bringing other varieties of fish with them. Following the salmon, these beggars are seeking an easy meal, mostly of salmon eggs. This phenomenon provides fish hatchery-like populations of fish at times.

The precise time of the run's return to a given watershed can't be predicted, but it will be within a few days of it's anticipated occurrence. The miracle of returning fish is almost exceeded by the marvel of how quickly the word spreads to waiting anglers. A whispered, "Reds are in the Russian," is heard seemingly simultaneously by thousands of waiting sportsmen. One day the stream is void of anglers and fish, the next morning the banks are lined with the hopeful. Every area along the road system in the state enjoys the same kind of angler's telegraph. Neighboring gas stations, restaurants, gift stores, and tackle shops know within an hour of when the first few fish are taken from any roadside water.

This is the most meaningful message of *Fishing Alaska*. If an angler is on the stream concurrent with the spawning run, it's almost impossible to not catch

It never rains on a fishing hole when the fishing is good, and Julie Kneen, holding a Dolly Varden, agrees.

fish, even if you use only basic fishing techniques. More important than all the how-to, where-to books and guides written, information obtained from local sources is the most reliable. The first time visitor, and those less knowledgeable about Alaska, will get more real angling assistance from those in the service industries than from a library of written material and a month of reading.

Filling station attendants, store clerks, and waitresses not only have the latest word on where the fish are, they're probably going fishing when their shift is over, and are willing to share their hot spot, if you ask. They will also readily give advice on what lure or bait to use and the correct method to fish the particular water. Coupled with the information obtained while eating lunch, filling the gas tank, purchasing a gift, or buying a new lure, anglers should spend the first few minutes on any given stream just watching. Almost invariably, a few people will be catching the most fish; sometimes one angler in the area will seem to be having all the luck. Observe what methods they're using and what bait or lure. Notice where they're fishing and how they cast and retrieve. If given the opportunity, talk to them and get pointers. Most Alaska anglers are willing to explain, and even help if you ask. The most productive advice we can give to assist first-time anglers, either to Alaska or a specific area, is to talk and observe, and then do the same thing those having success are doing.

Usually, following the above advice will require anglers to fish with crowds. During the height of the run, the most productive water will most likely be jam-packed with hopeful anglers. One way to avoid the congestion is to take advantage of the Northern Latitude's long hours of daylight. Fish from 8 p.m. to 7 a.m. Many of the day assemblage will be sleeping, and there may be only a handful of people fishing.

Another way to dodge the mob is to fish up or downriver. Some of Alaska's roadside streams have only a token number of their former resident fish. At least this is true near the highway, but any ambitious angler can find wilderness fishing by taking a short hike away from the road. A mile walk along the bank of most streams, or a hike over a hill to a lake, could lead to authentic wilderness angling.

Fishing Alaska is not a mystery, but it seems difficult to erase the misconceptions many people have about weather, cost, methods, means, and timing—mostly about weather. The most-asked question is, "What is Alaska really like?"

A couple of years ago, we were with an Alaska company as an exhibitor in a Sports and Travel Show in Houston, Texas. We had three booths side-by-side. On this fifty feet of wall space, we displayed thirty large, color photographs of Alaska's outdoors in summer. Two television sets continually played selections from our video library. An automatic slide projector projected a steady stream of images of summertime recreation. We'd been careful in choosing all of this material and did not include anything if it had even a hint of snow or ice. We were anxious to put our best summer foot forward.

During the course of the show, two school teachers approached the booth and greeted us with enthusiasm. They explained their classes had been studying Alaska the past several days and wondered if we had any interesting material they could take back to school to share with their students. Anxious to help, we explained each of the pictures hanging on the wall. We discussed the slide show and video presentations. We loaded them up with publications and filled their shopping bags with brochures and videos.

They were grateful, and we were thrilled to share with them and their students. Upon their departure, they thanked us graciously and prepared to leave. After taking a few steps into the aisle, one of them returned. In a quiet voice, almost a whisper, she asked, "Is it really cold, dark, and snowy there all the time? What's it really like anyway?"

Almost every call or letter our family receives contains a weather report inquiry. Is it really cold? Do you have snow? What's the temperature? People seem to refuse to believe the truth. Even in the face of hard evidence to the contrary, they persist in believing the misconceptions. It appears to be easier to re-tell the myths than accept the truth.

We've wondered if those two Texas school teachers don't represent part of the reason these false impressions continue. Unless we miss our guess, their students didn't get a true picture of Alaska and probably will grow up thinking Seward's Folly is nothing but icebergs and glaciers. Even with today's storehouse of information in print, on videos, and on television, a lot of people still think Alaska is synonymous with North Pole and Antarctica.

Don't worry about weather, it's the weather that provides the ingredients for the abundant fishing resources, and summer months are mild. Any angler can be successful in Alaska by following the advice in this guide, and particularly in this chapter. More importantly, don't judge the success of the trip on numbers and size of fish. If anglers have to catch fish to have a good time, they go for the wrong reasons.

An early morning walk on a deserted Kachemak Bay beach hunting colored rocks, and bringing home a trophy to show, is a real part of the Alaska fishing experience. Digging clams and pulling crab and shrimp pots is part. Taking pictures, keeping a campfire going, or watching a beaver tackle a twenty-four-inch-diameter cottonwood is part. Sometimes the most exciting thing to do is to do nothing. Taking time to just sit, relax, and enjoy the surroundings, breathe air so pure you can't see it, listen to the deafening silence of a still night, or feel the immense size of wilderness on a clear day with unlimited visibility, is part of the whole that makes the Alaska fishing experience.

The real reason to go fishing is found among the varied activities associated with the contrived excuses we used. Long after the thrill of landing a trophy is gone, the other things remain and are rehearsed in our minds and storied to others.

We're not speaking for ourselves. We go fishing in Alaska because it's our job. When others are enjoying their time afield and having fun, we're working.

THINK BEFORE YOU FISH

Fishing in Alaska is an exciting and enjoyable experience when anglers are properly prepared and follow necessary precautions. Failure to prepare and follow the rules of the road could mean a fishless trip, possible sickness, injury, and even death. Alaska is a wonderful place to fish, and the following information will help anglers safely enjoy Alaska and provide the basic information for a memory-building angling adventure.

Access

Access to Alaska is accomplished by using commercial airlines, riding the state ferry system, or driving the Alaska Highway. Once in the state, the highway system in Alaska differs from most other states. Southeast and southwest Alaska, the far north, and many other areas are not connected by roads. Many Alaska communities claim there are two places to drive if leaving town:

the end of the road, and the other end of the road.

Nearly all fishing spots mentioned in this guide are accessible by road. Although the numbers of highways may be limited, the list and variety of available fishing water isn't. On a single outing, an angler may wet a line in clear water tributaries, glacier-influenced streams, lakes, and even saltwater. The trip may involve fly-fishing, spin-fishing, trolling, surfcasting, jigging, and bobbing bait on the bottom.

It's helpful to know the road numbering system in Alaska.

Glenn Highway: mileposts begin in Anchorage.

Parks Highway: mileposts begin in Anchorage.

Richardson Highway: mileposts begin in Valdez.

Seward Highway: mileposts begin in Seward.

Sterling Highway: mileposts begin in Seward.

Edgerton Highway: mileposts begin at the Richardson Highway.

Animals

A large variety of wildlife may frequent fishing waters; some, annoying, others, dangerous. Most animals are friendly. Insects are the greatest nuisance: mosquitos, black flies, no-see-ums, black-socks, and white-socks. Alaska's insects do not transmit disease-causing agents, such as bacteria or viruses.

Mice, squirrels, martens, hoary marmots, beavers, and muskrats are friendly. Mammals, including bear, deer, goats, sheep, moose, and caribou are mostly friendly, but moose with young become very protective, and bears are unpredictable.

Three types of bears: black, brown, and polar, make Alaska special. Any angler may be lucky enough to see a bear; Alaska is bear country. Brown bears inhabit Alaska from the islands of Southeastern to the Arctic. Black bear inhabit most of Alaska's forests. Polar bear frequent the pack ice and tundra of extreme Northern and Western Alaska.

Most people who see a bear in the wild consider it the highlight of their trip. The presence of these majestic creatures is a reminder of how privileged we are to share the country's dwindling wilderness.

Bear Facts:

Polar Bear

Length: Eight to ten feet

Weight: Males 600 to 1,200 pounds, females 400 to 700 pounds.

Color: All white

Alaska population estimate: 4,000 to 6,000

Black Bear

Length: Five feet

Weight: Males 150 to 400 pounds, females 125 to 250 pounds

Color: Brown to black, white patch on front of chest

Alaska population estimate: more than 50,000

Brown Bear

Length: Seven to nine feet

Many anglers are concerned about bears. Taking precautions will greatly reduce the risk of a violent encounter.

Weight: Males 400 to 1,100 pounds, females 200 to 600 pounds
Color: Dark brown to blond
Alaska population estimate: 35,000 to 45,000

Bears rarely attack humans, but must be considered dangerous at all times. Fishing streams during salmon spawning season requires care. Make noise when in bear country and plenty of noise near creeks and waterfalls when fish are running. The State of Alaska Department of Fish and Game publishes a brochure, *The Bears and You*. It's available from their offices and other state agencies and visitor and information centers. First-time Alaska anglers, or those unfamiliar with bears, should read a copy before entering bear country.

Many anglers are concerned about bears and may even have an occasional bear encounter. Brown bears are an important part of the wilderness. Taking precautions will greatly reduce the risk of a violent encounter. The following tips can help prevent problems.

Minimize chances of trouble with bears. Odors attract bear. Before fishing in bear country, thoroughly wash packs, clothing, and other gear in an unscented detergent to be sure it is free of odors. Clean fishing tackle. Don't carry smelly foods like bacon or smoked fish, and leave scented soaps, lotions, deodorants, toothpaste, and other toiletries at home. The idea is to smell human, not delicious. Dogs may attract a bear. Leave them at home. Solo anglers are more likely to be attacked than members of a group. Where possible, fish with others for safety's sake.

Do things that prevent meeting bears in close quarters. Food attracts bear. Store all foods in sealed plastic bags or airtight containers. Take plenty of extra

Don't carry a gun unless you are fishing in areas of high brown bear concentrations, and then only if you are comfortable with firearms and trained in their use.

bags, including enough to double wrap all your garbage. Carry out all garbage that won't burn. Never bury it.

The best bear protection is to prevent a close encounter. Make lots of noise. Bears will usually avoid humans if alerted. Most attacks occur when people surprise bears at close range. Sows with cubs are particularly dangerous because they tend to see any intruder as a threat to their offspring.

Don't risk sneaking up on a bear. Talk, rattle pebbles in a can, or wear bells. Wind and running water muffle the noise. Entering thickets from upwind may let a bear smell danger and move away. Be especially careful and noisy along salmon streams, through willow thickets, berry patches, and areas with trails, prints, and droppings.

Watch for bear evidence. Droppings may look like a cow's, or like a pile of partially digested berries. Bear trails are common along streams, on ridgetops, and in berry patches. Watch for torn up patches of soil and vegetation. Bear dig up tundra hunting for rodents, roots, and bulbs. If you smell decomposing meat or discover an animal carcass covered with leaves and branches, leave immediately. You may have found a bear food cache, and a bear is probably nearby. Check around potential campsites carefully and, if bear sign is found, consider camping elsewhere.

Don't invite bears into camp. Keep food odors to a minimum. Cook and eat several hundred yards downwind from camp or, better yet, cook, eat, and then move on a mile or so to camp. Don't cook more than you can eat, and wash dishes immediately. Dump waste water far from camp. Store all food, soap, and any other smelly items well sealed and far from camp, high in a tree, if possible. Keep food and food odors off clothes. Never sleep in the same clothes you wore while cooking.

If you keep fish, clean it far from camp. Puncture the air bladder and throw the entrails far out into the water. Clean hands, clothing, and gear carefully before camping.

Know what to do if you encounter a bear. If you see a bear in the distance, alter the route to avoid it. Move out of its sight, downwind if possible. If the bear sees something curious, it may stand up and sway its head from side to side. It's trying to figure out what it's seeing. Help it! Speak loudly, hold arms up, and back slowly away. If the bear approaches, keep talking. Climb a tree, if possible. If the bear turns sideways, pops its teeth together, or makes a series of woofs, it's a warning. Retreat slowly. Never run; that could encourage the bear to give chase. Never imitate the sounds or postures of a bear, that may challenge it to attack.

If a bear charges, freeze, facing the bear. Most charges are bluffs. The bear will probably stop, turn, and run away. If it doesn't stop, drop to the ground and play dead. Lay on your stomach or knees-to-chest, with hands linked across the back of your neck. Leave your pack on. Keep silent and still. The bear may lose interest and leave.

It's legal to carry firearms in most National Parks in Alaska, except Sitka Natural History Park, Glacier Bay and Katmai National Parks, or in that part of Denali National Park formerly known as Mt. McKinley National Park. Don't carry a gun unless you're fishing in areas of high brown bear concentrations, and then only if you're comfortable with firearms and trained in their use. Without proper firearm training or practice, a firearm can be more dangerous than a bear. A suitable gun, properly used and kept handy, can be a little extra insurance. Rifles larger than 30.06 and 12-gauge shotguns loaded with rifled slugs are adequate. It's legal to shoot a bear in defense of life or property if reasonable efforts have been made to avoid the problem in the first place. The hide of a black bear or the hide and skull of a brown must be turned over to state officials immediately.

Birds and other animals

Golden eagles, hawks, grouse, and numerous varieties of songbirds nest in Alaska. Bald eagles are common throughout much of the panhandle and around Southcentral Alaska, especially near salmon spawning streams and tidal areas. Ptarmigan, the state bird, may be seen in alpine areas. Crows and ravens are common and may be seen and heard. A number of different waterfowl may be spotted near lake shores, sloughs, and ponds.

Now and then, fox and wolves may be attracted to campsites. Only under unusual circumstances do these canine creatures attack humans. They're shy, but if encountered and they appear tame or unafraid, they may be rabid. Don't attempt to handle them, they may bite. Rabies could be fatal; therefore, avoid exposure by avoiding sick animals.

Mosquito repellents containing diethyl toluamide (DEET) are most effective when used in roughly fifty percent concentrations of the active ingredient. Repellents for white-sox and no-see-ums are less effective. Breezes and low relative humidity deter insect activity, and should be considered when locating a campsite. A five-mile-per-hour breeze will ground most mosquitoes. Alaska has mosquitoes that winter as adults. They emerge from hibernation before snow has entirely disappeared. Insect population reaches its peak in June and declines thereafter. Mosquitoes are the most active at twilight and early morning.

Fires

Use extreme caution at all times with fire. Always thoroughly extinguish matches, cigarettes, cigars or pipe ashes before discarding. Permits for camp-fires aren't required in Alaska, except in Denali National Park and Katmai National Monument. As a rule, in areas where improved campsites exist, fires are restricted to established fire sites. Many of the soils in Alaska are rich in organic materials which may continue to burn unseen underground; therefore, extra care must be taken to extinguish campfires completely. Thorough soaking, stirring, and burying are best.

Use only dead and down wood for fires.

Keep fires small.

Don't hack into trees or stumps.

Disperse rocks from rock fire rings.

Use camp stoves in wilderness areas.

Be sure of the rules concerning campfires in each area you fish.

Fireworks are strictly prohibited in most areas of Alaska,
   particularly on public lands.

Help Others

Don't hesitate to stop and help others in need of emergency care. Alaska has a good samaritan statute, meaning state laws protect persons from liability for civil damages for acts related to rendering emergency care or treatment to injured persons.

Hygiene and Health

Wash dishes with soap and hot water away from streams or ponds. You shouldn't pour waste water from washing into a stream or directly onto the ground. It's best to pour waste water into a hole located away from water sources, so that it may disperse into the subsurface soil.

Defecate in intertidal zones away from streams or ponds or use a shallow hole on land at least 200 feet away from any water source. Burn toilet paper completely and carry out, or burn, all sanitary napkins or tampons. Wash and brush teeth on beaches away from tidal pools or streams. Use a good sun screen. Carry mosquito repellent and antidote for bug bites in a first aid kit.

Hypothermia

Even in temperatures above freezing, hypothermia is possible. Anglers exposed to wet, cold, and windy conditions can suffer hypothermia. Hypothermia is caused when body heat is lost faster than it's produced. Continued decline of internal temperature will lead to stupor, collapse, and possibly death. Hypothermia symptoms are: severe shivering, slurred speech, incoherence, clumsiness, lack of control of hands and feet, drowsiness, and exhaustion.

If you suspect or confront hypothermia, get dry and warm immediately. Remove all wet clothes and put on dry ones. Get in a warm sleeping bag and drink something hot.

Littering

Alaska's beauty can be greatly blemished by paper, cans, and other litter. Dispose of litter in roadside receptacles. Littering is punishable by a fine of not more than $1,000, imprisonment of up to ninety days, or both.

Planning

Planning is a practice that will make fishing in Alaska a pleasant, exciting, and fulfilling experience. Much of Alaska is untamed wilderness. A short drive from a city and just a few steps from the road can put anglers in real wilderness situations. Know your limitations and be prepared by carrying the following essential items: extra clothing, map, waterproof matches or a cigarette lighter, first aid kit, insect repellent, drinking cup, tide book, extra food, compass, knife, flashlight, rain gear, and water supply.

Plants

Opolopanex horridus, the scientific name for devil's club, explains much about this shrub. It's one plant all backcountry travelers learn to recognize and avoid. It grows to ten feet tall with huge maple-shaped leaves and stems covered with sharp, barbed spines. When a spine touches skin, it feels much like a bee sting and causes swelling. Because of the barbs, the spines are difficult to remove and continue to irritate. Wear gloves and long-sleeved shirts in areas where devil's club is abundant.

A number of poisonous plants occur in Alaska, but illness from them is uncommon and reports of death are extremely rare. Be careful to correctly identify berries before eating them, as some are poisonous. The most serious danger is to children, who may eat plants out of curiosity or because plants, flowers, or berries look tasty.

There is one very poisonous berry found in Alaska. The baneberry (*Acteaea rubra*) has either white or red berries and is commonly found in forests and thickets. It's a perennial that grows two to three feet tall. The leaves are large and lobed and coarsely toothed. Water hemlock, death camas, and certain species of mushrooms should be avoided.

Some individuals may develop severe allergic reactions from coming in contact with such plants as Indian rhubarb and nettles. Learn and avoid the common poisonous plants and eat only those known to be safe. In case of known or suspected poisoning from plants, call the nearest hospital, which will provide information regarding proper treatment.

Purchase a small guide titled, *Wild, Edible, and Poisonous Plants of Alaska*, available for $1 from local offices of the University of Alaska Cooperative Extension Service.

Water

Crystal, clear rivers and streams give the false impression that water is pure and safe to drink. Water clarity is not an indication of the presence or absence of bacteria or parasites. Beaver fever, *Giardia lamblia*, may be present in all streams and lake water, especially near beaver ponds or swampy rivers. It's carried by animal feces, including those of humans and dogs. It's not possible to guarantee which streams haven't been contaminated. Whenever you use surface water for drinking or cooking, steps should be taken to purify it through either of the following methods of treatment. Bring it to a full, rolling boil, not simply steaming. If the water has a flat taste, pour it back and forth between clean containers two or three times; or add four drops of household bleach, such as Clorox or Purex containing 5.25 percent available chlorine to each quart of water. Mix thoroughly and allow to stand thirty minutes before drinking; or treat water with tetraglycine hydroperiodide; or use a purification system with pore sizes of less than two micrometers.

Weather

Summer temperatures average fifty-five to sixty degrees Fahrenheit, and on bright, sunny days it may reach seventy-five to eighty degrees. Alaska weather is unpredictable. Even in summer months it can turn cold, wet, and windy. Anglers must be prepared for heat and sunburn and at the same time carry raingear, and warm clothing. Never enter Alaska wilderness without gloves, hat, warm coat, and raingear.

Fishing with Children

Taking a kid fishing in Alaska is an experience unlike no other. If the trip is timed with the run, the adventure may begin a lifetime of angling. Grayling are an excellent species on which to teach a youngster to fly-fish. If fishing Alaska for the first time it may be wise to use a guide, at least for a few days. Youngsters get bored easily. Plan to move often if the fishing is slow and be prepared with alternate activities between tides and slow action.

There's magic in fishing and a person's first catch, and it continues for a lifetime. The real magic is that the first time can be relived with emphasis by sharing another's first fish, and especially if the other person is a youngster who could not otherwise have the experience without your help. As with us all, we'll remember the first one and be eternally grateful to the person who helped us catch it.

I'll bet you remember your first fish. I remember mine like it was last week. It was up Oak Creek Canyon with Uncle Ivan on opening day of trout season. Our fishing equipment consisted of a ten-foot cane pole, no reel, a piece of line tied to one end, and night crawlers from a pork-and-bean can for bait. I have relived the innocent excitement of that moment for nearly five decades.

I recall Scoutmaster Hap Glad. I'm grateful for the lessons he taught and the appreciation he instilled in me for fishing, fresh air, forested mountains, camping, and other outdoor activities. I wish every youngster could have an Uncle Ivan or a Hap Glad who cares, teaches, and takes a kid fishing.

My youngest son Easten was a ten-year-old Webelo Boy Scout when he landed his first fish. Just after the snow melted and before the ice was off the lakes, I spent an afternoon on the front lawn with his den teaching them to cast a fly rod. A few days after casting instruction and practice, the ice went out of Green Lake. Easten's older brother, Lars, invited him to put his fishing lessons and practice to practical application.

I'll long remember the excitement of the two brothers returning home with stories of a mess of fish caught and released. They became the family entertainment for the afternoon, laughing and kidding each other about the day's events: the fish that actually jumped out of the lake onto the beach in search of Easten's fishing fly, Easten setting the hook so hard on a small one, the fish came out of the water and hit him in the chest, and on and on.

Don't limit your Alaska fishing excursions to boys. A fishing outing makes a great daddy/daughter date. On the last Friday before school started, Betty began bugging me. The clear, blue-sky weather, which followed three days of rain, was making her restless. She reminded me of the time passed since our last fishing date together and that I could preserve my image with her friends by taking a kid fishing: namely her. Then came the most powerful argument of all. She gave me a hug and told me how good a father I was. The next morning we were fishing the Talkeetna River for silvers.

Betty talked non-stop on the way to Talkeetna. She changed the subject after every breath. I got the low-down on everything. Music and musicians. Boys and brothers. Sisters, school, and summer. Clothes, cars, crystal, and charge cards.

Betty's outing was a serial of silver salmon fish-capades. Silvers are the most aerobatic of salmon, resembling the jumping, tail walking, skydiving antics of their cousin, the rainbow. Every dive, jump, and run trick pulled by a fish brought rock star audience squeals from the teenaged angler. It's amazing how the sound exploding from the lungs of a fifteen-year old daughter can affect a father. In front of the family room television set it's irritating. On the river bank,

This young girl waits for a strike.

exhilarating.

Back home that Sunday afternoon, during a fresh silver salmon dinner, Betty confessed, "It really isn't necessary to catch fish to have fun. What's important is that every chance you get, take your dad fishing." If you're a kid and want to fish Alaska, begin planning right now. Ask for a fishing rod and reel as a gift on special occasions. Save your money and give your dad or mom fishing equipment on their special days. Give a few flies or a new Dare Devil or two. Even take out the garbage and shovel the snow out of the driveway without being asked.

Let your folks know you won't cry with cold feet. Show them you'll take care of the fishing gear by taking better care of your things now, and keep your bedroom clean.

Call around or write and get brochures and information on different trips you

Joshua Constant shows off his king, and gets slapped in the process.

think they would like to go on. Determine the price. Find out which guides and what services will accept kids. See if they have special rates for you. Encourage making reservations early.

Fishing Alaska can be expensive. Try to earn money to help pay your way. Find out where it doesn't cost a lot of money, like the Russian River or the fishing hole on the Homer Spit. Study this guide and share the information with your parents.

Let other interested adults know you like to fish. Write a letter to grandparents telling of your interest in fishing. Send them a subscription to Alaska Outdoors magazine. Talk to neighbors who fish. Do something nice for them. Find out when National Fishing Week is. Ask your parents, grandparents, and neighbors, and find out who took them fishing when they were young. Get them to talk about their fishing experiences when they were growing up. Let them know how important it is to take a kid fishing.

Fishing fun is no respecter of age, price, or position. It's just right wherever you are. As long as I can be on the bank near the water, I'll take either the pork-and-bean can or the hand-crafted fly rod. It makes no difference to me if I'm catching with a hook or capturing with a camera. It's fishing. I'm thankful for the Uncle Ivans and Hap Glads in my early years and grateful my lot fell where I can fish Alaska.

Key to abbreviations used in The Angler's Guide to Alaska

KS	King Salmon	RS	Red Salmon	PS	Pink Salmon
SS	Silver Salmon	CS	Chum Salmon	H	Halibut
GR	Arctic Grayling	RT	Rainbow Trout	DV	Dolly Varden Char
LT	Lake Trout	BB	Burbot	WF	Whitefish
SF	Sheefish	NP	Northern Pike	KOK	Kokanee

Explanation of Fish Availability Charts

Fish Availability Charts are based on previous experience and should be considered as a guide. Fishing conditions, weather, and runs may vary. The information in the guide is our best guess but can't be relied on as absolute. The charts show when it's expected that fish will be available. If you desire only one specific species, we recommend you do your fishing at the peak of the run. By using the chart, anglers can time their trips to fish their species of choice at the peak of the run, and include other possibilities that may be available.

Timing is the key element to successful Alaska fishing, and fortunately the fish cooperate by returning with recurring regularity. It isn't a matter of *if* the fish will be there, it's *when*. More than matching the hatch, it's matching the time. Anglers must match their trip concurrent with the run. While a given lure may do better on a particular stream, it will always come up empty if you make the cast before or after the run.

The Alaska Department of Fish and Game did an outstanding job of studying and recording most of the fish runs. Their studies are available to anglers for the asking. Anglers writing or calling the Department's office in the area where the angler intends to fish will receive a wealth of information. Alaska Department of Fish and Game's mission is to help anglers enjoy Alaska's fishing possibilities, and they do an outstanding job. Anglers will find the department very helpful and central to their fishing success.

FISHING FORECAST

The following information has been compiled by field biologists of the Division of Sport Fish from the Alaska Department of Fish and Game. It's given as an overview of Alaska's varied fishing possibilities and when they occur. This, and all other information in *Fishing Alaska*, has been compiled using hundreds of sources and years of personal experience. This combined knowledge will aid inquiring anglers in their search for an ultimate Alaska adventure but can't replace the up-to-date data that anglers may obtain by asking locals. Tackle store personnel, gas station attendants, and Alaska Department of Fish and Game officials are still the angler's best source of current information.

Using this guide will enable first-time Alaska anglers to intelligently pick the season, species, and general location for their outing. It'll also give them the required knowledge to ask the right questions of prospective guides, outfitters, lodge owners, and even the local experts—store clerks. Anglers need not test the water to see if the fishing is up to par. They need only consult this guide and ask the guy already on the river. Alaska's fishing holes are not on trial. They're proven producers. It's up to the angler to be there at the right time, with the right gear, and hopefully for the right reasons. It's the wish of the authors that each reader's fishing excursion will be an event to remember. We trust it will.

Due to the size and variety of fishing options, we offer these fishing forecasts by region and species within the region. In many instances, we also provide the best time and method.

Southeast

Saltwater

King Salmon: King or chinook salmon are available from mid-March through October. The best period is from mid-May to mid-June, when big ones are available. The preferred bait is trolled or drifted herring. Some local hot spots are Bell Island, Ketchikan; Craig; Zimovia Strait, Wrangell; Scow and Pybus Bays, Petersburg; Saginaw Channel, Tee Harbor, Juneau; Sitka Sound near Sitka; and Yakutat Bay, Yakutat. Try reef edges where they drop off into deep water.

Silver Salmon: Silvers are available from late June through September, however the best fishing is in August. Herring or large spoons are used for bait and flashers are frequently used for attraction. Silvers usually run shallow but don't necessarily follow the shoreline. These fish average twelve pounds but can exceed twenty pounds.

Pink Salmon: Pink or humpy salmon are available from late June through August. Good fishing locations are Mountain Point and the mouth of Lunch Creek near Ketchikan; and North Pass, Amalgam Harbor, the Shrine, and Sheep Creek near Juneau.

Chum Salmon: Chum or dog salmon runs in Southeast Alaska are comprised of summer and fall runs, based on time of entry into inside waters and spawning streams. Summer chum salmon occur from a large number of systems and

State of Alaska
Trophy Fish Awards Program

Trophy fish awards are issued by Alaska Department of Fish and Game to give special recognition to anglers taking trophy-sized fish. Minimum-weight qualifications for each species are established by the Department and are listed in the current fishing booklet. Trophy fish rules and affidavits are available at all Department of Fish and Game offices. Affidavits must be signed by at least one witness (preferably two) and be accompanied by a picture of the fish, indicating size. Color pictures are preferred.

Attractive 8x10-inch parchment certificates suitable for framing will be presented to all contestants entering trophy-sized fish. In addition, an Annual Certificate of Record is presented to the individual submitting the largest (in weight) entry for each species during each calendar year and a Champion Certificate of Record is presented to anyone submitting an entry that establishes a new record as the largest fish of any species caught by a sport-fisherman in Alaska.

Entries should be mailed to:
**Alaska Department of
Fish and Game
Division of Sport Fisheries
P.O. Box 3-2000
Juneau, AK 99802**

SPECIES	STATE RECORD POUNDS	OUNCES	MINIMUM TROPHY AWARD WEIGHT
Arctic Grayling	4	13	3 Pounds
Chum Salmon	32	0	15 Pounds
Dolly Varden/Char	19	2.5	10 Pounds
Halibut	440	0	250 Pounds
King Salmon	97	4	
Cook Inlet			75 Pounds
Remainder of State			50 Pounds
Lake Trout	47	0	20 Pounds
Northern Pike	38	0	15 Pounds
Pink Salmon	12	9	8 Pounds
Rainbow/Steelhead	42	3	15 Pounds
Red Salmon	16	0	12 Pounds
Sheefish	53	0	30 Pounds
Silver Salmon	26	0	20 Pounds

Species Availability Calendar

Southcentral	Southeast	Western	Interior	Kodiak/AK Peninsula
January				
Burbot * Dolly Varden * Halibut Lake Trout * Rainbows * Rockfish Whitefish *	Ling Cod Sheefish *	Burbot * Dolly Varden * Kokanee * Ling Cod Pike * Rainbows * Rockfish Whitefish *	Burbot * Lake Trout * Pike * Rainbows * Land-locked Silvers * Whitefish *	Ling Cod Rainbows * Rockfish
February				
Burbot * Dolly Varden * Kokanee * Lake Trout * Ling Cod Rainbows * Rockfish Whitefish *	Ling Cod Steelhead Whitefish	Burbot * Kokanee * Dolly Varden * Lake Trout * Ling Cod Pike * Rainbows * Rockfish Whitefish *	Burbot * Lake Trout * Pike * Rainbows * Land-locked Silvers * Whitefish *	Ling Cod Rainbows * Rockfish
March				
Burbot * Dolly Varden * Lake Trout * Pike * Ling Cod Rainbows * Rockfish Whitefish *	Ling Cod Steelhead Rockfish	Burbot * Dolly Varden * Kokanee * LakeTrout * Ling Cod Rainbows * Pike * Rockfish Whitefish *	Burbot * Lake Trout * Pike * Rainbows * Land-locked Silvers * Whitefish *	Ling Cod Rainbows * Rockfish
April				
Burbot Dolly Varden Lake Trout Ling Cod Pike Rainbows Rockfish Whitefish	Brook Trout Cutthroat Trout Dolly Varden Kings Ling Cod Rockfish Steelhead	Pike Burbot Dolly Varden Halibut Kokanee Lake Trout Ling Cod Rainbows Rockfish Whitefish	Burbot * Lake Trout * Pike * Rainbows * Land-locked Silvers * Whitefish *	Ling Cod Rainbows Rockfish Steelhead (Kodiak only)
May				
Grayling Burbot Dolly Varden Halibut Kings Kokanee Lake Trout Ling Cod Pike Rainbows Rockfish Steelhead Whitefish	Brook Trout Cutthroat Trout Dolly Varden Halibut Kings Kokanee Ling Cod Rainbows Rockfish Steelhead	Grayling Burbot Dolly Varden Halibut Kings Kokanee Lake Trout Ling Cod Pike Rainbows Rockfish Sheefish Whitefish	Char * Grayling * Burbot * Lake Trout * Pike * Rainbows * Land-locked Silvers* Whitefish	Dolly Varden Halibut Ling Cod Rainbows Rockfish Steelhead (Kodiak only) Whitefish
June				
Char Grayling Rainbows Burbot Dolly Varden Halibut Kings Kokanee Lake Trout Ling Cod Pike Cutthroat Trout Reds Rockfish Steelhead Whitefish	Brook Trout Cutthroat Trout Dolly Varden Halibut Kings Kokanee Ling Cod Rainbows Reds Rockfish Steelhead	Char Grayling Burbot Dolly Varden Halibut Kings Kokanee Lake Trout Ling Cod Pike Rainbows Reds Rockfish Sheefish Whitefish	Grayling Burbot Lake Trout Pike Rainbows Land-locked Silvers Whitefish	Dolly Varden Halibut Kings Ling Cod Rainbows Reds Rockfish

* Indicates Ice Fishing

Species Availability Calendar

Southcentral	Southeast	Western	Interior	Kodiak/AK Peninsula
		July		
Char Grayling Burbot Silvers Cutthroat Dolly Varden Halibut Kings Kokanee Lake Trout Ling Cod Rockfish Pike Pinks Rainbows Reds Steelhead Whitefish	Grayling Brook Trout Cutthroat Trout Dolly Varden Chums Halibut Kings Kokanee Ling Cod Pinks Rainbows Rockfish Silvers	Char Grayling Burbot Chums Halibut Dolly Varden Kings Kokanee Lake Trout Whitefish Ling Cod Northern Pike Pinks Rainbows Reds Rockfish Sheefish	Char Grayling Burbot Chums Halibut Kings Dolly Varden Lake Trout Pike Rainbows Land-locked Silvers Sheefish Whitefish	Chums Halibut Dolly Varden Kings Pinks Lake Trout Rainbows Reds Rockfish
		August		
Char Grayling Burbot Chum Cutthroat Dolly Varden Halibut Kokanee Lake Trout Ling Cod Pike Pinks Rainbows Rockfish Silvers Whitefish	Brook Trout Chums Cutthroat Dolly Varden Halibut Kings Kokanee Ling Cod Pinks Rainbows Rockfish Silvers	Char Grayling Burbot Chums Dolly Varden Halibut Kings Kokanee Lake Trout Ling Cod Rockfish Pike Pinks Rainbows Reds Sheefish Silvers	Char Grayling Burbot Chum Kings Lake Trout Pike Rainbows Sheefish Silvers Whitefish	Dolly Varden Halibut Kings Ling Cod Pinks Rainbows Silvers Rockfish
		September		
Char Grayling Burbot Cutthroat Dolly Varden Halibut Kokanee Lake Trout Pike Ling Cod Silvers Rainbows Rockfish Sheefish Steelhead Whitefish	Char Brook Trout Chums Cutthroat Dolly Varden Halibut Kokanee Ling Cod Rainbows Rockfish Silvers Grayling Burbot Dolly Varden Halibut Kokanee Lake Trout	Char Grayling Burbot Dolly Varden Halibut Kokanee Lake Trout Ling Cod Rockfish Pike Pinks Reds Rainbows Sheefish Silvers Whitefish	Char Grayling Burbot Chum Kings Lake Trout Pike Rainbows Sheefish Silvers Whitefish	Dolly Varden Halibut Kings Ling Cod Rainbows Silvers Rockfish Steelhead (Kodiak only)
		October		
Burbot Dolly Varden Kokanee Lake Trout Ling Cod Pike Rainbows Rockfish Silvers Steelhead Whitefish	Dolly Varden Ling Cod Rockfish Silvers Steelhead	Burbot Dolly Varden Kokanee Lake Trout Ling Cod Pike Rainbows Whitefish	Burbot * Lake Trout * Pike * Rainbows * Land-locked Silvers * Whitefish *	Dolly Varden Ling Cod Rainbows Rockfish Silvers Steelhead (Kodiak only)
		November		
Burbot * Dolly Varden * Kokanee * Lake Trout * Ling Cod * Pike * Rainbows * Rockfish Whitefish *	Ling Cod Rockfish Steelhead	Burbot * Dolly Varden * Kokanee * Lake Trout * Ling Cod Pike * Rainbows * Whitefish	Burbot * Lake Trout * Pike * Rainbows * Land-locked Silvers * Whitefish *	Ling Cod Rainbows Rockfish Steelhead (Kodiak only)
		December		
Pike Burbot Dolly Varden Lake Trout Ling Cod Rainbows Rockfish Silvers Steelhead Whitefish	Ling Cod Rockfish Steelhead	Burbot * Dolly Varden * Kokanee * Lake Trout * Ling Cod Pike * Rainbows * Whitefish *	Burbot * Lake Trout * Pike * Rainbows * Land-locked Silvers * Whitefish *	Ling Cod Rainbows * Rockfish

* Indicates Ice Fishing

spawn about the same time, or slightly earlier, than many pink salmon runs. Fall chum salmon are restricted to fewer systems, where there are up-welling water sources required for late spawning. Large mainland river systems in northern southeastern Alaska produce the majority of the fall chum salmon.

Most chum salmon are taken incidentally by saltwater anglers targeting other salmon, and many ocean-bright dogs are mistaken for silver salmon. Many anglers can't tell the differences between chums and silvers. This is a good indication of the desirability of these fish.

Halibut: These fish are common throughout the entire area from May to October, peaking in inside waters in late August. Preferred baits are octopus and herring. Fine catches are also made jigging with large spoons and jigs. The large ones exceed 300 pounds and, because of their size and tenacity, can be dangerous in a small boat.

Freshwater

Silver Salmon: These fighters, also known as coho, are found in streams open to fish migrations throughout the area. They're available from August to early November, with the peak occurring in September. Bright, shiny spoons and flies are favored. Outstanding locations include the Situk, Lost, and Itlaio Rivers at Yakutat, Chilkat River near Haines, and Petersburg Creek near Petersburg.

Chum Salmon: Chum salmon fishing has become popular with roadside anglers near Haines, where the Chilkat River chum salmon are easily accessible. Although the quality of these fish does not equal that of ocean-bright fish, they offer excellent catch-and-release fishing. The flesh of keepers is suitable for canning or smoking.

Steelhead: Two separate runs of this trophy fish occur in Southeast. In southern Southeast a fall run enters creeks having an accessible lake in the system. The fall run occurs during September and peaks in October. These fish remain all winter and offer excellent fishing. The Naha River and Fish Creek near Ketchikan are highly recommended. An excellent northern Southeast fall run enters the Situk River near Yakutat in October and November.

Throughout Southeast, a spring run enters the larger creeks in April and peaks in May. Some of the better streams are Ikawock and Eagle creeks and Karta River on Prince of Wales; Snake Creek on Etolin; Kadake Creek on Kuiu Island, and perhaps best of all, Situk River at Yakutat. Eggs are the preferred bait with spoons and flies running a close second.

Dolly Varden: Dollies are found year-round as freshwater residents and migratory species. Resident fish are available throughout the year. The size range is wide, with fish up to seven pounds.

Sea-run fish are found in creeks and streams from April to early June and again from late July to November. The best fishing occurs during late August and September. To catch these fish, use eggs, flies, and spoons. Good locations are Chilkoot Lake and Chilkat River near Haines; Nakwasina and Katlian Rivers near Sitka; Duncan Canal Salt Chuck and Castle River near Petersburg; Salmon Bay Creek at Wrangell; and Bostwick Inlet and Wasta Creek near Ketchikan.

Rainbow Trout and Eastern Brook Trout: These fish have been successfully stocked in selected waters throughout the area. Eastern brook trout can be found

Probably the most popular one-day fishing trip is a guided riverboat charter. From Anchorage, you can fly or drive south to Soldotna or Homer or drive north to the Susitna River. In Southeast Alaska, most areas offer guided fall fishing for silvers, like this beauty taken by guide Paul Lemmert from the Situk River.

in numbers at Salmon Cheek Reservoir near Juneau; Green Lake near Sitka; and Grace and Perseverance lakes near Ketchikan. Rainbows are found in Blue Lake near Sitka; Swan Lake near Petersburg; Walker and McDonald lakes near Ketchikan; and Avoss, Rezanof, and other lakes on lower Baronof Island. Eggs, spoons, flies, and shrimp are the favored baits.

Native rainbow trout occur in lakes which also contain steelhead. Some of the better lakes include Mountain and Situk lakes near Yakutat; Heckman and Jordan lakes near Ketchikan; and Karta and Luck lakes on Prince of Wales Island.

Grayling: Southeast anglers have grayling fishing available in Antler Lake near Juneau; Beaver Lake near Sitka; Tyee Lake near Wrangell; Marge, Miller, and Summit lakes on Prince of Wales Island; and Big Goat, Manzoni, Orton, and Snow lakes near Ketchikan. Small flies, shrimp, and spinners are the way to take these sail-finned beauties.

Copper River and Prince William Sound

Saltwater

King Salmon: The best catches of this trophy fish are made near Valdez and Cordova in late winter and early spring. Large trolling lures and herring make the best bait.

Silver Salmon: Silver salmon become available in late July and remain present through mid-September. Excellent fishing occurs in the bays adjacent to Valdez and Cordova. A boat is required for best results and charter boats are available. Spoons and herring are proven lures for this scrappy fish.

Pink Salmon: Excellent pink salmon fishing is found in Prince William Sound throughout the summer. Pinks take a wide variety of lures, including golf tees, spinners, and spoons. The best lure is a Pixie.

Chum Salmon: Chums are available during July and August and frequently taken while fishing for pinks and silvers.

Halibut: Generally, small bays are the best areas to fish. Jigging with large lures and bait can be very rewarding.

Dolly Varden: Sea-run Dollies can be found in most of Prince William Sound during salmon runs and during fall. The best areas to fish are in the vicinity of creek and river mouths. These fish will bite on eggs, flies, and a variety of lures.

Freshwater

Grayling: Grayling fishing should be excellent in most small roadside streams along the Glenn and Richardson highways. The best fishing in these streams will be in May and June, during ice breakup. When water is muddy, eggs are the best bait; later in the year, flies and small lures work well. Lake fishing for grayling is good throughout the summer. Some hot spots to try are Mae West, George, Junction, Gillespie, Dick, Kay, Tolsona, Arizona, and Twin lakes. Gulkana River has excellent grayling fishing throughout the summer. There are several automobile access points, as well as a number of foot trails leading to the river.

Lake Trout: The best catches of lake trout are generally made immediately after ice breakup and just prior to freezing. Fishing for lakers should be good in Louise, Susitna, Beaver, Dog, Paxson, Summit, Swede, Tanada, and Copper lakes. Several small roadside lakes along the Denali Highway offer good lake trout fishing for the shore angler. Deep trolling after the water warms up is the best way to take these big lunkers, using spoons, red-eyes, or Alaska plugs.

Rainbow Trout: Good rainbow trout fishing is expected in such roadside lakes as Blueberry, Worthington, Sculpin, Buffalo, and Van.

Silver Salmon: Good catches of silver salmon are expected in Eyak River and other streams along the Copper River Highway in the fall. Landlocked silvers can be taken at Strelna Lake on the McCarthy-Chitna Road with flies and small spoons during summer and eggs during winter. Tex Smith and Buffalo lakes are also good for small silvers.

Dolly Varden: The best Dolly Varden fishing will be found in streams near Valdez and Cordova.

Red Salmon: Excellent red salmon fishing is available during late June and July in the Gulkana and Klutina Rivers. Fishing with streamer flies is very effective and furnishes considerable sport and enjoyment.

King Salmon: King salmon will be available in fair numbers in the Gulkana and Klutina Rivers during June and July.

Cook Inlet

Saltwater

Cook Inlet, north of the forelands, is not suitable for successful sport fishing because of silt-laden waters. Strong currents and extreme tidal fluctuations also reduce sport fishing opportunities.

Freshwater

Silver Salmon: These spectacular game fish enter the area in mid-July and remain until September. The peak of the run occurs in August. Excellent fishing takes place on the Deshka River, Lake and Alexander creeks, Chuit River, Talachulitna River, and Quig Creek. All of these streams are on the west side of the Susitna River and are accessible only by plane or boat. Silvers are also available in east-side tributaries of the Susitna River. These tributaries are accessible by car from the Parks Highway. Tee spoons and Mepps spinners are the lures most frequently used, and egg clusters are always a sure thing. Stocked landlocked silver salmon are also available in Echo, Victor, Lucille, and Finger lakes.

King Salmon: This highly prized sport fish enters upper Cook Inlet waters in early June. Anglers should consult the current sport fishing regulations for comprehensive information regarding open seasons, specific waters, and bag limits. This largest of all Pacific salmon can be caught on a variety of spinning lures, oakie drifters, and egg clusters.

Pink Salmon: Even-numbered years generally offer the best fishing in the Cook Inlet area. Mid-July through mid-August is the best time in such streams as Bird Creek, Deshka River, Alexander Creek, Lake Creek, Talachulitna River, and several east-side tributaries of the Susitna River. Small Daredevils and #1 red-and-white Mepps are proven lures for these fish.

Chum Salmon: Chum salmon are scattered sparingly throughout the streams of Cook Inlet from mid-July through mid-August. Anglers may tie into a chum salmon in such locations as Willow, Alexander, Sheep, and Montana creeks while fishing for pinks or silvers. Preferred chum lures are similar to those used for silvers.

Rainbow Trout: From late May until September 1, the Deshka River and Lake and Alexander Creeks offer fly-in fishermen some of finest rainbow fishing available in Cook Inlet. Anglers will find excellent fishing in the headwaters of the Deshka River and Peters Creek. Stream fishing for rainbow trout is available along the Parks Highway on such east-side tributaries of the Susitna River as

Willow and Montana creeks. Egg clusters and artificial spinning-type lures are preferred. Consult fishing regulations regarding the use of bait after September 1 in flowing waters.

Selected waters in the area have been stocked with rainbow trout and provide the nimrod with many hours of enjoyable fishing. The better rainbow lakes include Matanuska, Knik, Wasilla, Big, Lower Bonnie lakes, and the lakes of the Kepler-Bradley complex near Palmer. In the Anchorage area, Jewel, Campbell Point, Beach, and Sand lakes have good trout fisheries.

Grayling: This fish may be taken during late May and early June in the Deshka River and tributaries, Alexander Creek, and the lower stretches of Lake Creek. For the fly-in angler, the upper reaches of Lake Creek, the Talachulitna River, and Cola Creek provide excellent grayling fishing for most of the May-through-September period. Salmon eggs are excellent bait in the spring or during high water, whereas flies and small spinners produce well during summer and fall.

Some east-side tributaries of the Susitna have grayling and are accessible by automobile. Several Matanuska Valley lakes, such as Seventeen Mile, Harriet, and Long lakes, also offer grayling. Fishing is generally tops right after ice breakup in May. Small spinners, spoons, or flies are effective in these waters.

Dolly Varden: This white and pink-spotted relative of the lake trout is not abundant in most Upper Cook Inlet tributaries. However, Lewis River and Coal Creek near Cola Creek Lake, northwest of Tyonek, produce nice Dollies, and they may be occasionally encountered during the summer months in the Theodore, Chuit, and Talachulitna rivers. Effective lures are eggs, brightly colored lead-head jigs, and small spinning lures.

Lake Trout: Shell Lake, near Skwentna, provides an excellent lake trout fishery for fly-in anglers who have small motor-propelled rafts for trolling. Medium-sized red and white spoons and blue-tinted, minnow-type lures trolled to thirty-foot and greater depths provide the action these fish like.

Kenai Peninsula

Saltwater

King Salmon: Saltwater angling for these monarchs of the sea is available in Lower Cook Inlet from early May through late July. The best king salmon fishing occurs in that portion of the inlet located south of Deep Creek. Trolling of bright spoons and herring is the most popular method. King salmon in this fishery are large with many exceeding fifty pounds. In Kachemak Bay, a hatchery king salmon return has been established at Halibut Cove Lagoon and the Homer Spit. In Seward, a hatchery enhanced king salmon run returns to the areas of Lowell Creek and the small boat harbor. These hatchery fish are generally available from early May through early July in Kachemak Bay and from early June through late July in the Seward area.

Silver Salmon: Angling for fresh aerial acrobats is available from the road system in three areas of the peninsula: 1. Resurrection Bay, Seward, where they become available in early July, with the run peaking in mid-August and terminating in early September; 2. Kachemak Bay, Homer, where these fish are present primarily during August—silvers are taken here from the shore in Maud Bay on high tides; 3. Cook Inlet, and the beach, from late July through August between Cape Ninilchik and Anchor Point. Best results require a boat with herring, spoons, or spinners trolled near the surface.

Pink Salmon: Pink salmon fishing can be found throughout Kachemak Bay at Homer in July and early August. Pinks can be caught by casting small lures from the Homer Spit and from many beaches in the south side of the bay. One of the most popular areas is Tutka Bay Lagoon. Pink salmon are also abundant in Resurrection Bay at Seward on even-numbered years during this same time period.

Dolly Varden: Dolly Varden are available throughout Kachemak Bay from early spring through fall, with peak catches during July and August. Dollies are caught by shore anglers on the Homer Spit and can be taken from most south side beaches and stream mouths.

Halibut: Halibut are available throughout the season and can be best caught by fishing bait or jigging large, silver lures near the bottom. Lower Cook Inlet, from Deep Creek south to Kachemak Bay, offers good halibut fishing. Razor clams or herring fished on a sandy bottom work well.

Clams: Razor clams are sporadically abundant along sandy beaches between Kasilof River and Anchor Point. Roads at Clam Gulch and Deep Creek provide access to the beach. The most popular area is Clam Gulch, located twenty-two miles south of Soldotna. These tasty bivalves can be dug throughout the spring and summer on minus tides. At least a minus three-foot tide is recommended for beaches farther south around Deep Creek and Happy Valley. Hard-shell clams can be taken along the southern beaches of Kachemak Bay, with McDonald Spit being a popular site. Cockles can also be found on the east side of Homer Spit. A free booklet on Cook Inlet razor clam digging is available upon request from any Department of Fish and Game office.

Freshwater

King Salmon: King salmon season on Anchor River, Deep Creek, and Ninilchik River is open for short periods from late May through mid-June. The Kenai River, from Skilak Lake downstream to Cook Inlet, is also open for a portion of the season, as is Kasilof River from the Sterling Highway bridge downstream to Cook Inlet. King salmon can be taken on a variety of spoons and spinners, with salmon egg clusters preferred by many anglers. A boat is recommended when fishing the large, glacial Kenai River. Shore fishermen are successful on the lower streams and Kasilof River. King salmon fishermen should consult the current sport fishing regulations closely prior to fishing. Also, because the harvest of king salmon is closely regulated, field emergency closures may be issued, changing the seasons listed in the regulation summary.

Red Salmon: Red or sockeye salmon fishing is available in the Russian River from early June to late August. Colorful streamer flies used with spinning gear is a proven method for taking reds on the Russian River which is a fly-fishing only stream. Because of special regulations, consult the current sport fishing regulations before fishing these waters. Russian River is also subject to frequent field emergency closures during the season. Another location offering red salmon fishing is the Kenai River, with most of the fishing effort occurring from Skilak Lake downstream to Cook Inlet. Red salmon are generally available from mid July through early August, with streamer flies being the preferred terminal tackle. Angling for landlocked red salmon or kokanee can be found in Hidden Lake on Skilak Loop Road.

Silver Salmon: These flashy fighters enter most peninsula streams in late July, with runs peaking during late August. Silver salmon are most abundant in the Kenai River and are chiefly present from late July through October. This run has two peaks, which occur in early August and early September. Other popular streams for silvers are the Anchor River, Ninilchik River, Deep Creek, Russian River, and Swanson River. Salmon egg clusters are the preferred bait in glacial waters, while bright spoons, spinners, and flies work well in clear waters.

Consult fishing regulations closely, as bait fishing is prohibited in most Kenai Peninsula streams after mid-September. Landlocked silvers, stocked by the department, can be taken in numerous Kenai Peninsula lakes. A free brochure describing these lakes is available from Department of Fish and Game offices in Anchorage, Soldotna, and Homer. The most popular bait is single salmon eggs.

Pink Salmon: Pink salmon are very cyclic in most Kenai Peninsula streams, with strong runs occurring on even-numbered years. The largest run occurs from late July through August in the lower Kenai River below the Skilak Lake outlet. Resurrection Creek, near Hope, is also a popular fishing stream during this same period of time.

Steelhead: This highly prized sea-run rainbow trout enters freshwater from mid-August through October, with the peak of the upstream migration occurring in September. The most popular steelhead streams are the Anchor River, Deep Creek, and the Ninilchik River. Salmon eggs, Spin-N-Glow, and Oakie Drifters take the most fish. For the fly-fisherman, fluorescent flies have proven effective on this species. Consult fishing regulations regarding the use of bait after mid-September.

Rainbow Trout: Rainbow trout are found in most waters of the western Kenai Peninsula and are available throughout the year. Swan Lake and Swanson River Canoe Systems on the Kenai National Moose Range offer good fishing on native populations. Other good rainbow producers are the Kenai River and Russian River drainages. Consult fishing regulations closely when fishing this species, as regulations vary from drainage to drainage and differentiate between lakes and streams. Numerous Kenai Peninsula lakes contain stocked trout. A free booklet describing these lakes is available at the Anchorage, Soldotna, and Homer Department of Fish and Game offices. Trout may be caught using salmon eggs, flies, and small lures.

Dolly Varden: These sea-run char abound in most coastal streams from July through November. When Dollies are in, fast action can be expected on the Anchor River, Ninilchik River, Deep Creek, Quartz Creek and Ptarmigan Creek. The Kenai River offers the best chance at lunker Dollies. A small, landlocked variety called goldenfins is abundant in Upper and Lower Summit lakes and in streams connecting them. Grouse Lake, near Seward, and Jerome Lake, near Moose Pass, have reported excellent catches of this species. Dolly Varden are readily taken on salmon eggs, wet flies, nymphs, and small, bright lures.

Arctic Char: These close cousins of the Dolly Varden occur in lakes of the Swanson River drainage. Arctic char are popular with winter fishermen and are also taken during the spring and fall.

Warmer summer waters restrict these fish to cool depths where they can be taken by deep trolling. Salmon eggs, spoons, and spinners all work well for char. Arctic char are available in Stormy, Finger, Fish, and Dolly Varden lakes, as well as many other lakes in the Swanson River and Swan Lake Canoe systems.

Lake Trout: Also char, lakers or mackinaw, are present in all glacial lakes in the Kenai River system. The inlet and outlet of Skilak Lake are recommended just prior to freeze-up and shortly after ice breakup. Tustumena Lake outlet produces fair catches of lake trout immediately after the ice goes out. The mountain lakes along the Resurrection Pass Trail system also have populations of lakers. Good catches are common from Hidden Lake during the spring and fall months by trolling the shallows with spoons or flatfish. During winter, jigging with spoons under the ice is usually productive in this lake.

Arctic Grayling: This species has limited distribution on the Kenai Peninsula, as they are not indigenous to the area. Arctic grayling, however, have been introduced to the following waters which, while not adjacent to the road system, are accessible by trails: Grayling Lake near Seward; Bench Lake near Moose Pass; and Filler and Crescent lakes near Cooper Landing. These fish have also been successfully established in Twin Lakes and Upper and Lower Paradise lakes, which are accessible by float plane. Grayling are abundant at the outlets of these lakes from June through September and are most easily caught on flies and small spinners.

Eulchon: Smelt, commonly called hooligan, are slender but tasty little fish which are taken by long-handled dip nets during the May spawning run. Hooligan are abundant in Placer and Twenty Mile Rivers near Portage and at the mouth of Resurrection River near Seward. A personal-use gill net fishery for these fish occurs in the lower Kenai River during late May. Only Alaska residents are allowed to dip net eulchon.

Kodiak Island

Saltwater

Halibut: Halibut are caught in this area throughout the year, however, fishing in the offshore Kodiak area is best during summer months, as fish are more active. Halibut are plentiful but most are taken from deep water areas off Long and Woody Islands.

Dolly Varden: Dollies are plentiful along rocky beaches from about June through July. Herring strips and small- to medium-sized lures work well.

Pink Salmon: The first pinks move to local beach areas in late June to early July. Fishing is usually poor until after July 4 but picks up by mid-July and is good to excellent until mid-August.

Chum Salmon: Chums usually arrive in the area in late July and early August. Most chums are taken incidental to pink and coho salmon fishing.

Silver Salmon: Silvers are taken off Pasagshak Beach in mid-August; however, the best beach fishing is during early September.

Freshwater

King Salmon: Karluk River has the only run readily accessible to Kodiak anglers and is seventy air miles from the city. Kings start into the river during early June; however, fishing is usually poor in the upper river areas until the last week in June. About ninety percent of the kings will be in the river by July 4 and spawning will peak in mid-August.

Silver Salmon: Silver salmon enter most of the larger streams during high water in late August and early September. Good fishing is available through September in the Buskin, American, Pasagshak, Karluk, and Afognak rivers. These fish average about ten pounds and are readily taken on salmon eggs and lures.

Red Salmon: Red salmon are in Afognak, Uganik, Buskin, and Saltery rivers in June and in Karluk River from June 15 to August 1. Streamer flies and small lures fished very slowly work best.

Pink Salmon: Pinks are abundant in all streams on Kodiak and Afognak islands. July and early August are the best times to find these fish in peak condition.

Dolly Varden: These fish are available in large numbers in all area streams. Popular fishing spots are the Buskin, Afognak, Saltery, and Pasagshak rivers in May and again in September. Salmon eggs, wet flies, and small lures are effective.

Grayling: These arctic fish have been successfully introduced into Cascade, Aurel, Abercrombie, and Long lakes. Shoreline fishing with flies is recommended.

Rainbow Trout: Favorite waters near the city are: Bell Flats Lakes, Cliff Point Lakes, Woody Island Lakes, Pasagshak Point Lakes, and Genevieve, Margaret, and Abercrombie lakes. Good trout fishing during early June may be found in most river-lake systems on Afognak and Kodiak Islands.

Steelhead: Karluk River in October is a long-time favorite with local anglers. Frazer, Ayakulik, and Saltery rivers also have runs of steelhead. Spinners with bucktails, streamer flies, golf tees, and daredevil-type spoons are effective.

Bristol Bay/Lower Kuskokwim

Freshwater

King Salmon: These tackle-busters are at their best from mid-June through July. The better spots are Naknek River near King Salmon, along Nushagak River downstream from the village of Portage Creek, Togiak and Knaektok rivers, and throughout the length of the Alagnak River. Bait is illegal on Naknek River from March 1 through November 14.

Silver Salmon: Silver salmon are available in Bristol Bay streams from late July through September. The mouth of King Salmon Creek on the Naknek River is one of the good spots. Alagnak River, and the Igiugig area in the Kvichak watershed also produce silvers. Silvers are found throughout the Nushagak and Togiak drainages, the Kanektok and Goodnews rivers, in the Ugashik system at the narrows, at the outlet of Lower Ugashik Lake, and in Mother Goose Lake. Lures, such as gold tees or egg clusters, work.

Grayling: Grayling may be taken readily from May through October. They are abundant throughout the entire region, but the record-breakers are found in the outlet of Lower Ugashik Lake during July and August.

Rainbow Trout: Connecting streams, outlets, and many tributaries of all Bristol Bay watersheds, except Egegik and Ugashik Lake systems, offer rainbow fishing that's difficult to beat. Big silvery rainbow, often mistaken for steelhead, may be taken in Kvichak and Naknek drainages. The best periods are spring and fall. Rainbow trout in the western portion of the area are at their best in late August and September. To protect spawning trout, angling in Kvichak and Naknek watersheds is closed from April 10 through June 7.

Though good numbers of rainbows are taken all summer, these beauties will increase in abundance from late August until freeze-up. Some of the best locations are the Kvichak River at Igiugig, Lower Talarik Creek during September and October, and Newhalen, Iliamna, Gibraltar, Kanektok, and Goodnews rivers.

Angling in the Kvichak watershed is also restricted to unbaited artificial lures from June 8 through October 31, and in the Naknek River from March 1 through November 14.

Fairbanks and Northern Alaska

Freshwater

Grayling: Grayling are common in nearly all clear, flowing streams throughout interior Alaska. Grayling are available from early April through September in many streams along the road system near Fairbanks.

Delta Junction and Tok have hook and release regulations during the spring spawning period. Be sure to consult the current sport fishing regulations for the appropriate season. Popular fishing spots are the Chatanika, Chena, Delta Clearwater, Goodpaster, and Salcha rivers and the Tangle Lakes system. Large grayling are available in the Sinuk, Niukluk, and Fish rivers near Nome, Unalakleet River in Norton Sound, and in the Clearwater tributaries of the Yukon River. Dry-fly patterns such as the mosquito, black gnat, royal coachman, or blue upright, are often used to take grayling, as are small spinners.

Northern Pike: Pike are common in many lakes and streams in the Tanana, Yukon, and Kuskokwim River drainages, as well as in some waters of the Seward Peninsula and Northwest Alaska. Waters of the upper Tanana River, near Tok, such as the Chisana and Nebesna rivers, and Tetlin, Mansfield, George, and Volkmar lakes, are good producers. The Minto Flats area west of Fairbanks, while closed to pike fishing during winter months, is still popular with many area anglers. Numerous fly-in lakes located in the Yukon Flats north of Fairbanks offer excellent pike fishing opportunities as do the many sloughs and clearwater tributaries of the Yukon and Kuskokwim rivers. Medium-sized lures, spinners, and spoons are commonly used for pike, and while fishing is generally best in June, good catches occur during winter ice fishing.

Rainbow Trout: This popular sport fish species is not indigenous to the Yukon or Tanana River drainages. Rainbow trout, however, have been successfully introduced in many landlocked lakes throughout the Fairbanks and Delta

The state record for rainbow trout is forty-two pounds three ounces. This one was caught by Shelby Stastny in the Kvichak River.

Junction areas. Excellent rainbow fishing is available in Birch, Quartz, Chena, Bluff Cabin, and Donna lakes, which are accessible by road or trail system. Koole, Rainbow, and Dune lakes offer good fishing for the fly-fisherman as they provide the area's only rainbow trout fishing in flowing waters. Small spinners and spoons work well as do both streamer flies and dry flies. Bait, such as salmon eggs and shrimp, works well in the winter. Indigenous rainbows occur in Kuskokwim Bay streams, Kanektok, Goodnews, and Arolik rivers, and in lower tributaries to the Kuskokwim River: Kwethluk, Kisaralik, Aniak rivers. Natural populations don't occur above the Aniak River. Access to these streams is by air or boat.

Sheefish: These fish are taken year-round in the Kotzebue Sound/Selawik Lake area. Ice fishing on Hotham Inlet and Selawik Lake is good in late spring. During summer and fall, Kobuk River in the Kiana, Amber, and Kobuk areas, Selawik Lake, Selawik River, and Tuklomarak River provide some of the best sheefish fishing. They're also available in the Holitna and Hoholitna rivers at Sleetmute, and in the Koyukuk and Nowitna rivers, which are tributaries to the Yukon River. Limited numbers are available in fall in the upper Chatanika River near the Steese and Elliott highways, and in Forty Mile Lake on the Taylor Highway. A few sheefish are being taken from the Chena River in the Fairbanks area. Spoons are most commonly used to take sheefish. Sheefish may also be found at the mouths of clearwater tributaries of the Tanana River, although fishing may be sporadic.

Arctic Char/Dolly Varden: These fish are available in most coastal streams throughout the season. Most streams and many lakes on the Seward Peninsula contain arctic char and/or Dolly Varden in August and September. Some small resident Dolly Varden are available in the Nenana River tributaries near Nenana and in Tanana River tributaries near Tok. Trophy-sized Dolly Varden are present in the Wilik and Kivalina rivers and tributaries of the Noatak River, all near Kotzebue. The best fishing occurs in September.

Lake Trout: Some of the better lakes for fishing lake trout in the Brooks Range include Shaini, Chandler, Kurupa, Elusive, and Itkillik lakes on the North Slope and Selby-Narvak, Wild Helpmejack, Chandalar, Squaw, and Walker lakes on the South Slope. Lake trout are also available in limited numbers in Fielding and Tangle lakes near Paxson and in Harding Lake.

King Salmon: Chinook, or king salmon, are available in the coastal areas from June 1 to July 30. King salmon first arrive in the Fairbanks area in early July. The daily bag and possession limit is one king salmon. Popular areas open to king salmon fishing include the lower Chena River, the lower Salcha River, and the entire Chatanika River.

Chum Salmon: As with king salmon, the summer run of chum salmon first arrives in Fairbanks areas in early July. The fall run arrives in mid-August and continues until mid to late October.

Silver Salmon: Naturally occurring runs of coho or silver salmon are found

State of Alaska Marked Fish Recovery Program

The Department of Fish and Game wants the heads of all sport-caught coho, chinook, or steelhead missing their adipose fin—the small, fleshy fin on the salmonid's back, just in front of its tail. These fin-clipped fish carry a coded-wire tag in their heads that provides essential information about Alaska salmonid. The microscopic tag is implanted in the nose cartilage of both hatchery and wild stocks. Hatchery fish are tagged one to three months prior to their release, whereas wild salmonid are captured and tagged in their natural rivers during rearing or downstream migration. The adipose fin is clipped to serve as a visual identifying mark. Over 20 million salmonids are marked by Canada and the United States each year.

Information derived from coded-wire tag studies provides an understanding of the many aspects of salmonid biology. When combined with catch information provided by sportfishermen, it's possible to establish general migratory habits and basic biology of West Coast salmonids, stock strength and distribution by various systems, and the relative success of various enhancement strategies, such as hatchery diets and release timing. In more specific terms, this knowledge helps larger and stronger sport-fishing salmonid stocks.

If your coho, chinook, or steelhead is missing its adipose fin, please: Cut off the fish's head and return it to any State Department of Fish and Game office.

in selected spring-fed tributaries of the Tanana River in September and October. The Delta Clearwater near Delta Junction and Clear Creek near Nenana are two of the most popular sport fishing spots from Fairbanks to the Canadian border. Birch, Quartz, Chena, and Little Harding lakes are some of the better producers.

Pink Salmon: Pinks are available in coastal streams from June 15 to August 15, but peak in July. There is excellent fishing in the Unalakleet River, Norton Sound area; and in the Nome, Snake, and Niukluk rivers near Nome.

WILDLIFE SAFEGUARD

Anglers having concern for proper use and protection of our wildlife resources can play an important role in protection of these resources. Citizens observing fish or game violations are encouraged to report the violation to the Division of Fish and Wildlife Protection through the Wildlife Safeguard Program.

Violations can be reported on the toll-free number (800) 478-3377, twenty-four hours a day. Anonymity is guaranteed and rewards will be offered for information leading to the arrest or conviction of persons for poaching or other serious offenses.

When observing a violation, collect the following information for Wildlife Safeguard:

Who—Names and addresses of offenders, if known. Number and description of offenders. Car license, boat or airplane registration numbers, etc. Any other identifying characteristics.

What—Type of illegal activity—hunting out of season, over bag limit, etc. Number of fish taken.

When—Time violation was observed.

Where—Name of place. Description of location. River, harbor, milepost, or road or highway, etc.

The information should be as complete as possible and should be reported as soon as possible after observing the violation.

RAINBOW TROUT

Rainbow trout, *Salmon gairdneri*, are one of the most respected and sought after Alaska native game fish. Serious anglers from around the world are drawn to Alaska's wilderness waters for the thrill of challenging this hard fighter. Rainbow occur as both freshwater resident and sea-going travelers, known as steelhead.

In most areas, best rainbow fishing occurs during a few weeks in spring and again in fall. Rainbows will be there all summer long but almost impossible to catch because of the great number of salmon. When the stream is jammed with thousands of migrating salmon, it becomes almost impossible to get down to feeding rainbows without hooking a salmon.

Rainbow trout are voracious feeders and strong swimmers, willing to hit a wide variety of lures, baits, and flies. Weighted spinners are preferred by many anglers. The wobbling spoon is another fine rainbow getter. Fly-fishermen find that streamers, muddlers, and egg patterns fished near the bottom are dependable to do the trick. Black and red, especially fluorescent red, seems to add value. When salmon eggs cover stream bottoms, and rainbow are not interested in anything else, the hatch to match is eggs.

Rainbow trout are native to waters throughout Southeast Alaska, west to Kuskokwim Bay, and as far up the Kuskokwim River as Sleetmute. The clearwater lakes and streams draining into Bristol Bay provide outstanding rainbow fishing. Rainbow trout occur naturally on the Kenai Peninsula, throughout the fresh waters of Upper Cook Inlet, on Kodiak Island, and in the Copper River drainage. Release of hatchery-reared Alaska rainbow trout has extended the range of resident rainbow to specific lakes and streams in the Tanana River drainage near Fairbanks.

The Iliamna drainage is considered by many to be the world's top producer of large rainbow. Fish over six pounds are not uncommon. The state record is forty-two pounds three ounces. Minimum state of Alaska trophy award weight is fifteen pounds.

During summer, good trout fishing skills are required to fool these predators into taking a lure. Bigger trout seldom stay in a stream's center during bright sunlight. They hide in the cover along the bank. Wise anglers will wade the center of the stream and cast to either bank.

Late fall is the time of year for fly-fishing. Fall will produce more fishing memories for hardy anglers than the rest of the year put together. The sight, sound, and smell of fall, combined with a picture of a rainbow breaking the surface, paints a memory forever inscribed in the mind.

Rainbow trout possess the well-known streamlined salmonid form, but body shape and coloration vary widely and reflect habitat, age, sex, and degree of maturity. The body shape may range from slender to thick. The back may shade from blue-green to olive. There is a reddish-pink band along each side about the mid-line that may range from faint to radiant. The lower sides are usually silver, fading to pure white beneath. Small black spots are present over the back above the lateral line, as well as on the upper fins and tail. In some locations, the black spots of adults may extend well below the lateral line and even cover the entire lower side.

Rainbow trout are positively identified by the eight to twelve rays along the anal fin, a mouth that does not extend past the back of the eye, and the lack of teeth at the base of the tongue. River or stream residents normally display the most intense pink stripe coloration and heaviest spotting followed by rainbow from lake and lake/stream systems. Spawning trout are characterized by generally darker coloration.

During late winter or early spring, when water temperatures are on the increase, maturing adult rainbows usually seek out the shallow gravel riffles in suitable clearwater streams. Spawning takes place from late March through early July, depending upon location and severity of winter. The female uses her tail to prepare a redd or nest, four to twelve inches deep and ten to fifteen inches in diameter. From 200 to 8,000 eggs are deposited in the redd, fertilized, and covered with gravel.

Hatching normally takes place from a few weeks to as much as four months after spawning, depending upon water temperature. A few more weeks may be required for the tiny fry to emerge from the gravel. Upon emergence, the small trout assemble in groups and seek shelter along the stream margins or protected lake shore, feeding on crustaceans, plant material, and aquatic insects and their larvae. Rainbow trout rear in similar habitat for the first two or three years then move into larger water of lakes and streams and turn more to a diet of fish, salmon carcasses and eggs, and even small mammals.

Sexual maturity varies between individual fish, due primarily to such factors as population density, productivity of the aquatic environment, and genetic makeup. In the wild, male and female spawners as young as three and five years, respectively, have been found, but the majority of both sexes mature at six to seven years. Spawning frequently ranges from annually to once each three years. Among resident rainbow, those living in or migrating to large lakes with sockeye salmon runs generally grow faster and larger than fish which remain year-round in streams.

Alaska manages rainbow trout fisheries for the health of the species and for a diversity of recreational angling experiences. Wild trout are abundant over most of their range, but daily bag and sex limits are intentionally conservative. Artificial lure-only regulations are commonly used to reduce angling mortality. Many heavily fished waters are closed to trout fishing during the spawning period to further protect these valuable fish. Specific trout waters have been designated catch-and-release or trophy fisheries to help enhance the quality of the fishing experience and preserve an abundance of large fish.

My favorite fall outing is to hike up one of the rivers beyond the normal fishing holes and try virgin water not customarily fished. This provides an economical trip with many of the advantages of an expensive fly-in excursion.

Casting for rainbows on the Talkeetna River.

Steelhead

There are few fish carrying the mystique of the steelhead. Many anglers talk about steelhead, but few actually pursue these sea-run rainbows. Maybe it's poor weather or lack of knowledge that keeps most of us away from open water when sleek, silver-sided rainbow enter or exit their spawning stream.

Steelhead, like Atlantic salmon, may spawn more than once. As these sea-run rainbows return to spawn, they keep growing. Most steelhead overwinter underneath ice and spawn during spring and early summer.

Steelhead in Southcentral Alaska are almost all fall-running fish. A few spring-run trout enter some streams, but most appear in fall. Fall is the time for great steelhead fishing in the Anchor River. Catch-and-release is in effect, and

Alan Kajikawa knows the thrill of fighting and capturing a Kasilof River steelhead. Guide Ken Robertson and Lars Swensen look on.

only artificial lures may be used. Use a woolly bugger, green butt skunk, or purple egg-sucking leech.

Steelhead begin arriving in the Kasilof River the last week in April or first week in May. The Kasilof is developing into a respectable steelhead stream, thanks to the state's steelhead enhancement program. Most successful anglers will enjoy a mixed bag of hatchery and wild stock.

I lived in Alaska for over thirty years before I learned of steelhead fishing on the Kasilof. The Kasilof is an excellent stream for early steelhead. Many fish actually enter the stream under the ice. My first Kasilof steelhead hunting trip was just a few days after the ice went out. We had to cross shore ice and snow drifts to get the boat into the river. It looked like it was going to be cold, but there wasn't any wind, and when the sun came up it carried a good deal of heat. It was rather pleasant. Ken Robertson, my guide, had radiant heaters on board but they weren't required. I've experienced colder, wetter days in the middle of summer.

Ken uses a drift boat for early spring steelhead fishing on the Kasilof. He fishes with 9-foot fly rods and a personally designed and constructed gig on the terminal end. He rows the boat, holding it in place at the top of the holes, and moves back and forth across the water. He claims he covers a good deal more bottom than casting or trolling. According to Robertson, you've got to keep the lure on or near the bottom. Steelhead just won't move very far to strike. The lure must come right to them.

Anglers who want the season's first fish will eventually find the Situk River near Yakutat. Early spring, beginning in April, will find those who can't wait for summer and salmon runs checked into a Yakutat hotel or lodge and climbing over snow drifts to cast.

There are a host of rivers in Southeast Alaska supporting strong steelhead runs but most are difficult to fish because of limited lodging and related services. Maybe you're tough, but I want a cabin and a stove when I fish the Panhandle, especially in spring. There's an operator who uses a comfortable boat for headquarters and cruises the Inside Passage near Ketchikan for steelhead. If desired, clients fish a different stream each day and have the luxury of a warm, dry place to socialize and swap fish stories. The boat comes equipped with hot showers.

I've received reports of steelhead in Prince William Sound, and contrary to published information, even in some Bristol Bay streams.

I'm not a steelheader but I keep hearing how tough anglers are who pursue them. Those who fish for steelhead appear to enjoy the cold and wet as they chase their quarry. If you're a steelheader and enjoy punishing yourself in the pursuit of your sport, here's something you may want to attempt. Kasilof River and Crooked Creek are open to steelhead fishing during late winter and early spring, and fish are over-wintering.

There are two good ways to fish at this time of year. If the weather warms and open water appears, you can try any of the traditional methods. Should the weather remain cold and ice remains on the water, you may want to drill a hole and attempt ice fishing. I suspect there are steelheaders who have already thought about what it would be like to have a steelhead on under the ice. If you attempt to ice fish these two streams or any other flowing water, please be very careful and be sure of the ice thickness before you walk out. I'd like to hear how you do, but don't call me to go with you. I'll just stay by the fire and listen to your fish tales.

ARCTIC GRAYLING

Arctic grayling, *Thymallus arctucus*, is a rare freshwater game fish symbolic of clear, cold streams of northern wilderness. Grayling occur throughout the Arctic as far west as the Kara and Ob rivers in Russia and east to the western

Grayling are often easy to catch, with a tendency to eat almost anything.

A fishing trip in Alaska is standing in crystal-clear water, drifting a fly past a grayling that has never seen anything artificial.

shores of Hudson Bay in Canada. Once common as far south as Michigan and Montana, the arctic grayling has almost disappeared from the northern United States because of over fishing, competition from introduced species, and habitat loss.

Arctic grayling, sailfish of the north, is an elegantly formed cousin of the trout. With its sail-like dorsal fin dotted with large iridescent red or purple spots, it is one of the most unusual and beautiful fish of Alaska. Arctic grayling are generally dark on the back and have iridescent gray sides. They have varying numbers of black spots scattered along the anterior portion of both sides. The adipose, caudal tail, pectoral, and anal fins are dusky brown and the pelvic fins are often marked with pink to orange stripes.

Grayling have evolved many strategies to meet the needs of life in what is often a harsh and uncertain environment. Grayling can be highly migratory, using different streams for spawning, juvenile rearing, summer feeding, and overwintering. In other areas, they can complete their entire life without leaving a short section of stream or lake.

Winter generally finds grayling in lakes or the lower reaches and deeper pools of medium-sized rivers such as the Chena and Gulkana, or in large glacial rivers like the Tanana, Susitna, and Yukon. Their tolerance of low dissolved oxygen levels allow grayling to survive the long winters in areas where many other salmonids would die. With the coming of spring, grayling begin an upstream migration to spawning grounds. Like salmon, grayling faithfully return every year to the same spawning and feeding areas. Grayling spawn for the first time at an age of four or five years and a length of about eleven to twelve inches.

About one month after spring breakup, adult grayling begin their post-spawning migration to summer feeding areas. Depending on where they've spawned, the distance traveled can be up to 100 miles. By the middle of summer, grayling will segregate within a stream according to age and maturity. Older adults will be found in upper reaches of river and stream systems, sub-adults in the middle, and juveniles in the low ends. Grayling fry hatch about three weeks after spawning and tend to occupy the quieter waters near where they were spawned. In early fall, grayling again begin a leisurely downstream migration to reach overwintering areas.

During the Ice Age, grayling survived in unglaciated areas of Alaska in the Yukon River Valley and the North Slope. From there, they've spread throughout Alaska, except Kodiak, Southeast Alaska, and the Aleutians. Grayling have since been stocked into a few lakes in Southeast Alaska and Kodiak Island.

Grayling are generalists in their food habits, but drifting aquatic insects, especially mayflies, stoneflies, and caddis flies are their primary food items. At times, grayling will gorge upon the eggs of spawning salmon, out-migrating salmon smolt, terrestrial insects that have fallen into the water, or even an occasional vole or shrew.

The tendency of grayling to eat almost anything endears them to the angling public. Any fishing technique, including bait, lures, and flies, will work at one time or another. Grayling are especially popular because of their willingness to rise to a dry fly. Fly-fishing techniques for grayling are similar to those used for any trout species.

Grayling are often easy to catch, but, as with other species, the most skilled anglers with the best knowledge of feeding patterns and how to fish the water will be most successful. Generalized insect imitations, such as the dry fly, Adams, and the hare's ear nymph are usually effective patterns for grayling. However, when feeding on specific insects, grayling can be very finicky and the angler will be challenged to match the hatch.

The largest grayling fisheries occur along the road system in interior Alaska, however, larger size fish are generally caught in less heavily fished areas. Over seventy percent of the trophy grayling greater than three pounds registered by the Alaska Department of Fish and Game come from the Ugashik Lake and the river system of Bristol Bay. The state record grayling, twenty-three inches long and weighing four pounds, thirteen ounces, was caught in the Ugashik narrows. Minimum state of Alaska trophy award weight is three pounds.

Grayling are good fish to start youngsters fly-fishing. These fish will frequently take a fly. Often they come out of the water and strike on the way down. Experienced anglers will attempt to set the hook when they see the fish, and pull the fly away. It takes discipline to wait for the bite, rather than when the fish comes out of the water. New, inexperienced fly-fishermen are not so quick to set the hook, and, when what would be a lost fish if angling for other species, allows them to catch grayling.

My son, Jesse, got hooked on fly-fishing while sitting on my shoulders. He wasn't big enough for his own hip boots so he used mine, with me still in them. We were fishing in Otte Lake. He would cast to the right and I to the left. Many times we had an Otte Lake arctic grayling double. He caught a greater number of fish than his limited knowledge of math permitted him to count. A couple of them made breakfast in the camp frying pan. The rest were released to grow bigger and to thrill another angler.

Since Otte Lake, Jesse, now with two boys and two girls of his own, has fished a lot of water and stood in his own hip boots. I trust he recalls his early fishing and other outdoor experiences as he shares similar times with his children.

DOLLY VARDEN CHAR

Dolly Varden char, *Salvelinus malma*, is a widely distributed freshwater fish in Alaska. Dollies spawn in freshwater streams in early fall and often spend their entire lives in freshwater streams and lakes, although in some places they return to saltwater in the spring. Survival depends on maintenance of suitable stream- and lake-rearing areas, especially during winter. Dolly Varden vary greatly in size from less than one pound to over thirty pounds.

These fighting fish readily hit small spinners, single eggs, and salmon roe. Two distinct populations of char are in Alaska. Resident char are those fish which spend their entire life in fresh water. Anadromous char spend their first few years in fresh water and then migrate to the ocean to feed. These fish return annually to spawn in the fall, remain in fresh water through the winter, and then return to the ocean the following spring.

Called a trout, the Dolly is really a char. Char and Dollies are often taken in the same watershed. Fishermen argue which is which. Dollies generally have markings smaller than the pupil of their eye, while arctic char have much larger spots. The debate still continues streamside, and around the fireplace in the lodge. Records for Dollies and char are the same. The state record is nineteen pounds two-and-a-half ounces. Minimum state of Alaska trophy award weight is ten pounds.

Fishing for Dollies on light tackle is great sport. They hit with real intent and fight with fortitude. Because of the size variation in Dollies, an angler may be caught off guard after taking a few small fish and then have a trophy-sized one hit the lure.

If a hooked, trophy-sized fish is heading for a snag or downriver uncontrolled, quickly open the reel's bail or flick the level-wind into free-spool. Once the pressure is off, it often causes the fish to turn around quickly in the current. It's a calculated risk; ofttimes the fish will spit the hook as the pressure is released, but generally it works. As soon as the fish turns, take up the slack and reapply pressure.

I was fishing for reds on the Russian River when the biggest Dolly I've ever hooked took my streamer fly and headed downriver. My cast, using spinning gear, had been in fast water in the legal area just below the falls. The strike and subsequent run was so rapid and unexpectedly strong I lacked time to react. The fish was fifty yards downriver before I realized what had happened.

These Dollies and a silver were taken in Crescent Lake by Dana Dodge.

More from reaction than planning, I opened the bail and let the fish take most of the remaining line. It turned and I quickly took up the slack and began working the Dolly back upriver. Finally it settled in the original hole and I started thinking the fish was mine. As I raised the tip and pulled the line toward shore the fish felt the pressure and repeated its earlier downstream run.

I was ready this time and opened the bail as before. The fish stopped and mocked me by spitting the hook just as I applied pressure. The result was a sinker-weighted line, followed by the red and white blur of a coho fly traveling toward me at mach speed. I ducked and the fly tangled itself in the lower branches of a stream-side spruce tree. The Dolly continued to belittle me by making five quick jumps, and then it was gone. I was left with an empty creel and the memory of one smart, strong Dolly.

My daughter, Carrie, became an official angler on the spit at English Bay. She was fishing in saltwater when a fourteen-inch Dolly took her bait. Only girls display uncontrolled excitement when a fish starts taking out line. She screamed and shouted for her dad's help. Before I could get to her side, she solved the problem by herself. Her method of playing and landing her catch was backing up the beach while hollering her lungs out for her dad's help.

My daughter Kathryn's first fish came to her on a silver fishing trip. Although she caught a legal limit of silvers, her first fish was a Dolly Varden. She was pleased about it, and the fact she out-fished her dad for the day. She wrote a couple of paragraphs in her journal about her feelings and appropriately called it "My Dolly and My Daddy."

Most girls aren't the kind to go and do stuff with their fathers. Well I am the exact opposite. I love doing stuff with my dad and he always has courage to take me fishing. When I say he has courage, I mean I always out-fish him. Even though he knows it, he still takes me. Often we will take bets on the biggest fish, first fish, and most fish. I still out-fish him and always win. Sometimes I think he purposely lets me win, but I still enjoy it.

Every time I win my dad in the fishing bets, he says he is never going to take me again. But as soon as you know it, he is asking me to go with him. Once I went fishing with him and I only caught a small Dolly Varden and still won the bet. Another time when I went with my dad, we stayed at a lodge. We didn't catch anything but we still had fun taking pictures, going for walks, and taking boat rides.

It seems every day my dad and I don't go fishing the weather is kind of gloomy. When we do go, the weather is really sunny and warm. Of course it is always sunny with my dad around. I love my father a lot and I hope you love yours too.

The author took this northern pike from the wing of Jack Hayden's floatplane.

NORTHERN PIKE

Northern pike, the most popular game fish in North America, occurs throughout Central, Western, Interior, and Northern Alaska. Pike are not present on Kodiak Island or in Prince William Sound. Except for a population in five lakes about twenty-three miles east of Yakutat, pike do not occur in Southeast Alaska. They're the only naturally occurring pike in Southeast Alaska and are probably remnant populations that survived only because the most recent glacial advance missed the pike lakes area. Little information is available on the life history and population of these isolated populations.

Catching a large northern pike can be a tremendously exciting and satisfying fishing experience. Pike fishing is becoming a year-round activity for many Alaska anglers. Pike are sought by more and more fishermen as an ice-fishing target. Where opportunities to catch large fish of other species are limited, as in Interior Alaska, pike are popular. A large proportion, more than half, of the statewide harvest of pike is taken from waters of the Tanana River Valley.

Northern pike are relatively long-lived. In the Tanana River Valley, large individual pike exceed twenty years of age and weigh in excess of thirty pounds. There are anecdotal reports of larger fish taken, even an unsubstantiated report exists of a pike weighing seventy-five pounds. Individual fish exceeding twenty pounds are not uncommon in Interior Alaska. For example, pike tend to be heavier for a given length the further north they're found. Inch for inch, Alaska's northern pike are heavier than those from Minnesota or Alberta. Life expectancy tables for northern pike suggest that fewer than one fish in a million reaching one year of age will survive until age twenty-four when it will weigh about thirty-two pounds and exceed forty-eight inches in length. In general, a higher proportion of the oldest and largest northern pike over thirty inches are females, indicating that males grow slower after maturity and have lower survival rates. The state record is thirty-eight pounds. Minimum Alaska trophy award weight is fifteen pounds.

Northern pike reach sexual maturity by the age of four or five, at which time the fish are from sixteen to twenty-two inches in length. Female northern pike generally mature later and at a larger size than males within the age and size ranges mentioned above. Bag and size limits are structured so that fish have an opportunity to spawn at least once before they attain legal size for harvest.

Pike spawn in the spring, typically as the ice is melting from local lakes, sloughs, and rivers in mid-May. Prior to and during spawning, fish congregate in shallow weedy areas, sometimes in coves or backwater areas. Female pike broadcast their eggs, up to 300,000 per female, over aquatic vegetation and other matter. Eggs are adhesive, sticking to vegetation and other materials. Free-swimming fry emerge after about twenty days. Preparatory to spawning, sexually mature fish, primarily females, may spend the late winter and early spring actively foraging for food. Female pike are especially vulnerable to sport fisheries at this time, as well as immediately after spawning.

Radio tracking studies show that pike remain within 200 yards of where they were the day before. Northern pike prefer weedy areas and depths of less than fifteen feet. They're more active during daylight hours and occupy deeper areas during sunny periods than during dark or cloudy intervals. Pike are usually found in deeper locations during storms and windy periods than during calm periods.

Overwintering areas in Interior Alaska are located in main river channels of the Tolovana, Chatanika, and Tanana rivers, not in the shallow lake complexes where oxygen concentrations during the winter are extremely low. After ice break-up, and even before complete ice-out, pike migrate in large numbers from over-wintering areas into the lakes via streams and sloughs draining the lakes. The short Alaska growing season and comparatively cool average temperatures cause slow growth of northern pike in Alaska, but Alaska pike generally live about a third longer than southern populations.

In addition to the Minto Flat area west of Fairbanks, pike occur in the Wood River/Tikchik drainage, along the Kuskokwim and Yukon rivers, and almost every major river system in Interior Alaska. Several lakes in Southcentral have populations of pike.

Pike are a delicious, white-fleshed fish. Filleting pike and rolling the meat in flour or corn meal and pan-frying in butter make a pleasant change to a diet of salmon. Larger pike may be stuffed and baked. Very large pike can be cut into steaks.

Caution should be exercised when removing hooks or releasing pike. Their teeth are designed for cutting and tearing prey. Save your fingers, use pliers.

I accomplished three, "I've never done that before!" things on one pike in a Southwest Alaska lake. It was a windy day. Too windy to fly fish. I was prepared for big pike with a nine-foot, number 9 rod, and a piece of fifty-pound monofilament line as leader. Pike were present, but it was far too gusty to throw a fly.

My companions and I tried to wait out the storm by sitting out of the wind behind a high bank. I'd never caught a pike, and obviously hadn't taken one on a fly. In my fly box was a huge deer-hair mouse fly I'd carried for several years without even a hint of a strike. The longer we stayed behind the bank, the stronger the gusts were and the more restless I became.

More to be doing something, than actually fishing, I set up my rod and put on the old deer-hair mouse. As I approached the lake's edge I raised the rod as far as I could reach and let the fly act like a kite. The wind caught the bulky body of the mouse and carried it and my fly line for thirty yards. I played the line out as far as it would go until it touched the water. The moment it settled on the surface it was violently attacked by a mouse-hating pike.

I yelled, "Fish on!" as loud as I could, but the wind grabbed my words and sent them sailing unheard across the lake. Battling the old Ice Age survivor to the lake's edge, I continued yelling for an audience, but my companions could not hear above the wind.

My first pike lay in shallow water among some reeds. I bent over to remove the hook and remembered their sharp teeth. Not wanting to end up as a casualty, I caught the leader three feet from the fish's mouth and began to pull the fish to shore. As the line's tension increased, the pike flipped it's ugly head from side to side. The motion caused the fish's teeth to act like a buzz saw on my leader. It was severed, and the pike escaped with my deer-hair mouse.

I tried to explain to my fishing partners what I had done, but they would not believe me. They just made jokes and I could not convince them that I had caught a pike on my big deer-hair fly. I crossed my heart and hoped to die but received only a, "Ya sure."

"I'm telling you I got my deer-hair mouse fly out in a fifty-mile-an-hour gale, perhaps the world's singular northern kite fishing event. It was taken by a hungry pike and I brought him to shore, where he escaped with my fly. Honest!"

SHEEFISH

Inconnu, tarpon of the North, known to locals and knowledgeable anglers as sheefish, is a French name meaning unknown. It's found in Alaska from the Kuskokwim River north, throughout the Yukon River into Canada, as well as in Canada's Northwest Territories, and in Asia. The Inconnu is a member of the salmon subfamily, *Coregoninai*, and is the only predator member of the whitefish group in North America. In coastal areas, this fish is anadromous, but has become strictly a freshwater fish in many inland lakes.

Sheefish are aggressive predators. Large spoons, of one ounce or larger, resembling smelt, least cisco, or whitefish, are the best fishing lures. Chrome and gold with prism tape in various colors seem to work best. Lures, such as Krocodile, Little Jewel, Hot Rod and Daredevils that have a lot of flash can be fished slowly on or near the bottom, are definite winners. Irregular variations in the slow, deep retrieve is also effective at times.

Sheefish have a hard, bony mouth and the power to twist cheap hooks into a useless clump of metal. It strikes with an intensity that has the lure deep in its mouth before an angler can normally react. It is best to remove treble hooks and thin-wire hooks from lures before fishing for sheefish, replacing them with an extra-strong single hook with an oversized split-ring. This not only allows uninjured fish to be safely released but also gives better hookups in the hard, bony mouth.

Sheefish spawn in late September or early October. Their upstream migration begins in early spring and may last a few short weeks, as in the Kobuk River, or several months, as in the Yukon River drainage. Other possible rivers are Aniak, Holitna, Hoholitna, and Chatanika. These can produce twenty-five-pound fish, but most will run ten to twenty pounds. Kobuk River produces the largest fish.

Most anglers specifically seeking sheefish choose the Kobuk River. Other watersheds are generally fished as an add-on option by lodges or guides. It's almost impossible to fish for sheefish without the services of a guide, outfitter, or air taxi operator. It may be possible to travel to Kotzebue, which has direct commercial airline service from Anchorage, and then use one of the scheduled daily commuter services to villages along the Kobuk. Prior arrangements should be made with village residents for camping space and assistance.

Sheefish grow slowly. A trophy may be fifteen to twenty-five years old. Almost unfished, other than by locals, sheefish are not a threatened species, but as their popularity increases more pressure will be placed on them. Their flesh is considered by many as the finest, most succulent table fare among all fish. This, combined with their unusual appearance and fighting ability, may lead to an over-harvest. This is one species of fish that anglers have an opportunity to preserve through catch-and-release before regulations restrict fishing, or the stocks dwindle beyond return. Take a trophy if you desire, and perhaps one or two for the table, and release the rest. Super fighting sheefish, tarpon of the North, could well provide generations of fishermen with endless enjoyment if anglers will show a little sporting restraint.

Sheefish is the only recognized Alaska sport fish I haven't taken. I've interviewed many successful sheefish anglers and had the pleasure of presenting two sheefish World Record Line Class awards on my television show. Weather has been my problem. Each time I've attempted sheefish, the elements have conspired against me. Like many years before, I say again this season, this is the one for sheefish. This really is the year!

LAKE TROUT

Lake trout, *Salvelinus namaycush*, are really members of the char family and not a trout at all. They're Alaska's largest freshwater fish, the largest representatives of the char family, and are closely related to Dolly Varden and brook trout.

Lake trout are deep gray in color often with an olive tone. The fish have large, light spots along their sides. They're narrow at the base of the tail and the tail is deeply forked.

Jigging with spoons under the ice is usually productive in winter; however, the best catches of lakers are generally in shallow water immediately after breakup and just prior to freezing. After the water warms up, deep trolling, using spoons, red-eyes or Alaska plugs, is the best way to take lunkers. During summer months, lake trout will be found in deep, cold water.

Lake trout have a body shape similar to that of trout or salmon. They generally have small, light, irregular-shaped spots on a silvery-to-dark-gray background, but color can vary considerably at different seasons and between populations. Males and females are similar, with males having a slightly longer, more pointed snout. Lake trout can be distinguished from other char by the absence of pink spots and their deeply forked tail. The flesh of lake trout varies from creamy white to deep orange.

In Alaska, lake trout are present from the Arctic coast, south to the Alaska Peninsula. They inhabit the deeper, lowland lakes along the central Arctic coastal plain, as well as waters in the Brooks Range and Alaska Range. They're not found in the Yukon-Kuskokwim lowlands or the coastal drainages of Southeast Alaska. Lake trout inhabit clear, mountain lakes in northern Alaska as well as turbid glacial lakes on the north side of the Chugach Range and Kenai Peninsula.

Lake trout prefer large, deep, cold lakes in which they spend their entire lives. Spawning takes place over clean, rocky lake bottoms from September through November. Males reach the spawning sites several days before the females, and use their snouts and fins to clean the substrate. Spawning takes place at night, with peak activity occurring after dusk. Eggs hatch early in the following spring.

Little is known about the early life history of lake trout, which are thought to be reclusive while feeding on plankton during the first few years of life. Spawning occurs for the first time after seven or eight years. Lake trout spawn every other year, or less frequently in northern Alaska, while in some southern populations, such as those on the Kenai Peninsula, spawning may occur annually.

Lake trout growth varies from place to place, depending on diet, water temperature, altitude, and genetics. Alaska lake trout can live longer than forty years. The average ages are around twenty years. The maximum size attained in some Alaska populations probably exceeds fifty pounds, and eight to ten pound fish can be taken in many of the state fisheries. The state record forty-seven-pounder was caught in Clarence Lake in July 1970. Minimum Alaska

Lake Trout are really members of the char family and not a trout at all. The state record is forty-seven pounds.

trophy award weight is twenty pounds.

The lake trout diet varies with age and size of fish, locality, and food availability. Food items commonly include zooplankton, insect larvae, small crustaceans, clams, snails, leeches, several kinds of fish, mice, shrews, and even occasional young birds. When available, lake trout feed extensively on other fish, such as whitefish, grayling, sticklebacks, and sculpin.

A general knowledge of lake trout habits can pay dividends to the angler. In spring, when lake waters are cold, trout can be found near the surface and along the shoreline. As the season progresses, lakers go deeper and finally reside beneath the thermocline. Most successful lake trout anglers use both spinners or spoons while fishing from shore or near inlet and outlet streams. Trolling slowly through deep, colder water layers and along steep rock walls or drop-offs produces good catches of lake trout. Large spoons, often in combination with cut bait, is effective when fishing through winter ice.

Natural mortality is low in most lake trout populations; however, slow growth, alternate-year spawning, and older ages at maturity combine to make lake trout populations susceptible to over-harvest by commercial and recreational fisheries. The practice of good conservation ethics will go a long ways toward ensuring healthy trout populations for future Alaska anglers.

Our video production group was shooting a fireside scene on the shores of Lake Clark one evening. The lake was calm under a clear sky, and a building sunset added the desired effect. The sequence called for two Native Alaskans to explain the history and heritage of the area to a newcomer. Lake Clark is where the lands of the Eskimo and Indian meet.

The video, my favorite, eventually was titled the Kijik Experience. Kijik, in the native tongue, means "at peace with the land," or "at peace with nature." Either meaning fit the occasion as Grandpa Hobson and Uncle Pete drew descriptive pictures in beach sand around the fire. Their student, Cecil, listened as they told of ancient hunting parties and fishing excursions. As the sun dropped below the horizon and the fire turned from flames to embers, the director called it a wrap and turned off the cameras.

Cecil, an avid angler, had noticed lake trout feeding in the shallows near shore. Now dismissed from his acting role, he put on his hip boots, picked up his rod, and waded twenty feet offshore to where he thought the fish would be. He had correctly chosen the site and began picking up lakers and practiced good conservation ethics by releasing them.

As the twilight darkened, I observed the fire dying to an ideal fish-roasting bed of coals. It had been a long time since lunch, and the thought of roasted lake trout prompted me to suggest Cecil keep one for the fire. Almost as I spoke, he began working a good-sized fish toward shore. I waded as far out as my knee-high boots would permit in an attempt to assist the landing of our impromptu dinner. Members of the cast and crew soon gathered and tossed in their words of encouragement.

Cecil worked the fish to my position three yards from shore, and I took hold of the line to steady the fish until I could get a good grip on the fish. As I reached for our would-be dinner, the laker spooked, twisted in a mid-air leap, and gained its freedom. The cheering section on shore quickly turned to hungry hecklers.

Cecil turned back to the fishing hole while commanding instructions over his shoulder for me to go sit by the fire. His attempts to land another laker failed as the fish had moved on and the hole was stone cold. The hungry hecklers continued persecuting me for losing dinner. My feeble attempt to explain that I was only practicing good conservation ethics fell on deaf ears. They would not listen to my catch-and-release tale as the fire turned as cold as Cecil's fishing and we returned to our camp without the benefit of a lake trout snack.

Unknown to me the cameraman had filmed the entire sequence and it eventually became part of the Kijik Experience video. When you see the video I trust you'll agree with me. I was only practicing good conservation ethics of catch-and-release.

HALIBUT

Pacific halibut, *Hippoglossus stenmolepis*, can be found throughout most of the marine waters of Alaska. Halibut are the largest of all flat fishes and are distributed along the continental shelf of the North Pacific from Southern California to Nome, Alaska, and along the coasts of Japan and the Siberia. Halibut are found on or near the bottom over mud, sand, or gravel banks. While halibut have been recorded at depths of 3,600 feet, most are caught at depths of ninety to 900 feet. Halibut generally are in deeper water during winter, where

Jesse Swenson hauling in a halibut near Homer. Many people prefer to use the services of a charter service in hunting halibut.

they spawn at depths of 600 to 1,500 feet during November through March. Following spawning, halibut begin to migrate to shallower coastal summer feeding areas.

Male halibut become sexually mature at approximately eight years old, while females typically are not mature until age twelve. A female can release from one-half million to four million eggs, depending on the size of the fish. After spawning, the eggs float near the bottom and hatch into larvae after approximately fifteen days. These larvae are free-floating and are subject to movements by deep ocean currents. As the larvae mature, they move higher in the water column, where surface currents move them to shallower coastal water. These currents generally carry eggs and larvae in a northwesterly direction.

Bill Bass won the Ketchikan Halibut Derby with this 196-pounder. He was assisted by Dave Ausman.

Halibut larvae begin life in an upright position similar to other fish, with an eye on each side of the head. During metamorphosis, one eye migrates to the other side. Adult halibut have both eyes on one side of their head, one colored eye and one blind, unpigmented eye. Young halibut take on features of adult fish approximately six months after hatching. They now have both eyes on the pigmented, olive-to-dark-brown side of the body, while the underside is white.

Halibut can live up to forty years, grow to over eight feet long, and weigh over 500 pounds. Most sport-caught halibut are eight to fifteen years old and weigh between ten and 100 pounds. Female fish are larger than males. Males seldom exceed eighty pounds. The oldest halibut on record was a forty-two-year-old female. A halibut's age is determined by a bony structure in the inner ear called an otolith. As the fish grows, annual growth rings are formed on the otolith, similar to rings in a tree. Halibut undergo intensive geographic migrations. Fish tagged in the Bering Sea have been caught as far south as the coast of Oregon, a migration of over 2,000 miles.

Halibut are opportunistic carnivore feeders, eating almost anything they can catch. They assume the coloration of the ocean floor background. With only its eyes protruding, it lies motionless on the bottom until prey passes, then leaps to catch its dinner. The best time to fish for halibut is just before, during, and after slack tide when it's easiest to keep bait on or near the bottom, which is the key to successful halibut fishing. A tide book is necessary halibut fishing gear. June through September is the most productive time of year.

These barn-door-sized, tasty flatfish can be found along the Southeastern coastline, and in Kachemak Bay, Cook Inlet, and Resurrection Bay. A forty-inch halibut will weigh about twenty-nine pounds round weight. A sixty-inch fish will be about 108 pounds and seventy-two-inch halibut will tip the scales at around 196 pounds. Minimum Alaska trophy award weight is 250 pounds. The state record is 440 pounds.

Most sources, including Alaska State Department of Fish and Game publications, suggest stout tackle is required. They say to use a five- to seven-foot rod equipped with a level-wind reel holding up to 300 yards of thirty- to eighty-pound test line.

My experience tells me that much of the reason for heavy gear is brought about by the use of heavy gear itself. To land a halibut, an angler must coax the fish to the surface, where it can be dispatched with a gaff, by shooting, harpooning, or combination of these, depending on the size of the quarry. The quicker an attempt is made to bring up a hooked halibut, the more they fight. The natural thing for both angler and halibut to do when a tug-of-war with heavy gear begins is to pull with all their strength and capacity of gear and line. The firmer the angler pulls and more rapid the accent, the harder the hooked halibut resist.

I was in company with Steve Rajeff, world champion caster and avid fly fisherman, when he took a thirty-four-pound halibut on twelve-pound test line. Steve claimed he could have done the deed with six-pound gear. He simply nursed the fish to the surface. Other experienced, knowledgeable halibut anglers I know claim they use light gear and bring their catch to the surface by

Halibut Weight Chart
Relationship Between Length and Weight

Length	Weight	Length	Weight	Length	Weight	Length	Weight
21	3.6	42	34.3	61	114.8	80	276.8
22	4.2	43	37.0	62	1211	81	287.8
23	4.9	44	39.9	63	127.5	82	299.5
24	5.6	45	42.9	64	134.2	83	311.5
25	6.4	46	46.0	65	141.1	84	323.5
26	7.2	47	49.3	66	148.2	86	349.5
27	8.2	48	528	67	155.6	87	362.8
28	9.2	49	565	68	163.3	88	376.5
29	10.3	50	60.3	69	171.2	89	390.6
30	11.5	51	64.3	70	179.4	90	404.9
31	12.8	52	68.5	71	187.8	91	419.7
32	14.2	53	72.8	72	196.5	92	434.8
33	15.7	54	77.4	73	205.5	93	450.3
36	20.8	55	82.1	74	214.8	95	482.5
37	22.7	56	87.1	75	224.3	96	499.1
38	24.8	57	92.2	76	234.1	97	516.2
39	27.0	58	97.5	77	244.3	98	533.6
40	29.3	59	103.1	78	254.7	99	551.5
41	31.7	60	108.9	79	265.4	100	584.3

Data provided by the International Pacific Halibut Commission

pulling gently and slowly. As the word spreads, more and more guides and other bottom fish pursuers are switching to lighter gear, making halibut angling a real sport rather than a pulling contest.

When I hooked a halibut in Yakutat Bay, I tried Steve's method of urging the fish to the top. The guide was sure I was either pulling in a small halibut, crab or bait-stealing cod. He was unprepared when the dark image of a forty-eight-pounder came into view. Later in the day, to the amazement of a surprised guide, I landed an eighty-pounder using the same method. By using lighter gear and coercing the fish to the surface with its cooperation rather than dragging it against its will, halibut fishing, for me, has become an exciting sport instead of bobbing boredom and hard work.

When fishing for halibut, other bottom fish may add to the variety of the catch. Rockfish are probably the most prevalent keeper. They are a variety of the species *Sebastes*, all dwelling in saltwater. They are excellent eating, usually running three to four pounds, but possibly reaching weights to fifteen pounds. The many varieties vary a great deal in coloration, but overall they have a bass-like body, large, rough scales and spines often found along their dorsal fins and gill covers.

Some rockfish are schooling fish. Some are bottom dwellers. As such they are available to sport anglers at many depths. Pieces of herring or other fish flesh work well for bait as do saltwater jigs. Currently, sportfishing regulations have no limit to the number of rockfish you can take.

KING SALMON

Fossilized remains of an ancient sabre-toothed fish, eight feet long and weighing 400 pounds, found in old Oregon sandstone, had two six-inch-long teeth protruding out of its jaw. A large relative of the sabre-toothed salmon still lives. Known as king salmon—*Oncorhynchus tshawytscha*—it is the largest fish encountered in Alaska's fresh water.

The biggest king ever captured was a 126-pounder caught in a fish trap near Petersburg in 1949. This modern cousin to the saber-toothed salmon was 53.5 inches long, had a girth of 38.5 inches, and a tail 17.5 inches across. The current Alaska sportfishing record, a ninety-seven pound, four ounce fish, was taken by Les Anderson in the Kenai River in 1985. Larger fish have been taken, tagged, and released by Alaska Department of Fish and Game biologists. Guides and experienced anglers claim to have hooked even bigger fish, but they busted the line or pulled free and escaped. These same guides and anglers search with the zeal of a religious fanatic in search of the 100-pounder they are sure swims under their boat each season.

The king or chinook is Alaska's state fish and symbol of the north—an over-sized fish for an over-sized state. For many, landing a king is the ultimate fishing experience. Not many active anglers can rest until they have done battle with, and subdued, the king.

In North America, kings may be found all along the Pacific Rim from San

Francisco to Point Hope, Alaska. Asian kings range from Anadry River to Kamchatka and the Japanese island of Hokkaido. Kings only spawn in the United States in 380 rivers. By comparison, pink salmon frequent nearly this number of streams on Kodiak Island alone. Kings only go to big streams, like the Kenai and Susitna rivers in Cook Inlet, Copper River in Prince William Sound, Situk River near Yakutat, and Kvichak, Naknek, and Nushagak rivers in Bristol Bay. Kings spawn close to saltwater in rivers like the Karluk on Kodiak Island, or they may travel 2,000 miles up the king-sized Kuskokwim and Yukon rivers.

Least numerous of the five Pacific salmon, kings in the sea have steel blue backs and heads and silver or white on their sides and bottom when at sea. Kings have large black spots on their dorsal fins, backs, upper sides, and upper and lower lobes of the tail, and a distinct black gum line on the lower jaw. No other salmon has the black gum line. In fresh water they turn bright red, purple, and sometimes black. Males assume the brightest colors, and develop a hooked kype. The generic name, *Oncorhynchus*, means hooked snout.

Kings begin showing up along Alaska's shorelines by mid-March and move to the mouths of their natal streams. Kings first enter freshwater late in May and continue through June and July. Like all Pacific salmon, kings quit feeding when they leave saltwater.

Kings, like all Pacific salmon, die after mating. After becoming exhausted in the mating process, they drift into quiet backwater and die. Their wasted carcasses wash ashore and are picked over by bears, foxes, eagles, and ravens. Only a small percentage of eggs hatch and grow to adulthood and live to return to their spawning streams.

Kings have the longest life cycle of Pacific salmon. Some are mature after only two years, others take as long as seven, and most probably return after four or five years. The longer they remain at sea, the bigger they get. Legendary large second run kings on the Kenai River are six- and seven-year-old fish.

Traveling kings orient themselves by terrestrial landmarks, celestial navigation, and by taking readings off the earth's electromagnetic field. Kings find their natal stream by smell. Each river has a distinctive odor caused by soil, minerals, and supportive makeup of its watershed. By using such clues, kings return to the exact pool in which they were hatched.

Alaska's premier king fishery is the Kenai River on the Kenai Peninsula. Kenai kings arrive in two distinct runs, the first from mid-May to late June, and the second from late June through early August. Other road-accessible Kenai king rivers are the Anchor, Ninilchik, and Kasilof rivers, and Deep Creek. Saltwater fishing for kings is off the mouth of Deep Creek and south to Anchor Point.

North of Anchorage, the Susitna River, and Willow, Montana, Caswell, Little Willow, Sheep, Goose, Sunshine, and Birch creeks have king runs and are accessible by road. On Kodiak Island, remote Karluk and Red rivers receive good king runs. Bristol Bay streams having king runs, include Togiak, Kvichak, Alagnak, Naknek, Nushagak, and Wood rivers. These systems are remote and best fished using the services of a guide, lodge, or outfitter. Kings are also present in Prince William Sound and Southeast Alaska waters.

Again, the state record is ninety-seven pounds four ounces. Minimum Alaska trophy award weight is seventy-five pounds in Cook Inlet and fifty pounds for the rest of the state. These tackle-busters will strike herring or plugs trolled in saltwater, or on the Kenai River. A variety of spoons and spinners, as well as egg clusters can work in freshwater. Many anglers use twenty to thirty-pound test line, though the more adventurous chance lighter tackle.

Battling a king salmon for the first time is an unforgettable event. An angler who has challenged and subdued the noblest of game fish, walks a little taller. He has sampled the ultimate fishing experience.

King salmon are born into the world without knowing their parents and die without meeting their children. This may be the reason why they fight so hard. Perhaps they are mad for being raised orphans and dying before their children are born. At any rate, when hooked they seem to be mad and determined to take it out on the hook. Since the hook is attached to a line connected to a rod and reel held by a thrill-seeking fisherman, the battle for freedom brings sore arms, a tired back, and heart-pounding and stress-erasing recreation.

Often, when the fishing slows up, an unconventional or new method will heat up the action. I was fishing with a guide and the fishing was dead cold. Mike, the guide, was doing everything he could to make it happen, but either the fish were not there or they all had lock jaw.

It was a cold morning, and the lack of action made it seem worse. Mike told us that his dad taught him, "The fishing is always better if you're miserable." Mike said he was uncomfortable, but maybe not miserable enough that the fishing would pick up. "Dad always claimed," Mike said, "that if you're not catching fish, you're too contented. I guess I'll sit on my pocket knife," Mike laughed. "Maybe it'll get better."

Mike took out his knife, put it in his hip pocket, and sat down. He had hardly reached the seat when a king hit, then another, and then another. Three of the four lines out had hook-ups. I fished with Mike after that on several occasions. We always had good luck, and I wondered if Mike was sitting on his knife.

Winter Kings

Think bait, birds, and structure when fishing for feeder kings. Feeder kings, averaging eight to sixteen pounds are caught throughout the winter, which give them their nickname. Winter kings use the food source rich saltwater of Alaska as a giant grocery store. These fish may have been born in any river in the Pacific rim. Tagged fish from Oregon and Canada to Russia have been taken. Many of these fish spend all year in Alaska waters and are caught even in summer by fishermen who mistake them for spawning salmon.

The most important thing to consider when fishing for feeders is where to fish. Most anglers try the spots where they would normally find spawning kings. These fish are here for an entirely different purpose and will be located in areas anglers may not suspect. Spawning fish have a master plan keeping them on a course to their river of birth. Feeders frequent the area just to eat and grow.

Fish for feeder kings around kelp beds where bait is located, or watch for birds feeding on the surface. Where birds are feeding there's generally bait, and where there's bait, usually a predator will be found. If the predator is a king, perhaps he can be captured.

Doing battle and subduing the king salmon, Alaska's largest sportfish, is one of the most rewarding experiences an angler can have.

If a likely feeding spot is located, have each member of the party rig up with different lures, and fish various depths until attracting fish. Different than fishing for migrating fish, where anglers remain in one area and wait for them to come by, feeders must be chased. If a hook-up doesn't occur in a reasonable time, then move to a new spot and start over. Fish areas where water from two directions come together. Fish like to hang out in slower water between these two moving currents and watch the grocery store go by. It's much easier for them to remain in slack areas than to buck the current. In many places, there's a lot of food going by. Fish the outgoing tide.

Mooching and trolling are the two most productive techniques. Mooching is preferred when currents are running or the wind is blowing. Troll during slack tide in quiet bays and backwaters.

Use a two or three shelled-hook rig with 3/0 to 5/0 laser-sharpened hooks and a four- to eight-foot leader. Depending on tide and currents, a two- to six-ounce banana sinker should be attached to the leader. Use fresh herring. Use as fillets, whole, or cut-plug. Hook cut-plugs and fillets so the bait makes a slow roll as it descends and is carried by the current.

Use a depth sounder to look for schools of bait fish. Feeding flocks of sea birds will tell where the fish are feeding. Kings will hit as the bait descends. Lift your rod tip two feet, and drop it quickly, allowing the bait to flutter as it descends. Feeding kings will hook themselves. If a strike doesn't happen on the way down, keep the bait near the bottom and use a jigging action to attract feeding fish.

Jigging below a drifting boat is effective. Let the bait hit bottom, raise the rod tip two feet and quickly drop it. Reel in line slowly and cast again. If kings can't be found, or mooching is slow, try trolling. Use downriggers in deep bays and faster currents. Set the release tight so the king will hook itself. Try different spots and a variety of lures and methods.

Golf-tees, Tee-spoons, and spinners occasionally catch kings, but the best bait is herring. A favorite lure, summer or winter, is a Northern King. TruValue Hardware Store in Homer is the only shop in the state handling the product. It is the most productive lure used for feeder kings. The design of the Northern King keeps hooks from hanging up on kelp and other sea-going snags.

In Kachemak Bay, near Homer, most fishing will be from the surface down to about sixty feet. One good spot to try is just off Gull Island, between Moose Head Point, at the entrance of China Poot Bay. Work along the rocks off Moose Head point at the edge of the drop off. There's an upwelling in the water, off the shelf, where kings like to reside and watch for food. Fish the eddy at the tail end of Gull Island. There's a thirty-foot shelf feeders like to sit on and watch for groceries. You'll probably see birds and bait there, and it's close to the small boat harbor.

Another place is outside the small boat harbor, just in the mouth of the harbor. The water flooding out of the bay meets the current coming out of the harbor and creates a slack water area ideal for king feeding. Birds and bait may not be seen in this area but stop there on your way out and try a few passes. It may save going on a longer run and give more time for fishing. If fish are not connected with here after giving it a good going over, move on to other spots.

In addition to Kachemak Bay near Homer, saltwater in Prince William Sound's Orca Inlet near Cordova is a good place to try for feeder kings. Many areas in Southeast Alaska boost good locations for feeder kings. Generally the weather in Southeast Alaska is more mild than in Southcentral Alaska. The season can be lengthened and the fishing is more comfortable.

Feeding kings are a fine-tasting fish. They're in the prime of their life cycle. Catching these fish not only provides an opportunity to fish year-round in open water, but they're also great table fare. As the decision of where to go is made, think bait, birds, and structure when fishing for winter kings.

SILVER SALMON

Silver salmon, *Oncorhynchus kisutch*, are found in coastal waters from Dixon Entrance in Southeastern to Point Hope on the Chukchi Sea. They also occur up the Yukon River to the Alaska-Yukon border. Silvers, or coho, are characterized by their aggressive behavior. Juveniles can hatch and grow in almost any type of rearing environment. Adults feed on a variety of food organisms and grow extremely rapidly during their 1.5 years of ocean residency.

Adult silvers may grow up to weights of thirty-six pounds and lengths of thirty-five inches. An average full-sized adult will usually be about ten pounds and twenty-nine inches long. They're most easily distinguished from other

The Talkeetna River yielded this silver salmon.

species of salmon by several features. Silvers have a light-gray gum line, and black spots usually appear only on the upper lobe of the tail. Compared to king salmon, silvers are wider at the base of their tails. In stages of spawning coloration, both sexes turn dark, with a maroon-reddish color on their sides; males develop a pronounced hooked snout with large teeth.

Silvers enter spawning systems during periods of peak high water. Adults school in pools, ponds, or lakes for several weeks until ripe then move into shallow tributaries with clean gravel riffle areas to spawn. Spawning frequently takes place at night when females dig a depression by turning on their sides, using rapid body and tail motion. Females protect their nest area, and males frequently chase and combat each other for occupancy of this same area.

Spawning takes place when a male moves close beside the female, and the body vibrations simultaneously induce egg deposition and sperm emission. This spawning takes place from late September through January, with spawned-out silvers appearing in some streams as late as March.

Eggs develop slowly during cold winter months, hatching in early spring, with the embryo remaining in gravel until emerging in May or June. Young fry school in shallow areas along stream shorelines where they dart out to feed on adult surface insects or drifting insect larvae, which constitute its principal source of food. Juveniles spend one, two, or three winters in fresh water before migrating to sea as a smolt in early spring.

Last of the five species of Pacific salmon to enter Alaska rivers each year, they are not as large as kings, but silvers make up for the difference by their

Good scenery, good fishing. This silver was taken in Crescent Lake by Dana Dodge.

willingness to aggressively strike a lure or fly. They're the major sport fish in the state from July through October and are spectacular fighters and the most acrobatic of Pacific salmon.

In many areas of Alaska, silvers enter fresh water as early as July, with peak runs occurring in August. Silvers, as with all anadromous species, are not on a strict timetable, and runs can vary by a week or two.

Another wonderful attribute of silver salmon is their lack of preference for particular lures or flies. Spin fishermen do well with an assortment of spoons and spinners in different sizes and colors. Chartreuse and pink Pixies are popular. My favorite is an orange fluorescent Daredevil. A medium-weight rod, sporting a quality-made, mid-sized spinning reel, holding 150 yards of ten- to twelve-pound test monofilament will do.

Fly-fishermen use a seven- or eight-weight rod and a quality-made, single-action fly reel. A floating line on one spool and a fast sinking tip line on an extra spool will fill the bill. Silver salmon are tough on flies. Bright, flashy patterns like the wiggle-tail, flash fly, and outrageous, tied on a size two or larger hook, and weighted, are best for bottom-hugging silvers.

Silvers are often spooked by numerous casts into their holding water, and will often hold in water close to or beyond the obvious hole. When fishing a crowded pool, or if a number of casts have turned the fishing cold, try casting to water immediately above or below the main crowd or conspicuous holding area.

Once, while fishing the mouth of the Talachulitna River, the fishing stopped dead cold. My guide got nervous when his client ceased catching fish. He suggested we move across Skwentna River and try the mouth of Shell Creek.

Shell Creek is a small stream draining Shell Lake. It enters the Skwentna River 300 yards downriver from the mouth of the Tal River and on the other side of the river. A sandbar in the Skwentna at the mouth of Shell Creek grows and recedes with the season. Sometimes it nearly blocks the passage of Shell Creek. When this happens a small lake develops behind the sandbar, and at times this lake becomes a shallow-water holding area for traveling silvers.

My guide led me to the sandbar and the mouth of Shell Creek. Another party was already fishing the hole and had hit it pretty hard for nearly an hour. There was fish there, but they wouldn't bite. My guide moved me around a stand of trees, now in three feet of water, because of the sandbar growth. He pointed to a patch of water I would never have fished had I not been directed to do so. For an hour, I caught silvers, one after another. Meanwhile, the other group left the good, but now unproductive hole.

When our upper spot behind the trees cooled down, the lower hole was ready for another try. Thirty or more silvers cruised around and across the forty foot diameter pool. I again followed the guide's instruction and connected time and time again. The afternoon proved to be one of my most productive silver days.

From my home, I can see Mt. Susitna and the Alaska Range beyond. Somewhere between Susitna and the perennial snow-covered peaks of the Alaska Range flows a little stream out of Shell Lake. Although I can't see it from my home, I know it's there, and when fall comes I hope to be the first to warm up the mouth of Shell Creek.

RED SALMON

Oncorhynchus nerkus, red salmon, a beautiful fish in saltwater, is the color of chrome-bright, polished silver. During spawning in freshwater they take on a green or olive head and deep red body, giving them the nickname of Green Head. The male assumes a brilliant scarlet color with a pronounced hump on its back. The earliest species to arrive in spring, reds are powerful fighters and sought after more than any other species of salmon. They will take spoons but will answer to flies more readily. The state record is sixteen pounds. Minimum Alaska trophy award weight is twelve pounds.

Reds or sockeyes migrate to stream and lake systems from Southeast Alaska to the Aleutians, and north in the Bering Sea to Point Hope. Reds spawn in streams running out of lakes, seldom spawning in a stream not flowing from a lake, or in a lake itself. Stream-spawned red fry require a lake to spend their first year or two.

From the last week in May through mid-August, they move up rivers and streams to their spawning grounds. The female turns on her side, undulating her tail and body to excavate a nest up to a foot deep and four feet long. Then a dominant male, waiting nearby until the female builds the nest, rubs the dorsal fin of the female with his body and nudges her gently on the side with his nose. Then, they move into the nest and release their eggs and milt.

The female moves upstream and builds another nest while the male courts other females. Material from the new nest covers the fertilized eggs in the previous nest. The female's 3,000 to 4,000 eggs may take three to five nests and several days to deposit. About a week after spawning both die.

Six to nine weeks after fertilization the eggs hatch and the alevins live off their yolk sacs in gravel nests until April or May. They then move from the gravel, as fry, to a lake where they live for a year or two. In May or June, the fry move to the sea as smolts. Traveling mostly at night, they cover up to five miles per day. Once in saltwater reds hang close to shore feeding on water fleas and insects. The major food of young sockeye is minute planktonic crustacia. The first gill arch in the throat region of the fish has thirty to forty long, fine gill rakers which strain the food organisms from the water passing through the gills. Adult salmon stop feeding upon reentry to fresh water.

No one knows how salmon find their way back to the stream of their birth after their oceanic journeys. Speculation is that they use submerged, terrestrial landmarks and even celestial navigation. They home in on their natal stream by the distinctive odor caused by the soil, mineral, and vegetative makeup of their home water.

Red salmon have no spots, but may have a fine pepper-like speckling. They are generally smaller than chinook, coho or chums, and larger than pinks, averaging six to eight pounds. There are six to ten dark, oval parr marks on the sides that are about the same length as the width of the eye. The parr marks barely extend below the lateral line and are irregularly spaced along the side of the body.

Occasionally, a segment of red salmon fail to migrate to sea. This may occur out of choice or a physical barrier may prevent the normal seaward migration. When this occurs, a landlocked population of red salmon called kokanee may develop. These fish exhibit all the physical characteristics of red salmon except for size; kokanee rarely exceed fourteen inches in length. The life history of these landlocked salmon is the same as their anadromous counterparts; however, the ocean phase of their life cycle is absent. Kokanee salmon, highly valued as a sport fish, have been introduced into many lakes in Alaska.

Each year more and more people take up the challenge of fishing for reds. They're rewarded by fast action, beautiful scenery, and excellent eating. Reds are the most difficult salmon for the sport fisherman to catch, because they most often will not take bait or lures. Colorful streamer flies and small lures fished very slowly work best. The Russian and Kenai rivers on the Kenai Peninsula are two of the few places where reds will take lures and flies.

The Russian River was the site of my earliest Alaska fishing excursions nearly four decades ago. The legal limit was six fish per day with a two-day possession limit. Every other day during the run we would drive to the Kenai Peninsula after work and walk the two miles to our favorite hole on the Russian. Having great confidence in our ability to fish and the river's capacity to provide, we'd build a fire. Once the fire was set, we'd break out our rods.

The fish were stacked on top of each other and it didn't take long to bring the

The author took this red in the Togiak River.

first salmon in. Whoever was fortunate enough to draw first catch would immediately clean the fish, wrap it in foil, and put it under the coals of the fire. We'd fish for a couple of hours, and fill our limit.

By then the fire would be just a warm spot on the ground in the center of a circle of rocks. The foil wrapped around our first caught salmon was now blackened by the coals. Someone would fish it out with a stick and unwrap the package. We'd lay the perfectly cooked red out on a log, and everyone would help themselves to gourmet "red a la riverbank."

Next, we'd throw sleeping bags under one of the giant spruce trees crowding the shore and a take a couple hours of sleep. With the coming of dawn, the "cast, hook, play, land, clean, and put in the pack" process began. When the new day's limit was stored, each would shoulder packs and hike to the car for the drive home. A day later we'd repeat the process and continue until we felt we had enough to provide our family with required steaks, roasts, fillets, and kippered and smoked salmon.

The Russian River, thirty years ago, was mostly a subsistence fishery for local anglers. It was thought by most fishermen that reds would not take a fly or lure and must be snagged. Alaska Department of Fish and Game published regulations detailing what constituted a legal or illegal lure. Basically, the distance between the point of the hook and the shank had to be smaller than .5 inch, and no weight could follow the hook.

About the time I came on the scene, there were a few anglers beginning to learn that reds would indeed take a fly, if properly presented. I became an early disciple, preferring to use traditional fly-fishing gear; however, most anglers today use spinning gear with a fly as terminal tackle.

A medium to heavy spinning rod with fifteen- to twenty-pound test line is used. The angler faces the stream and casts upstream at a forty-five degree angle. They retrieve the line to tighten and keep the hook four to ten inches off the bottom. The current bows the line and exerts an inshore and downstream force, which helps draw the line to a fish's mouth. When the line gets caught in a fish's mouth, they lift the rod and tighten the line, bringing the hook into the fish's mouth. When the pressure is firm, they set the hook and the battle is on.

My son, Blake, went from spectator to angler with a Russian River red. He was too small for hip waders and did his casting from shore. Like most kids his attention span was short and he did a lot of fire stoking and rock throwing. He enjoyed helping Dad clean the fish and wrapping them for transporting home. He was one of the first to sample a streamside cooked red when the foil was taken off, and he would graze on the delicacy until it was gone.

Late one evening he managed to hook a red. The fish gave a spectacular battle. The several other anglers in the area backed out of the river and let Blake play and land his fish. One fisherman picked up his net and offered to help Blake. Between the two of them they were able to bring the fish to shore. Then it was discovered that it was foul hooked. The crowd of spectators was disappointed. So was Blake.

The man with the net told Blake, "Nobody cares if you keep this fish. Go ahead and keep it." He then laid the net down with the fish still trapped in it. Blake looked at me. His eyes asked the questions he didn't say. "Should I keep it?" I didn't comment but went back to my fishing. Blake removed the hook and turned the net inside-out, allowing the fish to swim away. The small crowd of anglers gave a hearty cheer for the young sportsman's act of outdoor etiquette. I don't think anyone fishing the Russian for reds that night considered keeping a foul-hooked fish.

PINK SALMON

Pink salmon, *Oncorhynchus gorbuscha*, also known as humpback or humpy, acquires a very pronounced hump on the back of the adult male before spawning. Pink salmon, found from Ketchikan to Kotzebue Sound, contribute substantially to the catch of sport anglers. Pinks are the smallest of Pacific salmon, averaging about four pounds and twenty to twenty-five inches in length. The state record is twelve pounds nine ounces. Minimum Alaska trophy award weight is eight pounds.

Returning adult fish are bright, steel blue on top with silvery sides with large black spots on the back and tail fin. The scales are small and the flesh is pink. Approaching spawning streams, the bright appearance of the male is replaced by a brown to black back and a white belly. Females become olive green with a light-colored belly. By the time males enter spawning streams, they have

Reeling in a pink salmon on the Susitna River. Eva Eckman decided to release this one.

developed the characteristic humpback and hooked jaws. Juvenile pink salmon are silvery without the dark vertical bars of the young of other salmon species.

Adult pink salmon enter Alaska spawning streams between late June and mid-October. Different runs with differing spawning times frequently occur in adjacent streams or even within the same steam. Most pink salmon spawn within a few miles of the coast, and spawning within the intertidal zone at the mouth of streams is very common. Female pinks dig a nest or redd with their tail and release their eggs into the nest. The eggs are immediately fertilized by one or more males and then covered by further digging action of the female. The process is repeated until all the eggs have been released. After spawning, the adults die, usually within two weeks.

Eggs hatch sometime during winter, and in spring they outmigrate to saltwater. Following entry into saltwater, juvenile pink salmon move along beaches in dense schools near the surface, feeding on plankton, larval fishes, and insects. Predation is heavy on the small, newly emerged fry, but growth is rapid. When one year old, juveniles are four to six inches long and move into ocean feeding grounds in the Gulf of Alaska and Aleutian Islands. Pink salmon almost invari-ably mature in two years.

A good pink spot may have been responsible for the cliche, "There were so many fish, you could have walked across the stream on their backs." They're excellent fighters on light tackle, taking a lure or fly without partiality. Pinks are an outstanding fish for kids and novice anglers. It can be fairly easy to catch a pink by casting small lures at the mouth of a spawning stream. Small Daredevils or Mepps lures are proven lures for these small, but tasty, salmon.

I was fishing a hole with a group of fishermen from Texas. It was in holding water less than 100 yards from the ocean. Hundreds of fish were trying to occupy the same spot in the stream at the same time. At first, my Texas friends were fascinated by their good fortune at being able to hook at least one fish on every cast. If a fish took the hook and got off, another would immediately take its place, or the escaped fish would bite again. After an hour of every-cast-a-fish fishing, they stopped for a snack. During the break, they conjured up a contest to see who could cast across the hole and get their lure back without bringing in a fish. It was late afternoon before a member of the group won the contest. I learned that catching a fish on every cast is far more boring than getting skunked all day. At least when I go fishless, I always think that the next cast is the one, and I look forward to the strike. A fish on every cast soon loses its appeal when the thrill of anticipation is gone.

The Texans finally noticed a shallow place off the main stream where a few pinks were swimming. One of the group broke out his fly rod and began casting to a single fish. The fish refused his every offer, and at once the challenge of fishing returned. Finally his target struck the fly, making a couple of air-borne jumps when the line tightened. He yelled, "Fish on!" and the thrill of ordinary fishing returned, replacing the mundane fish-on-every-cast boredom of the morning.

CHUM SALMON

Chum Salmon, *Oncorhynchus keta*, have the widest distribution of any of the Pacific salmon. Chum salmon are the least utilized of all Pacific salmon. They're often called dog salmon because native Alaskans use this fish to feed their dog teams during winter. Due to their size, many fishermen refer to chum as the little king. Ocean fresh chum salmon are metallic greenish-blue on the dorsal surface with medium-sized black speckles. They're difficult to distinguish from sock-eye and coho salmon at this time without examining their gills. Chum have fewer but larger gillrakers than other salmon.

Holding a chum salmon caught in the Alagnak River.

The state record for chum salmon is thirty-two pounds. Minimum Alaska trophy award weight is fifteen pounds.

Chum salmon often spawn in small side channels and other areas of large rivers where upwelling springs provide excellent conditions for egg survival. They also spawn in many of the same places as do pink salmon, such as small streams and intertidal zones. Chums in the Yukon River travel over 2,000 miles to spawn in the Yukon Territory. These have the brightest color and possess the highest oil content of any chum salmon when they begin their upstream journey.

Chum salmon spawning is typical of other Pacific salmon, with the eggs deposited in redds located primarily in upwelling spring areas of streams. Female chum lay as many as 2,700 eggs. Chum do not have a period of freshwater residence after emergence of the fry as do chinook, coho, and silver salmon. Chums are similar to pink salmon in this respect, except that chum fry do not move out into the ocean in the spring as quickly as pink fry. Chum fry feed on small insects in the streams and estuaries before forming into schools in saltwater, where their diet usually consists of zooplankton.

By fall, they move into the Gulf of Alaska, where they spend one or more winters of their three- to six-year lives. In Southeastern Alaska, most chum salmon mature at four years of age, although there is considerable variation in age at maturity between streams. There is also a higher percentage of older chum in the northern areas of the state. Chum vary in size at maturity from four to over thirty pounds, but usually range from seven to eighteen pounds, with females usually smaller than males.

Sport fishermen only occasionally hook chum salmon in saltwater, and usually as they're trolling for other Pacific salmon. After entering fresh water, chum are seldom highly palatable unless smoked. In the Yukon and other rivers in Arctic Alaska, however, chum salmon remain an important year-round source of fresh and dried fish.

While fishing for chum salmon, my son, Alan, tied a handful of Las Vegas Showgirl flies for our use. The Showgirl is my favorite chum fly. As we approached the river Alan said, "Dad, throw me your line and I'll tie a Showgirl on for you."

I flipped the line's end to Alan, and he tied on the fly. We could see chums rolling in a stretch of slow water behind a big rock. I made a couple of casts before the freshly tied Showgirl did its work. The chum hit hard and headed for fast water beyond the protection of the big rock. As the fish turned in the current, the hook pulled loose. No matter, the hole was choked with fish.

I returned to the hole, offering the Showgirl to any takers. Several fish accepted my invitation, struck the hook and quickly dove for fast water. Each time a fish bit the hook, it escaped as the first one did. They'd strike, immediately put pressure on the line as they moved away into the swift water, and then, as they turned facing me, they spit the hook.

Finally, Alan, having observed the action, shouted above the sound of the rushing river water, "Dad, why don't you check your hook. It looks like it may be dull."

I reeled in the line and looked at the new-made Showgirl. It was a perfectly tied fly, complete with shiny, metallic-looking streamers that give the fly its name. I noticed something peculiar with the hook, however. The point was missing. There was just enough bend for an attacking chum to get a grip on the fly, but with the point gone there was not enough angle to penetrate a chum's hard mouth, especially with the sharp point of the hook gone.

At first I suspected that I'd caught the fly on a rock, and the hook's point had broken off. I couldn't remember getting snagged, and I examined the fly closer. The metal showed signs of sabotage as the markings of cutters were clearly visible. Alan kept on fishing and didn't even look my way.

"Alan, you vandal, you cut off the point of my hook."

"Dad," he said, hiding a grin, "I wouldn't do a thing like that." He never admitted to the vandalism, always claiming his innocence.

ALASKA'S SHELLFISH

Not normally classified as fishing, digging for clams or bringing in crab or shrimp provides sportsmen with tasty table fare and can break up the monotony of landing too many fish. Nearly all Alaska saltwater is home to shrimp, crab, or clams. All three may be taken in the same area. Like saltwater fishing, you never know what will be caught.

Razor Clams

Razors are long, narrow clams, sometimes growing to seven inches in length. Species of razors differ mainly in coloration and length of siphon. In Cook Inlet, in Southcentral Alaska, one species is found close to the sand surface, the other is deeper. They are equal in eating quality.

Clam Gulch is one of the most popular places to go clam digging. Shovels and buckets are the usual tools, and clam guns are also popular. Clams can be located by watching the damp sand for small siphon holes. Low tide is the best time to dig.

After capturing clams, and before eating, wash off all surface sand with sea water. Cover clams with clean sea water or two percent brine, one-third cup of salt to one gallon of tap water, and let stand for fifteen to twenty minutes to allow the clams to cleanse themselves of sand. Saltwater is necessary if clams are to open and discharge sand, which will then settle to the bottom of the container.

Butter clams at low tide on Kachemak Bay.

Kachemak Bay treats a clam digger to the makings for chowder and a panoramic view.

Change the water and let stand for fifteen to twenty minutes for two or three times. This step is important if clams are to be eaten from the shell or steamed.

In addition to clam chowder, successful diggers either fry or steam their catch. To fry clams, cover meat with flour, then dip in beaten egg, and roll in cracker crumbs. Fry in hot oil or butter, one minute on each side—no more. Drain on paper towel and serve hot.

To steam clams, use an inch or more of salt water in a large covered pan and bring to a boil. Place scrubbed clams in the water. They don't need to be covered with water. Return to boiling. Steam five to ten minutes or until shells open. Remove from the water. Don't overcook. Pick meat from shells with a fork. Dip in melted butter. Eat while hot. The broth or nectar from clams can be strained to remove sand particles.

Harvest only from certified beaches. Observe all TV, radio, and newspaper announcements concerning paralytic shellfish poison.

Abalone

Pinto abalone, *Haliotis kamischatkana*, the only species found in Alaska, is abundant along the outside coastal waters of Southeast Alaska from Dixon Entrance to Icy Straits. Abalone are marine snails, and related to clams, oysters, mussels, and squids. Pinto abalone is one of the smallest species of abalone. It grows to six inches in length, but is rarely found longer than 5.5 inches. The oval shell contains four to six holes, has an exterior of mottled colors, and is covered with sea growth which is similar to the surrounding habitat.

The shell interior of an abalone is an iridescent mother-of-pearl, which is pure on small abalone; larger specimens usually have a muscle scar or some discoloration. The shell muscle, or edible portion, is creamy-white in the center, mottled orange on the sides, and a deeper orange on the bottom of the foot.

Tentacles are attached around the entire foot. When the abalone is disturbed, the muscle and foot contract and adhere to the rock with such force the shell can be broken or torn completely off without releasing the hold of the foot. A small pry, such as a butter knife, works well to dislodge abalone.

Pinto abalone require the influence of deep ocean swells as they're not found far from the outside coast. They can be found in thick kelp beds and clinging to cracks and crevices in rocks where surging waves can't easily dislodge them. On more exposed islands and rocks, they're generally found on the lee side, where they can maintain their hold during violent wave action. In deeper water, they're found exposed in rocky boulder patches near kelp beds and sandy bottoms. Abalone can be hand-picked during extreme low tides but most are found from the low-water mark to about minus twenty to forty feet.

Abalone, called abs, are considered a gourmet food and are highly esteemed by those who relish their distinctive flavor. Pinto abalone, being of small size, are especially tender and have a delicate flavor all their own.

Dungeness Crab

Dungeness crab, *Cancer magister*, is a popular shellfish that inhabits bays, estuaries, and the near shore coast of Alaska. Dungeness crab is named after one of its representative habitats—a shallow, sandy bay inside of Dungeness Spit on the south shore of the Straits of Juan De Fuca that separates Washington and Vancouver Island. It's widely distributed, however, and can be found as far north as 61 North Latitude (Cook Inlet, Prince William Sound) and south to Magdelena Bay, Mexico.

Dungeness crab have a broad, oval body covered by a hard, chitinous shell, and two of its ten legs have large pincers. This species can be distinguished from other crab because its legs are much smaller and shorter in relation to its body size, and its abdominal flap is symmetrical instead of asymmetrical.

A Dungeness crab can be over 6.5 inches in shell width and can weigh between two and three pounds. A large male dungeness crab can exceed nine inches in shell width. The estimated maximum life span is approximately eight years or more.

Dungeness crab are widely distributed sub-tidally and prefer a sandy or muddy bottom in salt water. However, they are tolerant to salinity changes and can be found in estuarine environments. They're most abundant in waters less than ten fathoms, but they've been found in depths down to 100 fathoms.

Crab scavenge along the sea floor for organisms that live partly or completely buried in the sand. They're carnivores, and their diet can include shrimp, mussels, small crab, clams, and worms.

Residents of Alaska may harvest Dungeness crab for personal use. This fishery is often incidental to recreational boat outings. Crab pots similar to those used in the commercial fishery, ring nets, diving gear, dip nets, and hooked or

Shrimp, crab, and clams round out the catch at Kachemak Bay.

hookless hand lines can all be used to harvest crab for personal use. Dungeness crab are sometimes stranded by minus tides and can be picked up by observant beachcombers. Be forewarned, the mighty pincers of this crab can move quickly and catch you unaware!

Personal-use fishermen fish at depths between three and twenty fathoms, where more keepers, male crab greater than 6.5 inches wide, seem to be found. They usually bait their pots with the most convenient baits, fresh carcasses. The number of crab that can be kept varies from five to twenty per person, depending on what area is fished.

There are two good methods of cooking crab. Both methods require a large pot of seawater boiling over a constant source of heat. The first method is to cook the crab in boiling salt water for twenty minutes, and then cool it quickly, remove the back, and wash away the gills and internal organs. The second method is to butcher and clean the crab, then cook the two sections in boiling salt water fifteen minutes.

King Crab

King crab have tails, or abdomens, that are distinctive, fan-shaped and tucked underneath the rear of the shell. They also have five pair of legs; the first bears their chelipeds (pinchers or claws; the right claw is usually the largest on the adults), the next three pair are their walking legs, and the fifth pair of legs are small and normally tucked underneath the rear portion of their carapace (the shell covering their back). This fifth pair of specialized legs are used by adult females to clean their embryos (fertilized eggs) and the male uses them to transfer sperm to the female during mating.

Since a crab's skeleton is its shell, made mostly of calcium, it must molt its shell in order to grow. Juveniles molt many times in the first few years, then less frequently until they reach sexual maturity in four to five years. Adult males will often not molt every year, but frequently they'll skip a molt and keep the same shell for several years. King crab may weigh as much as twenty-four pounds, and live to twenty to thirty years old. The male's leg span may be nearly five feet across.

Clean the crab, then boil or steam the legs, in either salted or unsalted water for twenty to thirty minutes, and either eat the meat hot or cold, plain or with butter and garlic or seafood sauce; or use the meat in salads, in sandwiches, or in various dishes. Some people prefer to split the legs open and broil them.

Shrimp

Pandalid shrimp are among the few animals that exhibit protandours hermaphroditism, ie, each individual spends the early mature part of its life as a male and later transforms into a female for the balance of its lifetime. For example, a pink shrimp will typically mature sexually as a male, spawn one or more times, pass through a short transitional phase, and subsequently mature and spawn as a female.

Lightweight pots are fished from boats to collect personal-use shrimp. Small subsistence fisheries occur statewide.

Shrimp can be cooked many ways, though boiling in salted water for a few minutes is the preferred method for small shrimp. Shrimp can be split or butterflied and broiled with butter and garlic for a lobster-like feast.

CATCH-AND-RELEASE

Millions of salmon are taken for food by Alaska sport fishermen each season. The catch by Alaska's anglers represents less than one percent of the salmon harvest. Salmon, a reliable, renewable, and enjoyable food resource, isn't heavily impacted by sportfishing. With increased fishing pressure in many watersheds, wild stocks of sheefish, steelhead, lake trout, rainbow trout, arctic char, northern pike, arctic grayling, cutthroat trout, and Dolly Varden char, require a different approach than when harvesting abundant, renewable, salmon.

Angling tradition dictates killing the legal limit of fish as a gauge of the success of the angling outing. While salmon can sustain legal-limit harvests, wild stocks of slow-growing, native fish can't survive if anglers maintain a kill-your-limit mentality. To preserve the resource, it's imperative that the large-sized, brood stock of resident fish be released to perpetuate the numbers. Alaska anglers who kill these fish are destroying their own future angling opportunities.

Catch-and-release goes beyond what's legal. It represents a person's angler ethics, his personal code of behavior.

While releasing mature fish to reproduce, many anglers enjoy eating the variety of species Alaska offers sportsmen. One of the benefits of fishing is to be able to enjoy a streamside lunch of fresh-caught fish, or to take the catch home to share and savor later. A person's catch-and-release philosophy could include harvesting and eating smaller, generally more tasty fish. Those who enjoy eating fish for pleasure or for health, add to their pleasure by limiting their kill to pan-sized fish, and releasing larger, mature fish to provide for another angler's enjoyment.

Catch-and-release begins long before anglers put on their waders and make the day's first cast. Catch-and-release is more than periodically letting a fish go. Catch-and-release requires the use of correct terminal tackle and knowledge of how to fight, handle, and release fish. It means an inner commitment to maintain Alaska's wild fish resources for all anglers. Catch-and-release is a way anglers can directly impact their sport while enjoying it. It is the best way to provide additional sportfishing opportunity, to preserve wild stocks of fish, to develop trophy fish stocks, to relieve pressure on specific stocks, and to help maintain good fishing for all, now and in the future.

Catch-and-release goes beyond what's legal. It represents an angler's ethics, his personal code of behavior. It involves how one acts when no one is watching and how one obeys the law. An ethical angler would never crowd in on other fisherman, or enter private property without permission. An ethical angler is courteous, with a concern for the well-being of all, and his own long-term impact on natural resources. An ethical angler never leaves litter or uses crude, vulgar, or abusive language when others are present. Many fishermen have learned that catch-and-release is one of their highest outdoor ethics. In adopting a catch-and-release ethic, they learn to appreciate their sport and the environment more, and they no longer need to kill or even catch large numbers of fish to have a successful angling outing. To paraphrase Trout Unlimited, "Wild fish are too important to catch only once."

My son, Alan, then four years old, and I were fishing the Swanson River from our homemade, twelve-foot boat rightly christened Miss Shapen. It was his first trip. Alan fished without a bite for a few minutes, when a small Swanson River rainbow, took the single egg and retreated to cover. In one motion, Alan set the hook and jerked the fish into the boat. The excitement of landing his first fish caused him to trip over the tackle box, kicking lures across the bottom of the boat. He stumbled on the seat and fell into my lap. Quickly recovering, he searched the boat bottom and found his catch between the wooden slats.

To the eyes of a four-year-old, the five-inch rainbow looked like a trophy catch. He looked up at me and asked if he could keep it. I told him that we normally released fish that small, but he could decide for himself. He considered for a moment and then put the fish back in the water.

Alan, now a father of five, has fished many parts of the state since the day he released his first fish over the gunnel of Miss Shapen. He's captured and released many species and a host of fish—released them because they were too small, too big, or too many. Alan may have been too young to even remember the experience, but I remember, and am proud of the young man who, at an early age, displayed a mature outdoor ethic and appreciation for God's handiwork.

How to Correctly Release a Fish
- Land the fish quickly. Do not play it to exhaustion.
- Avoid removing the fish from the water.
- Don't touch the fish if possible.
- Keep hands away from and do not touch the gills.
- Handle the fish gently. Never squeeze the fish.
- Back the hook out. Remove the hook with pliers or similar instrument.
- If the fish is hooked deeply, cut the line close to the hook and leave the hook in place.
- Revive the fish by gently supporting it in the current with the head pointing upstream. Maintain the fish in this position until it swims on its own.

Fish Identification Chart

Large, flat fish with both eyes on right side of head, small scales, arched lateral line, dark color on top, white on bottom. **Halibut**

Stout, bass-like body, single spiny dorsal fin, some brightly colored, anal fin has three strong spines. **Rockfish**

Freshwater. Double dorsal fin, second fin elongated, barbel under jaw. **Burbot**

Anal fin has 13 or more rays. **Salmon**

Fish with no adipose fin.

Adipose Fin (fleshy, no fin rays)

Dorsal Fin

Vomer

Caudal Fin

Barbel

Fin Rays *Anal Fin*

Pectoral Fin

Pelvic Fin

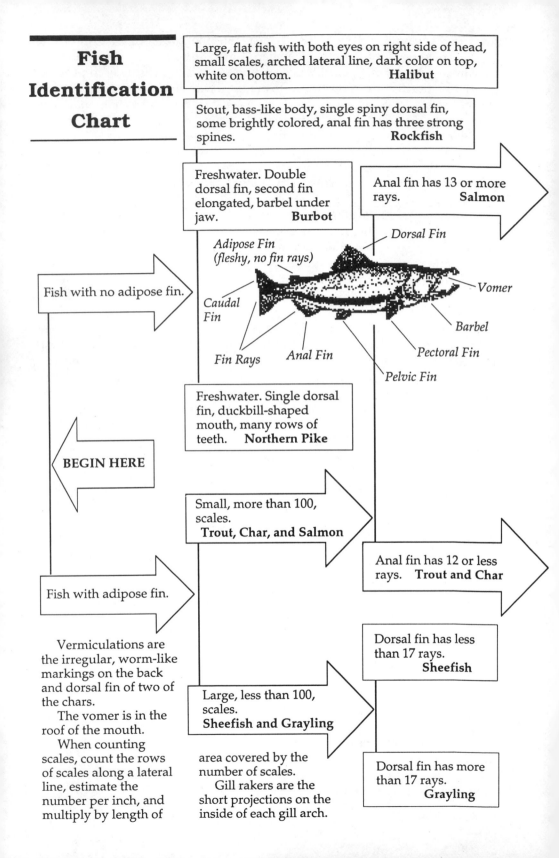

Freshwater. Single dorsal fin, duckbill-shaped mouth, many rows of teeth. **Northern Pike**

BEGIN HERE

Small, more than 100, scales. **Trout, Char, and Salmon**

Anal fin has 12 or less rays. **Trout and Char**

Fish with adipose fin.

Vermiculations are the irregular, worm-like markings on the back and dorsal fin of two of the chars.

The vomer is in the roof of the mouth.

When counting scales, count the rows of scales along a lateral line, estimate the number per inch, and multiply by length of

area covered by the number of scales.

Gill rakers are the short projections on the inside of each gill arch.

Large, less than 100, scales. **Sheefish and Grayling**

Dorsal fin has less than 17 rays. **Sheefish**

Dorsal fin has more than 17 rays. **Grayling**

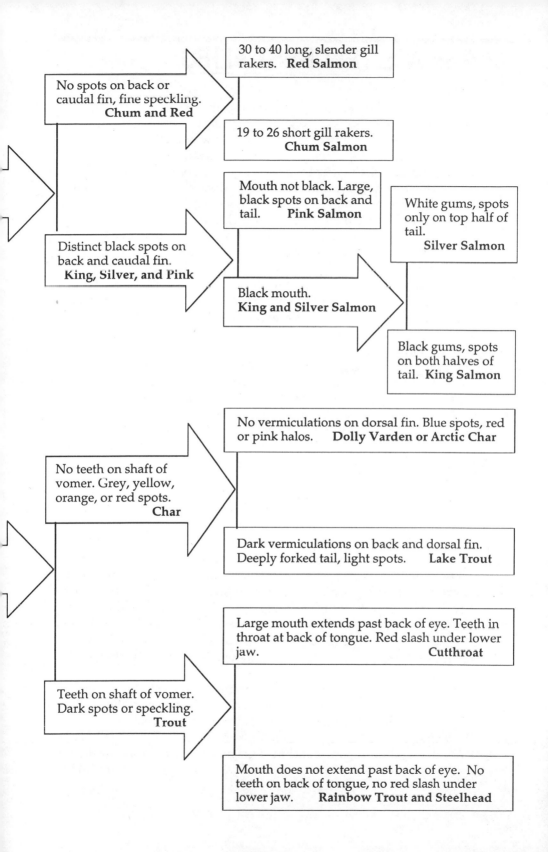

ALASKA'S TEN BEST FLIES

by Dan Heiner

These are the top ten fly patterns used in Alaska:

1—Egg-sucking leech and egg zonker. Called Alaska express by many. The egg-sucking leech is unquestionably the number one winner. Best tied in purple woolly-bugger style, the egg-sucking leech employs a pink egg tied at the head. Great for all species, including sockeye and grayling. Coming on strong is the egg zonker, which uses a mylar tubing body with a rabbit fur wing. Highly visible. Especially good for rainbows, char, and Dollies

2—Flash flies and Everglows. Silver salmon, chum salmon, pinks, and kings strike these attractor patterns with reckless abandon. Commonly tied on size 2 or 1/0 hooks, weighted, these attractors are deadly. Since salmon aren't in freshwater to feed and strike out of reflex or habit. A flash fly stripped through temporary resting or holding waters is extremely effective. Kings seem to be particularly prone to strike flies tied in chartreuse, with everglow tyings (a phosphorescent material which glows in the dark) being the first choice of many fly-rodders.

3—Leech patterns and woolly-buggers. Rabbit fur leeches are challenging the old favorite, woolly bugger. Where woolly buggers use a marabou tail to create a live effect, leech patterns do the same with rabbit fur. Black is the most popular color, with purple growing in popularity and white filling the niche for flesh flies, tied to resemble decaying salmon flesh.

4—Polar shrimp and babine special/two-egg sperm fly. Highly effective for salmon, trout, grayling, char, and Dollies, these two dressings continue to catch fish. Especially good steelhead patterns, these two continue to deliver success to Alaska's fly-rodders.

5—Comets. Designed initially for steelhead, these multi-colored patterns are excellent for all species. Highly visible flies, comets are available with and without bead-chain eyes that help them to sink deep.

6—Glo bugs and Iliamna pinkies. Alaska's version of matching the hatch. Yarn and chenille flies tied on short O'Shaugnessy hooks with a turn or two of lead wire for added weight. It's only natural these flies are continual producers, since Alaska's sport fishing begins, and peaks, with the life cycle of five species of Pacific salmon. A multitude of effective colors include champagne, pink, red, bright orange, and even black and white. Of these, champagne is considered most effective. These single egg patterns have a long and successful history of catching fish. Fat Freddie is the king-sized version of the single egg pattern for kings and silvers.

7—Sculpins. Bottom dwellers are an important food source for many fish. Tied on heavier wired hooks with wool for heads, artificials get down, and are noted for catching big fish. Tied with deer hair heads and unweighted, they make excellent surface patterns. Sculpins are great pike medicine in larger sizes.

8—Krystal bullets and sparkle shrimp. Designed for salmon and steelhead, these two newcomers use reflective krystal flash and mylar and are highly visible attractors. Both are available in chartreuse, orange, purple, pearl, black, and flame. Rainbows also like them.

9—Dry fly classics. Increased popularity of float-tube fishing has influenced a new generation of fly-rodders to take a good look at classic dry patterns. The virtues of Wulffs, humpys, mosquitoes, duns, gnats, elk hair caddis, and others have suddenly come to the attention of many fly-fishers.

10—Hares Ear nymphs and woolly worms. These old favorites work great in Alaska. Creeped along the bottom, stripped in a slow rise to the surface, or twitched on the surface, the hares ear is a favorite with float tubers. Woolly worms, in a variety of sizes and colors are effective for trout and steelhead: purple, pearl, black, and flame. Rainbows also like them.

ALASKA'S TEN BEST LURES

"Manufacturers make their lures for fishermen, not fish," the clerk commented as my fishing buddy, loaded with a zillion kinds and colors, headed for the checkout counter. I'd just met Rick, a first-time Alaska angler. He'd saved his money for several years, and was at the beginning of his once-in-a-lifetime trip to Alaska. We came together through a group of mutual friends. For the next week, we'd be floating and fishing a remote Alaska river. Rick, not wanting to be in the bush without the proper lure, stopped by the local tackle store and loaded up on terminal tackle. Had he asked me what he should take to the river instead of asking the clerk, his tackle box would not have contained nearly the variety of lures, sizes, or colors, nor would he have hauled so many back to California when his trip was over.

Early in my Alaska fishing career, I fished strictly with Daredevils. My tackle box was loaded with several different weights and as many different colors. My thinking was I would do better if I used a lure I was most familiar with and just change the color or size as water clarity, depth, and current velocity demanded. I did pretty well and caught at least my share.

My fishing habits changed when I began fishing with guides and discovered a new world of lures. Almost every guide had his favorite lure which he considered his secret weapon. When the fishing slowed, he'd dig in his bag of tricks and produce a strange new lure, claiming, "This one will break the curse. It always does. Just wait and see."

I'd put on his magic and most times my luck changed. The lure would be some off-the-wall piece of flash and glow, perhaps one purchased at California Rick's garage sale. When the fishing cooled, the guide would remove his secret and we'd return to an old standby. Here's the top ten old standbys used by the guides with whom I've fished.

Without a doubt, more guides hand a **Pixie** to their client than any other lure. Although Pixies come in a variety of colors, red seems to be the most popular. In Valdez, the little tackle store, Hook, Line, and Sinker is the area's pink salmon expert. The shop is under the world's largest pink salmon carving and inside the

An assortment of Pixies.

store is probably the state's largest display of Pixies. Pixies are sold by the handful, and anglers of all ages use them to catch their limits along the beach surrounding the Solomon Gulch Hatchery. When the silver run replaces pinks, other anglers stop by the store under the big pink salmon, and swallow the Pixie sales pitch, hook, line, and sinker.

Back in my **Daredevil** days I was silver fishing the mouth of Willow Creek. The run was in and I was casting to the sweet spot of the hole using a fluorescent Daredevil. All conditions: weather, water, and fish, combined to load my lure with a fish on every cast. Other anglers fishing the Willow weren't so fortunate. I held the hot rod, and, in-as-much as I had the only Daredevils, I announced, "Daredevils for sale, $5 each." No takers.

On the next cast, another silver met its match. "Daredevils, $6 each." No takers and nobody else even gets a strike. Another cast and another silver. "Daredevils, $7 each." So it went for the next thirty minutes. A silver, "Daredevils, $8 each," then "$9 each," and finally "$10 apiece."

One angler from across the stream shouted, "Okay, give me one of those things." I asked him to hook a $10 bill to his lure and cast it to my side of the hole, which he promptly did. I removed his lure and pretended to pocket the money. Next, I fastened a new Daredevil to his snap swivel and attached the $10 bill to his line with a rubber band. I threw his new lure in the water and he began to retrieve it. Almost simultaneously his line grew tight, the new fluorescent lure started its singular Daredevil wobble and a silver responded with enthusiasm.

The resulting battle terminated when the luckless fisherman netted his first fish. For a moment, the discovery of the $10 attached to his line left him with a puzzled look on his face and a question in his voice.

"You didn't keep the ten bucks?" he said, more of a question than a statement. "How come?"

"I was only pulling your leg," I said and tossed the other three guys a brand new fluorescent Daredevil. The animosity that was building because of my feigned arrogance was soon dispelled, and we all became friends. They laughed at themselves and me when they realized I'd taken them in hook, line, and sinker.

By day's end, I'd lost or given away nine new lures. Before saying goodbye and leaving the river with their limits of silvers, each one tossed something in my nearly empty tackle box. I thought they were returning their unused lures. When I packed up to leave, I found five $20 bills laying in the top tray. Those guys hadn't let me get the last laugh, even if it cost them twenty bucks apiece.

The next day I replenished my supply of Daredevils at a local sporting goods store. After paying the clerk, I realized I'd gotten all my lures replaced and made money on the deal. I really did take those guys in, hook, line, and sinker.

Anchor River Campground becomes Alaska's second largest city during king season. It hasn't always been that way. Before Alaska became a state, the feds were mishandling the resource and the king population was almost decimated. They allowed both sport and commercial fishing far above what the salmon stocks could stand. When the State of Alaska Department of Fish and Game took over, things changed. They closed the fishing and let the runs build to respectable numbers. The huge numbers of successful anglers on the Anchor now is a testimony to the Department's ability to correctly manage Alaska's fish and game populations.

I was fishing the Anchor one evening with a friend. We intended to catch a few Dollies for dinner. I put on a gold, number 14 hook and loaded it with a single salmon egg. It had been raining, and the river was a bit muddy. I didn't see an underwater snag and kept hanging up on it. I figured that's where the fish would be, but it was difficult to get my bait through the hole without hooking a snag. It didn't seem to be a cruel snag and always let go before I lost my set-up.

On one cast, my bait stopped and I thought I'd snagged again. I pulled on the line but it didn't come loose. I gently tugged again. The line stayed put. I pulled again. Nothing. I gave it as hard a jerk as I figured the line could stand and all hell broke loose.

A resting steelhead had slipped away from its hiding place behind the snag and sucked in my bait without me feeling the take. My last pull set the hook and the fish exploded into multiple bursts of dives and jumps. I was caught completely by surprise, and the fish was way ahead of my meager attempts to contain it. The steelie had me, hook, line, and sinker.

After a series of break-away vaults, the fish turned and charged directly at me. I ground the reel's handle as fast as I could, but was unable to keep up, and the line became slack. In a mighty bid for freedom, the steelhead dove to the bottom, turned upstream, and with all its energy, came straight off the bottom and cleared the surface by three feet. At the top of its mid-air flight, my rapid reeling paid off and the line tightened, pulling the fish toward a muddy river bar. The height of the jump and the snap of my tightening line swung the fish so it landed two feet up on the bar.

With a flip of its tail and a jerk of its head, the fish became unattached to my line and began sliding into the river. Without thinking of the consequences, my friend jumped over the bank and made a flying tackle on the steelhead. He was able to flip the fish to a more secure position on the bar. Mud covered both the fish and my friend as he held up the prize, my first steelhead.

Fishing on the Anchor has changed over the years, and so have I. Over three-and-a-half decades ago, when this incident took place, we killed the steelhead and ate it for dinner. Since then, I've matured and have found greater pleasure in releasing all rainbow, resident or sea-run, than in killing and eating. I still fish the Anchor, but now it's only catch-and-release.

The best way to fish the Anchor and other Lower Kenai Peninsula streams for kings is to drift **Spin-N-Glos** or **salmon eggs** or a combination of the two. Use either a fly rod or a standard steelhead drift rod. Attach a Spin-N-Glo by running the line through the Spin-N-Glo, then bait-loop your hook, and either drift bait or a piece of yarn behind the Spin-N-Glo. Use a number 5 or 7 splitshot or equivalent depending on the current and depth. Less than 1/16 of an ounce is needed. Put the weight twelve to sixteen inches above the hook. Cast upstream and drift through the hole.

The Talachulitna River is one of my favorite fishing holes, whether it be for rainbows or kings. The Tal has a respectable run of kings, and I've had them respond to **Tee Spoons** on more than one occasion. The best place for kings is at the mouth where the clear water of the Tal mixes with the muddy Skwentna.

Rex and I were fishing for Tal River kings. It was Rex's first king trip, and he was excited. Steve, our guide, boated us from the lodge to the mouth and let us off on a sandbar thirty yards upstream and thirty feet from the north shore.

Rex was a humble student and listened to every instruction Steve gave him. He applied his learning and was soon tied to his first king, Tee Spoon success story. After fifteen minutes of battle, Rex began to tire. "How long does this go on," he moaned.

"I've found that the fight lasts about a-minute-a-pound of fish," I quickly answered. "The biggest fish I've seen taken here has been a fifty-five pounder. We haven't seen your fish yet. You could be in for another forty minutes of battle."

Rex seemed to catch his second wind and continued properly playing the fish. We still hadn't seen Rex's fish fifty-five minutes into the battle. Rex's green eyes possessed an unusual glimmer as he exclaimed, "This must be a Tal record. It's at least fifty-five pounds and still going."

The fight continued. Seventy minutes and then ninety. We accused Rex of loosening the drag, and Steve confirmed its tension was correct. The rod bent as the king made a run at 110 minutes into the fight.

"A 110-pounder," Rex yelled as the fish moved deeper into the hole. "It's at least 110 pounds."

At the 137-minute mark, the fish went to the bottom and sulked. Rex couldn't make him move. He kept the pressure on, but the fish wouldn't budge. Finally, the king tired of it all and gave one gigantic pull and the line snapped.

Rex sat on the boat gunnel and nursed his arm. "A minute a pound," he mumbled. "A 140-minute battle, a 140-pound fish."

I've heard Rex tell the story many times of the 140-pound king that got away. He tells it with such authority that his listeners swallow it hook, line, and sinker.

Steve knew the fish had wrapped the line once around an old submerged log. The pressure on the log gave Rex the impression that he could not move the fish toward shore. After rubbing back and forth for an hour and twenty minutes, the line finally failed and Rex lost his world record. At least that's what Steve told me, and I believe him.

One lure that took Kenai River guides by storm was the **Tadpolly**. One season no one had heard of the lure, and the next it was the most popular lure on the river. A new guide to the area brought it with him. He caught fish and the other guides swallowed his Tadpolly success story. They still use it on the Kenai, and with great success, but nothing like the first year. Each guide has his favorites, but one of the lures in his arsenal will be always be a Tadpolly.

When Rick came away from the tackle store, he had a few **Mepps spinners**, a handful of **Rooster Tails**, several bubble packs of **Vibrax**, and even a **Krocodile** or two. He had some of each of the ten best lures, and like every angler before him, he took most of them home unopened.

I'm convinced I need them all, and my tackle box contains some of all ten. I've got Pixies, Daredevils, Spin-N-Glos, salmon eggs, Tee Spoons, Mepps spinners, Tadpollys, Rooster Tails, Vibrax, and even Krocodiles. I listen to the guides and tackle store experts, and accept their advice, hook, line, and sinker.

Best Bait or Lure by Species	
King Salmon	Eggs, Herring, Spoons
Silver Salmon	Herring, Spoons
Red Salmon	Flies, Spoons
Pink Salmon	Spoons
Chum Salmon	Flies, Spoons, Spinners
Rainbow Trout	Bait, Flies, Lures
Steelhead Trout	Flies, Spoons
Lake Trout	Plugs, Spoons
Arctic Char	Eggs, Spoons
Arctic Grayling	Flies
Northern Pike	Spoons, Spinners
Sheefish	Flies, Spoons
Halibut	Herring, Octopus
Burbot	Bait
Cutthroat Trout	Bait, Flies, Spinners
Dolly Varden	Bait, Flies, Spinners
Brook Trout	Eggs, Spinners
Kokanee	Eggs, Spinners
Ling Cod	Herring
Rockfish	Jigs, Herring
Whitefish	Eggs, Flies

The Kenai River is known for its world-record king salmon. After the kings leave, the silvers take their place. Betty Swensen and Steve Shepard show off their catch of silvers as guide Ken Robertson looks on.

ALASKA'S TEN MOST POPULAR RIVERS

Kenai River

Probably the most productive salmon water in the state is the Kenai River. It's not easily fished from shore in many places, but where it is, the fishing is generally superb. Record-sized king salmon, outstanding silver and red salmon, and rainbow trout fishing thrill anglers from around the world. Glacial-fed, the eighty-five-mile-long Kenai has given up the largest sport-caught king salmon in the world, a ninety-seven pound, four ounce fish. The river has two distinct king and silver runs, and some of its tributaries boast two red runs. The early king run usually contains smaller fish than those of the later run. Anglers fish for silvers from August through November, and have even taken fresh fish as late as January.

Karluk River

While not on the road system, the twenty-one-mile-long Karluk River is accessible to anglers by a short flight from the city of Kodiak. It's known for fall, overwintering steelhead runs and outstanding salmon fishing. Its shallow water is ideal for wading. Karluk steelhead fishing is best during October and again in May. Karluk king and silver fishing is noted for numbers of fish. It's not unusual for an angler to catch-and-release thirty kings or seventy silvers in a day. One Karluk River attribute is its summer-long red run. On almost any summer day the Karluk will reward anglers with reds in addition to Dolly Varden and rainbow. Most fishing is at the mouth, along the spit near the village of Karluk. It's also floated and fished via fly-in by floatplane to Karluk Lake, and exiting at Karluk Village, and returning to Kodiak by commercial airline. Karluk's variety and quality of fishing definitely qualifies it as a top ten river.

Situk River

Yakutat's twenty-mile-long Situk River empties into the Gulf of Alaska six miles east of Yakutat. Strong fall and spring steelhead fishing, great numbers of large-bodied silvers, and a strong red run is the Situk's hallmark. Even a few catch-and-release kings may be caught. Most people fly by commercial airline to Yakutat, stay in a local hotel or bed and breakfast, and hire one of the locals to drive them to the river. Many bring their inflatable boat, but others hire a guide or rent a boat. Like the Karluk, the Situk is ideal for wading and fishing from shore.

Susitna River

Southcentral Alaska's murky, glacial-fed Susitna River is not generally fished, but clearwater tributaries give anglers access to fine fishing. Guides and knowledgeable anglers have found a few places where fishing in the Susitna itself has proven to be outstanding. I believe there are methods and means, yet untried, that when applied will give this large, accessible river a more favorite fishing status.

Fourth largest of the state's rivers, the Susitna drainage receives strong runs of all five Pacific salmon. Clearwater tributaries contribute outstanding rainbow and grayling before and after the salmon runs. The Deshka and Talachulitna rivers, Lake, Willow, and Alexander creeks, and tributaries of the Talkeetna River are the most popular. The Susitna is accessed by air charter from Anchorage, Willow, and Talkeetna, or by charter or private boat from Talkeetna or Susitna Landing. Highway access is through the campground at the mouth of Willow Creek.

Kvichak River

Wild, steelhead-sized rainbow trout fishing puts the cap on Kvichak's angling season. Southwestern Alaska's Kvichak River flows from Lake Iliamna, Alaska's largest lake. It's one of the state's best big trout waters. Dolly Varden and grayling fishing add to the excitement. Pools, cut banks, and holding water are mostly fished by boat. Shore fishing is done at the mouth, at the lake outlet, or in the downriver braids. It's almost impossible to fish elsewhere without a boat and motor. A boat is needed for trolling the lake outlet and for transportation to downriver braids. Wading and fishing side channels produces unexpected results. The Kvichak is the conduit to the spawning grounds for the world's largest run of red salmon, and on even-numbered years, millions of pink salmon. It also provides outstanding silver salmon fishing.

Shelby Stasny is visibly happy and proud of his Kvichack River rainbow.

Naknek River

Another commercial airline-accessible rainbow and salmon river is the Naknek. Like the Kvichak, it empties a huge lake system. Fishing is generally from boats. Most fishing begins in the town of King Salmon. King Salmon, Alaska, was not named Silver Salmon or Rainbow Trout for good reason. The town earned its name because of its huge runs of Alaska's state fish, the king.

Talarik Creek

Upper and Lower Talarik Creek probably are responsible for more trophy rainbow trout than any other state stream. Lake Iliamna's big resident rainbow migrate into these trickles every fall. Fall fly-fishing in Talarik can be phenomenal. Shallow, with lots of holding water containing dozens of big rainbows, these creeks offer excellent wading and fly-fishing. Accessible only by floatplane, Talarik is most often fished using the services of a guide or fly-in lodge.

Ugashik Narrows

The state record arctic grayling, just under five pounds, was taken from Ugashik Narrows. Not a stream, but a short stretch of stream-like water it connects two lakes and is the state's most popular arctic grayling fishing area. Magnificent char fishing adds to its attraction. This Alaska Peninsula fishery is almost unused because of its remote location. I'm not usually one to claim that a new record may come from a given area. In the case of Ugashik, I make an

Mark Eaton displays his rainbow taken in the Lower Talerik as guide Greg Erickson looks on.

exception. I'm convinced that world-record-breaking grayling reside in these waters. Ugashik is simply not tested by serious, record-seeking anglers.

Wulik River

In Northwestern Alaska, the Wulik River drains the western Brooks Range into the Chukchi Sea, eighty-four miles from Kotzebue. In the fall, it receives enormous numbers of migrating arctic char. These fish visit the Wulik to spawn and overwinter. The Wulik holds the current arctic char state record of seventeen pounds, eight ounces. An average fall Wulik char will be between six and nine pounds.

Nushagak River

Last on the list of Alaska's ten most popular rivers is another river known for its king fishing. Receiving the third largest run of kings, the Nushagak River offers outstanding float fishing for rainbow trout, arctic grayling, and arctic char. This feeder of Bristol Bay has long, gravel beaches ideal for flyfishing. Nushagak kings are not as large as Kenai kings, but their numbers will make most anglers head for camp to rest, long before the fishing grows cold. Anglers not wishing to use the services of either a lodge or guide may float the Nushagak successfully on their own. Access is by commercial airline to Iliamna or Dillingham and then floatplane to the river.

In my opinion, these are the ten most popular rivers in Alaska. Many anglers will challenge my opinion, giving valid reasons for including their favorite. On any given day, I too, may have selected differently. I've fished with guides who have taken me to their secret spots where I've enjoyed Alaska's best. I'm grateful for their trust in sharing their hard-earned and sometimes expensive discoveries. Some special streams, and even sections of streams, I've found on my own and am selfishly keeping to myself. Additionally, the state is so large, and filled with so much fishable water, some awaiting the first fisherman, I'll leave these for the reader's own discovery. Every angler should have their own secret Alaska fishing hole.

I had the urge as I wrote this to tell what my favorite river was, but decided against it. I haven't fished my favorite stream for three years. The last time I was there, I got skunked, but it was an enjoyable trip with a group of old friends. It was more reunion than serious fishing outing. I knew, when I went, that it was too early for kings. Several in my party caught kings, or at least had them on; I didn't get a strike.

Compare my fishless trip to the day we made a television show on the same stream. On that trip the kings were in—really in. The cameraman and director would set up the shot, direct me to catch a fish and even tell me when—and I did. It was almost like shooting to a script—enter forty-pound king salmon stage right.

The filming took place from 9 a.m. until noon, and we had all the footage we required. After lunch, the filming crew picked up their rods and spent the day receiving fringe benefits. I'd done so well on camera with a fly rod, I decided to see how many kings I could capture and release in one day. When it became too dark to fish, I'd released thirty-seven kings. The strain of battling these brutes on a fly rod rendered my casting arm so sore and stiff that I was unable to fish the next day. It was several days before I could comfortably throw a fly again.

Often, it's not the size or numbers of fish that make the memories, it's who you're with. This same river produced my son, Lars', first fish and his first on a fly rod. He was having pretty good luck while fishing for pinks. He was hooking them but was unable to bring one to shore. He'd get close enough to touch the fish, and then it would dash off to deep, swift water and escape the hook. Casting to a group of fish moving slowly upriver along the opposite bank, he was surprised by a grayling; so surprised that he tripped, or slipped, on a boulder and went in over his hip boots. Recovering from the fall, he proudly

These dried salmon were taken from the Nushagak River.

stood and excitedly exclaimed, "Dad I still got him, I still got him!" We ate his catch for breakfast the next morning and relived the day with each bite.

ANCHORAGE AREA

Alaska Department of Fish and Game stocks Anchorage area lakes for the enjoyment of the city's residents. Streams to the south have salmon runs in season, but, like other populated areas, most anglers feel a need to travel some distance for better fishing. Local tackle stores have at least one knowledgeable person on staff aquainted with fishing in the local area. In addition, the Department of Fish and Game is helpful.

Although there's good fishing in the area, I suspect only a handful utilize the fishery. One fishing season I was approached by a float-tube manufacturer who offered a hands-on demonstration in Jewel Lake. Outfitted with a dry suit and an inflated float system, the manufacturer and I paddled the system toward hanging willows on the west side of the lake.

For thirty minutes, we caught and released a number of small rainbow before our allotted time expired. We got too busy fishing and forgot to look at the equipment. I still don't know all the features and reasons to fish with a float system, but I know there are rainbow trout in Jewel Lake. Even so, like so many others, I still head down Turnagain Arm when the fishing bug bites.

Turnagain Arm and Cook Inlet were named by Captain James Cook, who, searching for the Northwest Passage had to turn again. Cook Inlet still attracts people from all over the world, but now they turn again for photography, sightseeing, gold panning, and especially fishing. Tall mountains rim the area,

These fishermen are hoping that their day on Cook Inlet will be a rewarding one.

Anchorage Area Freshwater

Fish Availability Chart

Species	May	June	July	August	September	October
King Salmon		▓▓▓▓				
Silver Salmon				▓▓▓▓▓▓		
Red Salmon			▓▓▓▓			
Pink Salmon			▓▓▓			
Chum Salmon			▓▓▓			
Rainbow Trout	████████████████████████████████					
Steelhead						
Lake Trout						
Arctic Char	████			▓▓▓▓▓▓▓▓▓▓		
Arctic Grayling						
Northern Pike						
Sheefish						
Halibut						

████ = Available   ▓▓▓▓ = Peak

streams drain the valleys, and hanging glaciers line the shores of Turnagain Arm. The streams from the valleys are teeming with salmon runs.

The Seward Highway, the state's most heavily-traveled thoroughfare, takes anglers to the Kenai Peninsula and right past great fishing. Thirty minutes from Anchorage, Bird Creek enters the arm after crossing the Seward Highway. From mid-July and continuing through early August, the stream has a strong run of pink salmon. An occasional Dolly Varden may also be taken.

One hour from Anchorage, Twentymile Creek at the head of Turnagain Arm is not fishable, but clearwater tributaries carry four species of salmon. Red salmon run in mid and late July, pink and chums in late July and early August, and silvers arrive during September. Dolly Varden are available in July, August, and September. Good fishing begins a little over a mile upstream, and ambitious anglers, willing to hike, will be rewarded with good fishing.

Prior to the Great Alaska Earthquake, the land along the shore of Turnagain Arm was as much as eight feet higher. The earthquake slipped the earth's crust, allowing the land at the mouth of Twentymile Creek to sink. Both the highway and railroad bridge spanning the creek were destroyed. A combination of earthquake and bridge restoration left the creek without its former boat ramp—probably with good cause.

Prior to the earthquake, I fished the area many times a season. A one-hour drive from my home in Anchorage would put me on the creek. Ten minutes to slip the boat from its trailer and load up our gear, and another fifteen minutes of river travel put us at an excellent silver fishing hole at the junction of Twentymile and its first clearwater tributary.

Our habit was to arise early, drive to the creek, dash to the tributary, fish for a couple of hours, and return home in time for work. An alternate schedule was to leave after work, do our fishing and return home before it got dark. We did this several times a week during the silver run. The limit was six fish, and it didn't take long to supply our fillets and smoked salmon needs.

One such day my fishing partner, Max Marquiss, and I arrived at the fishing hole in the early evening. As we pulled into the tributary and slid the boat up on the beach, we discovered the water was boiling with migrating silver salmon. It was an evening when we almost had to bait our hook from behind a tree to keep the fish off until we could cast. In our exuberance, we forgot the time and fished until it was dark.

Wanting to remain over and catch the morning's first fishing, we justified staying by making the excuse that we didn't want to go on the river at night. We pulled the twelve-foot boat up on the beach, propped it up on its side for a lean-to, built a fire in front, and cooked a fresh-caught silver for dinner. Using spruce boughs for a bed, we slept until it was light.

With the first light of morning, we noticed that the water in the stream had come up during the night. We paid it little attention and went about fishing. Finally, running out of time, we left the stream so we could return home in time for work.

When we arrived back at our car, we discovered that it had been flooded by the year's highest tide. Fortunately, water didn't get into the gas tank, but the engine and seats were covered. We drained the crankcase and flushed it out with kerosene, then filled it with oil. It started up, and we repeated the process before sitting down on the wet seats and returning to Anchorage.

Immediately, the car was taken to a service station, given the full treatment and run through the car wash several times. It seemed to run all right, and except for a foul interior smell, it appeared that we'd escaped with only a minor expense and a little inconvenience. With the coming of winter, we soon learned we were mistaken. Windows wouldn't roll up or down. The transmission wouldn't shift, the interior fogged up and then froze.

Toward summer, inconvenience turned to tragedy. The U-joints broke, the door windows handles refused to work, and finally the front wheels fell off. We discovered that almost everything covered by the saltwater was rusted away or corroded beyond use or repair. We had to junk the car.

I suspect that after the earthquake, when the state and railroad fixed the road and repaired the bridges, consideration was given to unthinking river travelers like me. The reconstruction did not include a boat ramp that would allow a vehicle to be parked where it could be reached by the tide. It also didn't allow easy access to the river and its good fishing.

I've only been back upTwentymile once since the earthquake. The gravel beaches we fished from and camped on are now covered with mud. Because the land has lowered, the beach is now tide affected. No longer can Max and I siwash it on Twentymile and fish all night for silvers, even if we remembered to keep our car above the tide line.

ANCHORAGE AREA

Site Number and Name	Fish	Location and Accessibility
1 Mirror Lake	RT, KS, GR	East side of the Glenn Highway, at Mile 22.
2 Beach Lake	RT, KS	At the end of Beach Lake Road, off Birchwood Loop Road.
3 Lower Fire Lake	RT	East side of the Glenn Highway at Mile 17.
4 Clunie Lake	RT, KS GR	Fort Richardson. Check at gate for map and permission.
5 Eagle River	DV, RT	Mile 12.9, Glenn Highway.
6 Waldon Lake	RT, GR	Fort Richardson. Check at gate for map and permission.
7 Thompson Lake	RT, KS GR	Fort Richardson. Check at gate for map and permission.
8 Gwen Lake	RT, KS, GR	Fort Richardson. Check at gate for map and permission.
9 Otter Lake	RT, KS	Fort Richardson. Check at gate for map and permission.
10 Ship Creek	KS	Off Whitney Road.
11 Lake Otis	RT	West of Lake Otis Parkway, between Northern Lights Blvd. and 36th Avenue.
12 University Lake	RT	East of Bragaw, between Providence Drive and Tudor Road.
13 Cheney Lake	RT, KS	Between East Northern Lights Blvd. and Debarr Road, on Baxter Road.
14 Conners Lake	RT	Off Jewel Lake Road, between International Airport and Raspberry Roads.
15 Delong Lake	RT, KS	On the west side of Jewel Lake Road, two blocks north of the corner of Jewel Lake and Raspberry Roads.
16 Sand Lake	RT, KS	West of Jewel Lake Road, between Dimond Blvd. and Raspberry Road.
17 Campbell Lake	RT, KS, GR	Off Raspberry Road, 1.5 miles west of the intersection of Raspberry and Sand Lake Roads.
18 Sundi Lake	RT	Between Sand Lake and Jewel Lake Roads.
19 Jewel Lake	RT, KS	On the north side of Dimond Blvd., one mile west of the corner of Dimond Blvd. and Jewel Lake Road.
20 Taku Campbell Lake	RT	0.25 mile north of the corner of C Street and Dimond Blvd.
21 Campbell Creek	RT	South of Northern Lights Blvd.
22 Rabbit Creek	RT	Mile 117.3, Seward Highway.
23 Bird Creek	DV, PS	Mile 101.2, Seward Highway. Parking area. Campground 0.5 mile south of creek. Summer fishery.
24 Twentymile Creek	SS	Mile 80.7, Seward Highway. Campground.

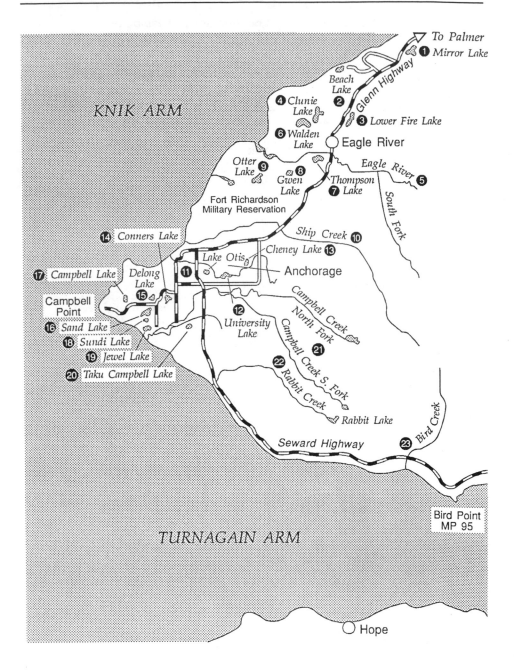

KNIK ARM

To Palmer
① Mirror Lake

Beach Lake ②

④ Clunie Lake

② Clunie Lake

③ Lower Fire Lake

⑥ Walden Lake

Eagle River

Otter Lake ⑨

⑧ Gwen Lake

Thompson Lake ⑦

Eagle River

⑤

South Fork

Fort Richardson Military Reservation

⑭ Conners Lake

Ship Creek ⑩

Cheney Lake ⑬

Lake Otis

Anchorage

⑰ Campbell Lake

Delong Lake ⑪

⑮

Campbell Point

⑯ Sand Lake

⑱ Sundi Lake

⑲ Jewel Lake

⑳ Taku Campbell Lake

University Lake ⑫

Campbell Creek North Fork

Campbell Creek S. Fork

⑳ Taku Campbell Lake

㉑

㉒

Rabbit Creek

Rabbit Lake

Bird Creek

㉓

Seward Highway

Glenn Highway

Bird Point MP 95

TURNAGAIN ARM

Hope

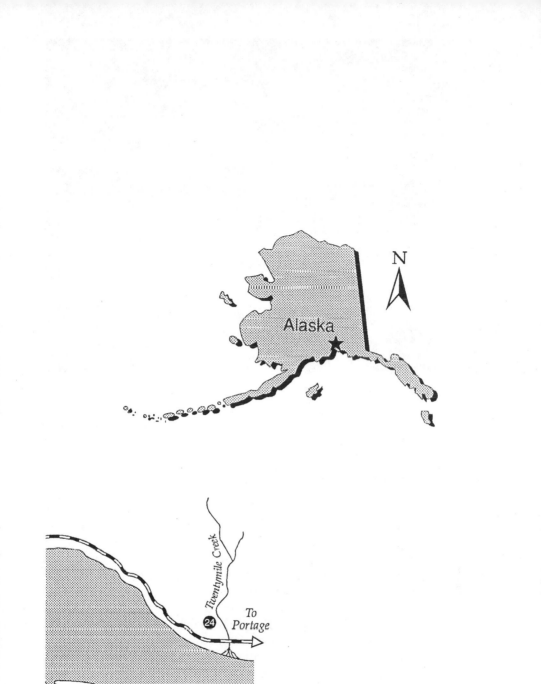

A crowded marina in Kachemak Bay.

KENAI PENINSULA

The Kenai Peninsula is the state's most heavily fished area. The Kenai River alone accounts for 230,000 angler days per year. Twenty five species of freshwater fish may be taken and all but one of the twelve recognized sportfish species. The expression "combat fishing" was born on the Kenai. At times, it can be crowded, particularly when one or more species of salmon is running. Some turn up their nose at the Kenai because of the numbers of anglers on a given stretch of water. I began my love affair with Alaska's fishing on the peninsula. I've fished its waters for over thirty-five years and enjoyed every trip. The reason so many people are on the Kenai, and why I like fishing it myself, is because a lot of fish are available and are caught. People who fish the Kenai have a good time, and there's an angler camaraderie on the peninsula.

The peninsula's most famous fishery is the river for which the area is named, Kenai. The Kenai River is a glacially turbid stream originating at the outlet of Kenai Lake. The river bisects the peninsula for nearly sixty miles before entering Cook Inlet near the city of Kenai. Most anglers direct their efforts toward nine of the twenty-five species found on the peninsula. King, red, silver, and pink salmon are in the river during their respective runs. Anglers also fish for both sea-run and resident Dolly Varden as well as rainbow trout. Lake trout are found in Kenai and Skilak Lakes, and pike are occasionally taken in Soldotna Creek, a tributary of the Kenai River.

At the end of a great day of fishing, these anglers put their boat back on the trailer.

The season's first fishing begins with May steelhead in the Kasilof River and a run of early kings in saltwater off Anchor Point and Deep Creek. Then, the run increases and divides and enters other rivers like Kasilof, Deep Creek, and Anchor River as many anglers go inland.

The Fishing Hole, a king salmon fishery on the Homer Spit has given many anglers an opportunity to catch a king without the use of a boat or guide. A similar fishery has been established in Halibut Cove, across Kachemak Bay, and at Seward in Resurrection Bay. These terminal fisheries allow less experienced and younger anglers as good a chance of landing a king as those guided by a professional. An enjoyable afternoon may be spent at the Fishing Hole just watching kids tying into fish as big as the angler.

On top of the king run, reds flock to the river mouths, then pinks, and finally, concurrent with fall colors, come the silvers. From the beginning of May through October, one or more species of salmon may be pursued on the Kenai. Hardy anglers even keep their rods busy as late as January. Following freeze-up, resident fish—rainbows and Dollies—lose their lock-jaw mentality and begin taking lures again. Anglers wanting to extend the season, and those desiring to fish away from the crowds take to the Kenai. The less vigorous put their rods away, guides store their boats, and sporting goods stores turn to skiing and other winter activities. Ardent Kenai anglers go into hibernation, waiting for spring and another season of plenty.

Kenai Peninsula Freshwater

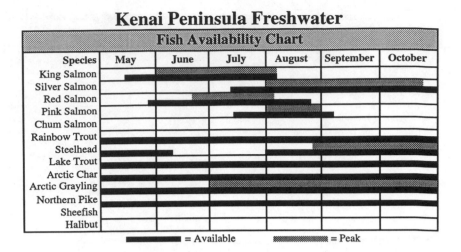

Species	May	June	July	August	September	October
King Salmon						
Silver Salmon						
Red Salmon						
Pink Salmon						
Chum Salmon						
Rainbow Trout						
Steelhead						
Lake Trout						
Arctic Char						
Arctic Grayling						
Northern Pike						
Sheefish						
Halibut						

= Available   = Peak

Kenai Peninsula Saltwater

Fish Availability Chart

Species	May	June	July	August	September	October
King Salmon						
Silver Salmon						
Red Salmon						
Pink Salmon						
Chum Salmon						
Rainbow Trout						
Steelhead						
Lake Trout						
Arctic Char						
Arctic Grayling						
Northern Pike						
Sheefish						
Halibut						

= Available   = Peak

Trophy King Lodge Recipe for Barbecued Salmon

Make a barbecue sauce by mixing equal amounts of Buttermilk Ranch Style dressing and Italian dressing. Fillet the fish and wash it clean. Apply an all-purpose seasoning to both sides of the fillet. Put the fillet on the grill, meat side down. When the fish is about half cooked, turn it over so the skin side is now down. Smother the meat side with the barbecue sauce and let the fish finish cooking. The end result will be some of the finest tasting gourmet delicacy ever invited to a cookout.

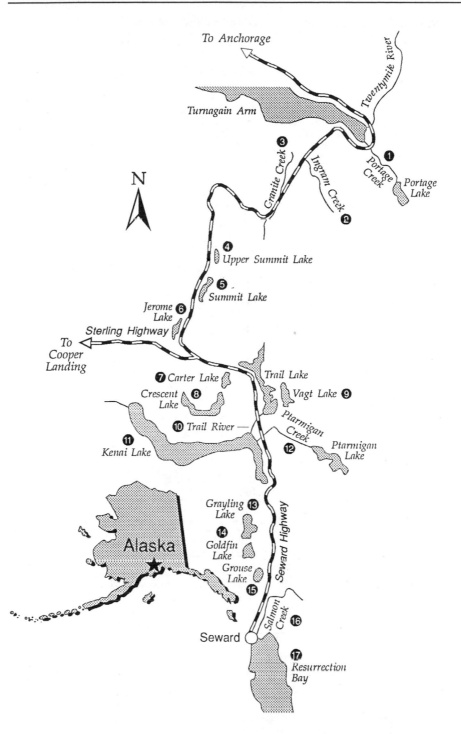

To Anchorage

Turnagain Arm

Twentymile River

Portage Creek

Portage Lake

Granite Creek

Ingram Creek

N

Upper Summit Lake

Summit Lake

Jerome Lake

Sterling Highway

To Cooper Landing

Carter Lake

Crescent Lake

Trail Lake

Vagt Lake

Trail River

Ptarmigan Creek

Ptarmigan Lake

Kenai Lake

Grayling Lake

Goldfin Lake

Grouse Lake

Seward Highway

Alaska

Salmon Creek

Seward

Resurrection Bay

PORTAGE CREEK TO SEWARD VIA SEWARD HIGHWAY

Site Number and Name	Fish	Location and Accessibility
1 Portage Creek	DV, SS, RS	Mile 79.4, Seward Highway. Campground.
2 Ingram Creek	PS, DV	Mile 75.3, Seward Highway. Summer fishery.
3 Granite Creek	DV	Mile 63.3 to Mile 64, Seward Highway. Numerous pull-offs. Summer fishery.
4 Upper Summit Lake	DV	Mile 46, Seward Highway. Campground and parking area. Year-round fishery.
5 Summit Lake	DV	Mile 44, Seward Highway. Campground and parking area. Year-round fishery.
6 Jerome Lake	RT	Mile 38.6, Seward Highway. Limited parking area. Year-round fishery.
7 Carter Lake	RT, GR	Mile 34, Seward Highway. Year-round fishery. Trail to lake.
8 Crescent Lake	RT, GR	Mile 34, Seward Highway. Year-round fishery. Trail to lake.
9 Vagt Lake	RT	Mile 28, Seward Highway. Year-round fishery. 1.5 mile trail to lake, along south end of Trail Lake.
10 Trail River	DV, RT, LT	Mile 25.3, Seward Highway. Campground. Summer and fall fishery.
11 Kenai Lake	RT, DV, LT	Mile 24, Seward Highway. Parking and boat launching area at Forest Service work center. Summer and fall fishery.
12 Ptarmigan Creek	RT, DV	Mile 23.2, Seward Highway. Campground area. Summer and fall fishery.
13 Grayling Lake	GR	Mile 10, Seward Highway. Year-round fishery. 0.5 mile trail to lake.
14 Goldfin Lake	DV	Mile 8, Seward Highway. 0.5 mile trail through Divide Ski Area. Year-round fishery.
15 Grouse Lake	DV	Mile 7.4, Seward Highway. Limited parking area. Spring and fall fishery.
16 Salmon Creek	DV	Mile 5.9, Seward Highway. Limited parking area. Late summer and fall fishery.
17 Resurrection Bay	SS, PS, DV, H	Mile 0, Seward Highway. The town of Seward. Campground and commercial facilities. Boat rental and charters. Spring, summer, and fall fishery.

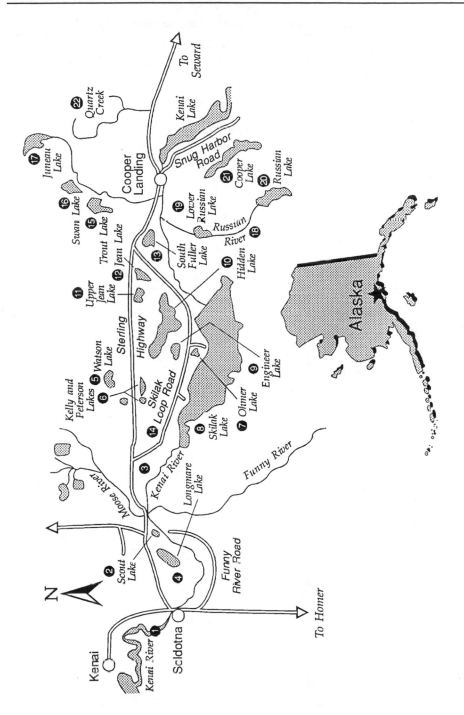

SOLDOTNA TO QUARTZ CREEK VIA STERLING HWY.

Site Number and Name	Fish	Location and Accessibility
1 Kenai River	RT, PS, SS, RS, DV	Soldotna Area. Two campgrounds. Summer and fall fishery. Charters abundant.
2 Scout Lake	RT, AC, SS	Mile 29, Swan Lake Road. Parking. Year-round fishery.
3 West Entrance, Skilak Loop Road	SS	Mile 75, Sterling Highway. Parking. Year-round fishery.
4 Longmare Lake		Mile 88, Sterling Highway. Parking area. Year-round fishery.
5 Watson Lake	RT	Mile 72, Sterling Highway. Turnoff plus one-mile drive. Campground area. Year-round fishery.
6 Kelly and Peterson Lakes	RT	Mile 70, Sterling Highway. Turnoff plus one-mile drive. Campground area. Year-round fishery.
7 Ohmer Lake	SS	Mile 8, Skilak Loop Road. Campground. Year-round fishery.
8 Skilak Lake	RT, DV, SS, RS	Mile 7, Skilak Loop Road. Campground. Year-round fishery. Two access roads at Mile 7 and 12 on Skilak Loop Road. Campground and boat ramps. Summer and fall fishery.
9 Engineer Lake	RT, DV, LT, Kok	Mile 3.5, Skilak Loop Road. Campground. Year-round fishery.
10 Hidden Lake		Mile 59, Sterling Highway.
11 Upper Jean Lake	SS	Mile 63, Sterling Highway. Campground. Year-round fishery.
12 Jean Lake	RT, DV	Mile 61, Sterling Highway. Parking area. Year-round fishery.
13 South Fuller Lake	GR	Mile 57.2, Sterling Highway. Two-mile trail leads to lake. Spring, summer, and fall fishery.
14 Skilak Loop Road		Mile 59, Sterling Highway. Many fishing spots.
15 Trout Lake	LT	Mile 53, Sterling Highway. Five-mile trail leads to lake. Campground area. Year-round fishery.
16 Swan Lake	RT, LT, DV, RS	Mile 53, Sterling Highway. Nine-mile trail leads to lake. Campground area. Year-round fishery.
17 Juneau Lake	RT, LT	Mile 53, Sterling Highway. Six-mile trail leads to lake. Campground area. Year-round fishery.
18 Russian River	RT, DV, RS, SS	Mile 55, Sterling Highway. Campground area. Year-round fishery. Check regulations closely before fishing this area.

Site Number and Name	Fish	Location and Accessibility
19 Lower Russian Lake	RT, DV,	Mile 53, Sterling Highway. Three-mile trail leads to lake. Campground area. Year-round fishery.
20 Upper Russian Lake	RT, DV,	Mile 53, Sterling Highway. Twelve-mile trail leads to lakes. Campground area Year-round fishery.
21 Cooper Lake	DV	Mile 49, Sterling Highway. Take turnoff, and lake is twelve miles from turnoff. Year-round fishery.
22 Quartz Creek	RT, DV	Mile 41.5, Sterling Highway. Campground area. Summer and fall fishery.

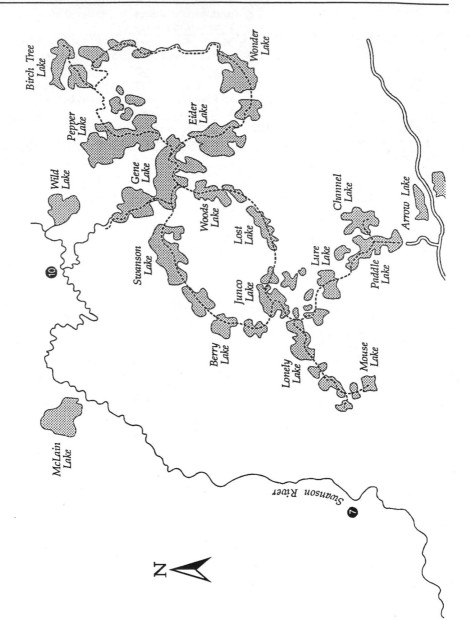

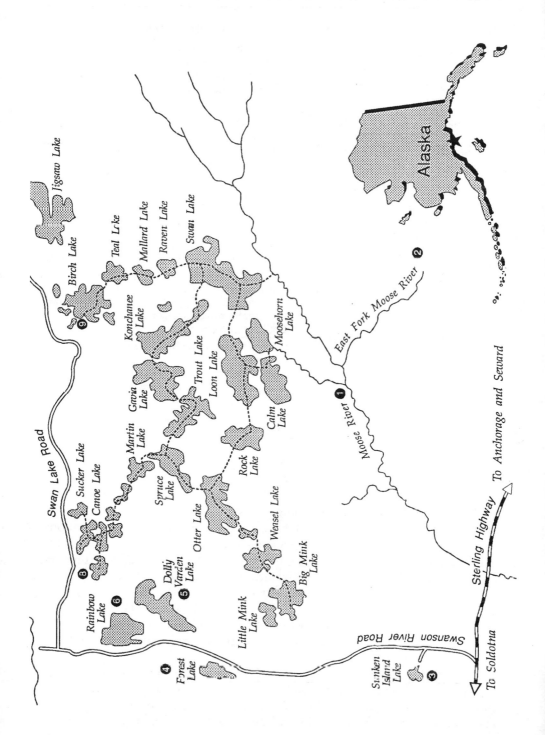

Jigsaw Lake

Birch Lake

Teal Lake

Mallard Lake

Raven Lake

Swan Lake

Konchanee Lake

Groin Lake

Trout Lake

Loon Lake

Moosehorn Lake

Martin Lake

Sucker Lake

Canoe Lake

Spruce Lake

Rock Lake

Calm Lake

Otter Lake

Wensel Lake

Dolly Varden Lake

Rainbow Lake

Little Mink Lake

Big Mink Lake

Forest Lake

Swan Lake Road

Sunken Island Lake

Swanson River Road

Moose River

East Fork Moose River

Alaska

Sterling Highway   To Anchorage and Seward

To Soldotna

107

STERLING HIGHWAY TO SWAN LAKE

Site Number and Name	Fish	Location and Accessibility
1 Moose River	RT, DV, RS	Mile 82, Sterling Highway. Parking and commercial campground. Boat rentals. Summer and fall fishery.
2 East Fork Moose River	RT	Mile 72, Sterling Highway. Parking area. Summer and fall fishery.
3 Sunken Island Lake	SS	Mile 4, Swanson River Road. Parking, campground. Year-round fishery.
4 Forest Lake	RT	Mile 9.5, Swanson River Road .Parking area. Year-round fishery.
5 Dolly Varden Lake	RT, AC	Mile 14, Swanson River Road. Campground. Year-round fishery.
6 Rainbow Lake	RT, AC	Mile 16, Swanson River Road. Campground. Year-round fishery.
7 Swanson River Canoe Route	RT, DV, SS	Mile 18, Swanson River Road. This is the west entrance to Swanson River Canoe Route. Campground. Summer and fall fishery.
8 Swan Lake Canoe Route	RT, AC	Mile 3.5, Swan Lake Road. This is the west entrance to Swan Lake Canoe Route. Parking area. Year-round fishery in Canoe Lake, the first lake in the system.
9 Swan Lake Canoe Route	SS	Mile 9.5, Swan Lake Road. This is the east entrance to Swan Lake Canoe Route. Parking area. Year-round fishery in Portage Lake.
10 Swanson River Canoe Route	RT, DV, SS	Mile 12, Swan Lake Road. This is the east entrance to Swanson River Canoe Route. Campground. Year-round fishery in Paddle Lake.

Swan Lake and Swanson River canoe routes, located in a nationally designated wilderness area, provide anglers an opportunity to fish in a true backcountry setting. Although fishing may be the purpose of the outing, a special adventure awaits anglers taking these routes. Designated as National Recreational Trails, backcountry travelers can expect to see a variety of wildlife. Mink, otter, loons, wolves, moose, muskrat, beaver, bald eagles, trumpeter swan, black and brown bears, and waterfowl are often observed.

The Swanson River canoe trail links more than forty lakes with forty-six miles of Swanson River. The entire eighty miles can be traveled in less than one week. Anglers can enter the headwaters of Swanson River, via Gene Lake outlet, and float to the access area, or continue twenty-four miles further to the North Kenai Road bridge.

From Paddle Lake, one day is required to reach Gene Lake by either the east or west routes. There are many shallow areas and two short portages along the Gene Lake outlet to Swanson River. Campsite are difficult to find along the low and marshy banks of Swanson River. The best sites are near hills or rises.

Waterways east of Pepper and Eider Lakes, as well as the upper Swanson River to Wild Lake are narrow and vegetated, providing difficult passage. Current in upper Swanson River is slow. The upper two miles may require additional effort to push through lily pads during late summer if the river is low.

Swan Late canoe trail connects thirty lakes with forks of the Moose River. The entire sixty-mile route can be traveled in less than a week. Anglers should allow more time for fishing.

Approximate Travel Time

Paddle Lake to Gene Lake	1 to 2 days
Gene Lake to Swanson River Campground	1 to 1.5 days
Swanson River access area to Cook Inlet	1 to 2 days
Paddle Lake via Eider Lake to Nuthatch Lake	2 to 3 days
Paddle Lake via Pepper Lake to Nuthatch Lake	2 to 3 days
Canoe Lake via Gavia Lake to Portage Lake	2 to 3 days
Canoe Lake via Loon Lake to Portage Lake	2 to 3 days
Portage Lake via Swan Lake to Moose River Bridge	3 to 4 days

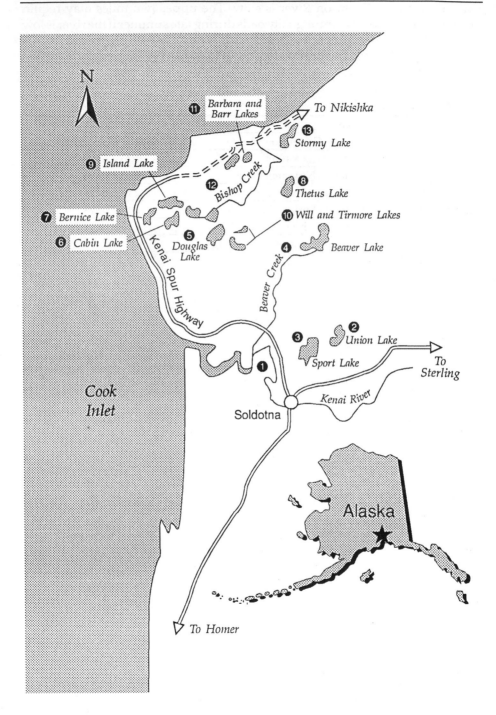

SOLDOTNA TO NIKISHKA VIA NORTH KENAI ROAD

Site Number and Name	Fish	Location and Accessibility
1 Kenai River	RT, PS, SS, RS, DV	Soldotna Area. Two campgrounds. Summer and fall fishery. Charters abundant.
2 Union Lake	RT	Off Kenai Spur Highway on Conner Road, past turnoff to Sport Lake. (below)
3 Sport Lake	RT	Kenai Spur Highway at junction 2.5 miles north of Soldotna leads 1 mile to lake. Parking. Year-round fishery.
4 Beaver Creek	RT, DV	Mile 6 on Kenai Spur Road. Limited parking. Summer and fall fishery.
5 Douglas Lake	RT	Mile 19.1, North Kenai Road. Turn right onto Miller Loop Road, then right on Hold Road. Douglas Lake is accessible by turning right on Baun Drive, or right on Douglas Lane, and right again on Drew Street.
6 Cabin Lake	RT	Take gravel fork right off Miller Loop Road approximately 1.2 miles from North Kenai Road. Gravel road forks left and ends at parking area.
7 Bernice Lake	RT	Turn right on Miller Loop Road at mile 21.3 North Kenai Road. Turn left on gravel road 1 mile from North Kenai Road. Parking at end of road.
8 Thetus Lake	RT	Proceed on Island Lake Road approximately 2.3 miles, and go left on Pipeline Road. Turn left at 0.75 mile on Moose Run. Bear right on Thetus Lake, bear left for east end of Island Lake.
9 Island Lake	RT	Go right on Island Lake Road at mile 25.9 North Kenai Road. Island Lake is on the left, 1.4 miles from North Kenai Road.
10 Will and Tirmore Lakes	RT	At mile 28.8, North Kenai Road, turn right on Lamplight Road. Turn right on Romanov Road and proceed to end of road for access. Tirmore Lake is on right side of Lamplight Road, approximately 2.4 miles from the North Kenai Road.
11 Barbara and Barr Lakes	RT	Right on Halbouty Road, at mile 29.7 North Kenai Road. Turn right 1 mile on gravel road for Barr Lake. Barbara Lake is on Halbouty Road about 2.2 miles from the North Kenai Road.
12 Bishop Creek	RT	Mile 35.1, North Kenai Road. Parking area. Summer and fall fishery.
13 Stormy Lake	AC, RT	Mile 36.5, North Kenai Road. Year-round fishery. Campground.

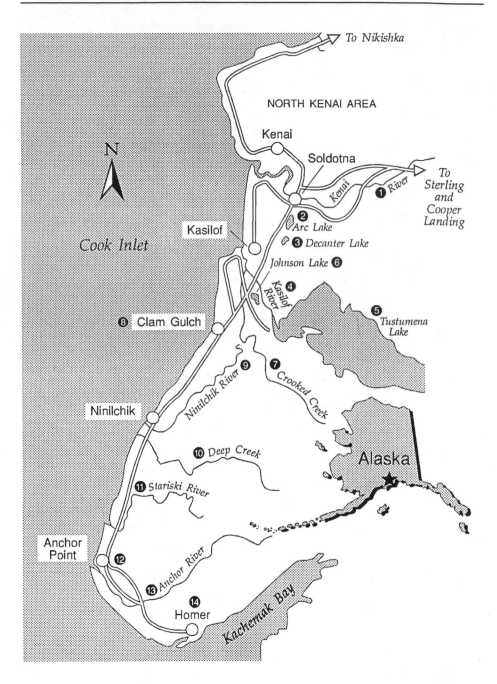

To Nikishka

NORTH KENAI AREA

Kenai

Soldotna

N

To Sterling and Cooper Landing

Kenai River ❶

Cook Inlet

❷

Arc Lake

❸ Decanter Lake

Kasilof

Johnson Lake ❻

❹

Kasilof River

❺ Tustumena Lake

❽ Clam Gulch

Ninilchik River ❾

❼

Crooked Creek

Ninilchik

❿ Deep Creek

Alaska

⓫ Stariski River

Anchor Point

⓬

⓭ Anchor River

⓮

Homer

Kachemak Bay

SOLDOTNA TO HOMER VIA STERLING HIGHWAY

Site Number and Name	Fish	Location and Accessibility
1 Kenai River	RT, PS, SS, RS, DV	Soldotna Area. Two campgrounds. Summer and fall fishery. Charters abundant.
2 Arc Lake	SS	Mile 98.2, Sterling Highway. Parking area. Year-round fishery.
3 Decanter Lake	RT	Mile 106.9, Sterling Highway. Short gravel road east side of highway leads to lake access.
4 Kasilof River	KS, PS, SS, RS, RT, DV	Mile 109, Sterling Highway. Campground area. Spring, summer, and fall fishery.
5 Tustumena Lake	LT, DV, SS	Mile 110.5, Sterling Highway. Turn off 5 miles on Tustumena Lake Road. Caution advised in boating because of wind—little shelter from it. Spring fishery at outlet.
6 Johnson Lake	RT	Mile 111, Sterling Highway. Campground. Year-round fishery.
7 Crooked Creek	RT, DV	Mile 114, Sterling Highway. Parking area. Summer and fall fishery.
8 Clam Gulch	Razor Clams	Mile 118, Sterling Highway. Access road leads 2 miles to clam beaches. Parking area. Spring, summer, and fall fishery. Minus tides are recommended.
9 Ninilchik River	DV, ST, KS, SS	Mile 136, Sterling Highway. Parking and campground. Commercial facilities. Summer and fall fishery.
10 Deep Creek	DV, ST, KS, SS	Mile 138, Sterling Highway. Parking and campgrounds. Summer and fall fishery.
11 Stariski Creek	DV, ST, SS	Mile 151, Sterling Highway. Parking area and campground 1 mile south. Summer and fall fishery.
12 Lower Cook Inlet	KS, RS, PS, SS, H	Campground and commercial facilities. Spring, summer, and fall fishery.
13 Anchor River	DV, ST, KS, SS	Mile 157, Sterling Highway. Campground and commercial facilities. Summer and fall fishery.
14 Kachemak Bay and Homer Spit	RS, KS, DV, SS, PS, H	Campground and commercial facilities Spring, summer, and fall fishery.

MATANUSKA/SUSITNA VALLEY

Many songs, poems, and other works proclaim that dreams can come true. The Matanuska/Susitna Valley is where many anglers' fishing dreams come true. The valley, close to the state's largest population center, easily fits the description, "Alaska is minutes away from Anchorage." The valley, bordered on the south by the Matanuska and Knik rivers, is surrounded by the Chugach, Talkeetna, and Alaska ranges. It is bisected by the glacier-fed Susitna River, which drains most of the valley's tributaries into Cook Inlet.

Towering Mt. McKinley, North America's highest mountain, watches over

Sportfishing is Alaska's number one sport and outdoor recreation activity. This rainbow trout was taken in the Talkeetna River.

the valley from the north. Melting, ageless glacier ice trickles from the slopes of 20,320-foot McKinley. The trickles join together, gaining size as they cascade from the dizzy heights of their beginning to the valley floor below. Larger streams are formed, some muddy with glacier silt, others clean and clear. Running water from McKinley marries with rivers and streams from the Chugach and Talkeetna mountains to form the Susitna River. Susitna, beginning on the slopes of McKinley, mixes with sea-level saltwater as it terminates in a muddy delta in Cook Inlet. Through the delta, millions of migrating salmon move into the Susitna to meet their fate as parents of orphans or at the end of an angler's line.

The Matanuska/Susitna Valley is blessed with great beauty, clear, clean air, abundant wildlife, and outstanding fishing opportunities. Many valley streams, accessible by road, may be crowded during the water's respective salmon runs, but the area is large, fishable waters are many, and road and water access easy.

Rumors run that when the sun shines in Alaska everyone closes up and goes fishing. Some Southeast communities claim only thirty-seven rain free days per year. Anglers from dryer climates would excuse truancy under these conditions and many would probably even encourage it.

Truth is, Alaska businesses don't close up and go fishing when the sun shines. Fishermen go fishing here just like everyone does everywhere else. They talk about it on sunny days, wonder why it forever rains on weekends, only clears up on Mondays, and wish they didn't have to fish in the rain. Alaska anglers fish after work, go out early mornings on week days, and fill their weekends and holidays with fishing.

The dream of every fisherman is to put a sign on the door, occasionally, and let the world know, for at least one day a year, priorities are right. One day a year the folks at the Alaska Sausage Company in Anchorage do just that. They close down for a day, put a sign on the door, "Closed. Gone fishing." The staff, management, spouses, and friends pack up and go fishing in the Matanuska/Susitna Valley. Last year's outing was spent fishing the tributaries of the Susitna

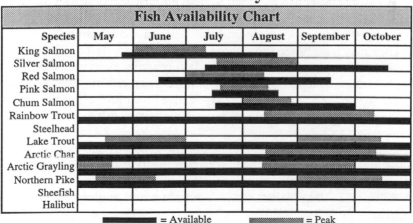

115

These Dollies were taken in the Talkeetna River.

River for silver salmon. The year before they flew in with Ketchum Air Service. Every year is different.

Many nationalities and races are represented on their staff: Blacks, Caucasian, Laotion, Polish, German, Chinese, Philippino, and Vietnamese. In addition to their common employment, they have one other thing in common—fishing. Their common interest brings them together each August when they have a slack time at the store, between major fish runs and hunting season.

Their outing last summer had all the ingredients of a fun time. They lost gear, broke rods, and one of the boats went up a wrong channel. The passengers had to get out, wade, and push the boat. Several employees confessed that the boat trip was the best part of the day, especially the shortcut up the wrong channel.

Customers love it when they find the "Closed. Gone fishing." sign on the door. They may have heard the rumors from Southeast Alaska or just wish they worked for a company that puts fishing before work, even for a day.

Herb Eckman, Alaska Sausage Company owner, explained one of the side benefits. "When we bring our fish in, we realize how much effort the customers took to get their fish, and we take better care of their catch. Our customers know the difference."

One angler summed up the feelings of the group as she explained, "Even though everyone caught fish, the best part of the day was being together in the good weather and sunshine."

Matanuska/Susitna Valley really is where many anglers' fishing dreams come true.

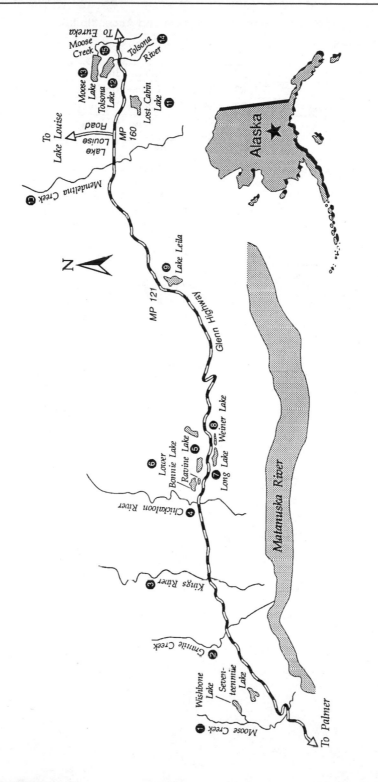

PALMER TO EUREKA VIA GLENN HIGHWAY

Site Number and Name	Fish	Location and Accessibility
1 Moose Creek	DV, RT, CS, SS	Mile 54.6, Glenn Highway.
2 Granite Creek	DV, RT	Mile 62.4, Glenn Highway.
3 Kings River	DV, RT	Mile 66.5, Glenn Highway.
4 Chickaloon River	DV, RT	Mile 77.7, Glenn Highway.
5 Ravine Lake	RT	Mile 83.2, Glenn Highway. Take the road to Bonnie Lakes. Ravine Lake public access is at mile 0.08.
6 Lower Bonnie Lake	RT, GR	Mile 83.2, Glenn Highway. Take the road to Bonnie Lake. Lower Bonnie Lake public access is off a dirt road, at mile 1.2.
7 Long Lake	GR, BB	Mile 85.3, Glenn Highway. Camping and picnic area. Boat launch, well water, and toilets.
8 Wiener Lake	GR, RT	Mile 87.9, Glenn Highway.
9 Lake Leila	GR	Mile 121, Glenn Highway. Gravel pit, parking, short hike to outlet.
10 Mendeltna Creek	GR	Mile 153, Parks Highway. Pull-off present, accommodations available.
11 Lost Cabin Lake	GR	Mile 166, Glenn Highway. 0.75 mile trail across from Atlasta House.
12 Tolsona Lake	GR, BB	Mile 170, Glenn Highway. Turn north at sign. Parking spaces provided by lodge.
13 Moose Lake	GR, BB	Mile 170, Glenn Highway. Turn north at sign. Parking spaces provided by lodge.
14 Tolsona River	GR	Mile 173, Glenn Highway. Adjacent to highway. Campground.
15 Moose Creek	GR	Mile 186, Glenn Highway. Adjacent to highway.

PALMER TO DENALI NATIONAL PARK VIA GLENN AND PARKS HIGHWAYS

Site Number and Name	Fish	Location and Accessibility
1 Echo Lake	RT	Mile 37.6, Glenn Highway. Public access on north shore within the highway right-of-way.
2 Bradley Lake	GR, RT	Mile 37.3, Glenn Highway. Public access for day outing. Commerical campground and boat ramp.
3 Kepler Lake	GR, RT	Mile 37.3, Glenn Highway. Public access for day outing. Commerical campground and boat ramp. Connects with Bradley Lake by a short stream. A bridge accross the stream allows access to both sides of the lakes.
4 Matanuska Lake	RT	Mile 36.4, Glenn Highway. Boat launch and picnic area.
5 Little Susitna River	DV, RT, SS, KS, CS, PS	Mile 57, Parks Highway. Highway crosses river. Publc access. Excellent roadside fishing for salmon and Dolly Varden.
6 Nancy Lake	RT, LT, NP	Mile 64.4, Parks Highway. Canoe rentals and marina.
7 Nancy Lake	RT, LT, NP	Mile 66.6, Parks Highway. Wayside and access road to Nancy Lake Canoe Trail.
8 Little Willow Creek	RT, GR, SS, PS	Mile 74.7, Parks Highway. Highway crosses river. Publc access. The best fishing is downriver from the bridge to the mouth.
9 Kashwitna Lake	SS	Mile 76.4, Parks Highway.
10 Kashwitna River	RT, GR	Mile 83.2, Parks Highway. The best fishing is downstream from the bridge. The stream may clear up in the fall for better fishing.
11 Caswell Creek	KS, SS, PS, RT	Mile 84.9, Parks Highway.
12 Sheep Creek	PS, SS, RT, GR, DV, WF, CS	Mile 88.6 Parks Highway
13 Montana Creek	HS, PS,	Mile 96.6, Parks Highway.
14 Talkeetna River	DV, RT, GR, SS, CS, KS, PS, RS	Mile 98.7, Parks Highway. Take the Talkeetna Spur road for 14 miles to Talkeetna. Good camping and boat launch.
15 Robideaux Creek	SS	Mile 104.6, Parks Highway.
16 Chulitna River	RT, GR, WF	Mile 132.8, Parks Highway.
17 Troublesome Creek	RT, GR, DV	Mile 137.3, Parks Highway.
18 Byers Creek	RT, GR, DV	Mile 143.9, Parks Highway.

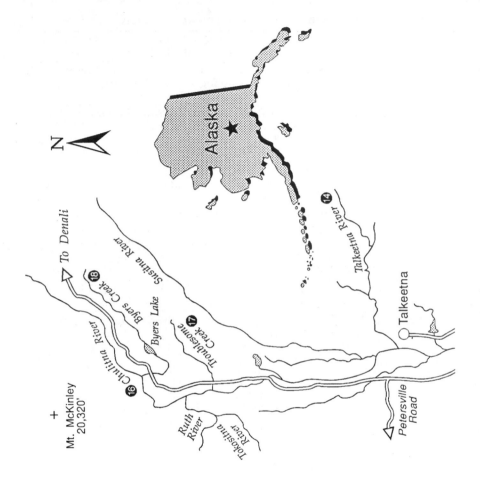

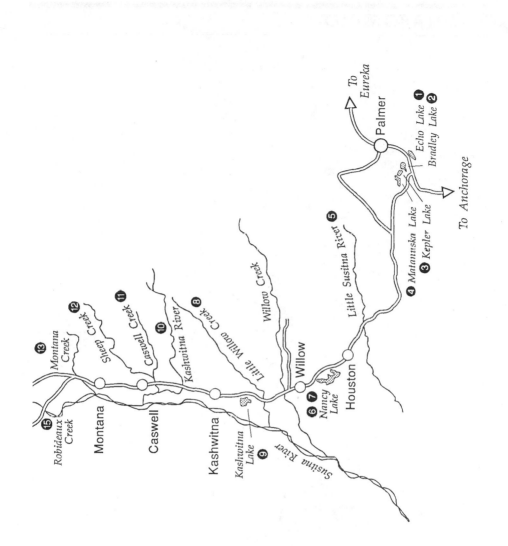

To Eureka

Palmer

Echo Lake ❶

Bradley Lake ❷

To Anchorage

❸ Kepler Lake

❹ Matanuska Lake

Little Susitna River ❺

Willow Creek

Willow

❼ Nancy Lake

❻

Houston

Little Willow Creek

Kashwitna Creek ❽

Kashwitna River

Caswell Creek ❿

Caswell Creek ⓫

Sheep Creek ⓬

Montana Creek ⓭

Montana

Kashwitna

Kashwitna Lake ❾

Susitna River

Robideaux Creek ⓯

⓯

121

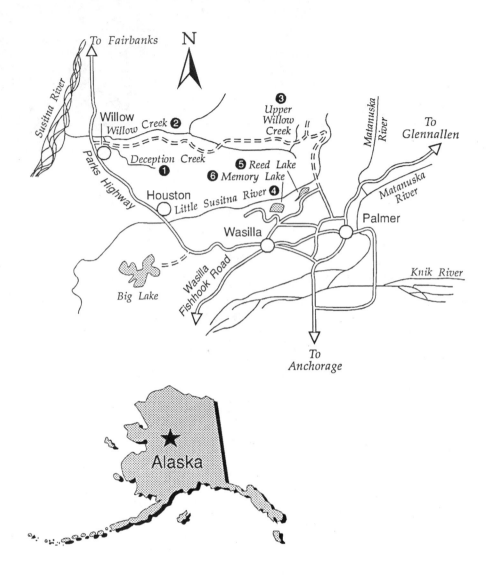

To Fairbanks

N

Susitna River

Willow
Willow Creek ❷
Deception Creek
❶

Upper
Willow
Creek
❸

Matanuska River

To
Glennallen

Parks Highway

Houston
Little Susitna River ❹

❺ Reed Lake
❻ Memory Lake

Matanuska
River

Palmer

Wasilla

Big Lake

Wasilla
Fishhook Road

Knik River

To
Anchorage

★
Alaska

WASILLA TO WILLOW VIA HATCHER PASS AND FISHHOOK ROADS

Site Number and Name	Fish	Location and Accessibility
1 Deception Creek	RT, DV, SS, PS, CS	Mile 1.0, Hatcher Pass Road. Camping and picnicking wayside.
2 Willow Creek	RT, GR, DV, SS, CS, PS, KS	Mile 0 to Mile 6, Hatcher Pass Road. Many pulloffs with stream access.
3 Upper Willow Creek	DV	Mile 6 and above rapids along Hatcher Pass Road. Good fishing for small Dollies.
4 Little Susitna River	DV	Hatcher Pass Road, Palmer side. Numerous pulloffs present above the canyon near Mother Lode Lodge. The water is cloudy but Dolly fishing is good.
5 Reed Lake	RT	Mile 1.2, Fishhook Road, Wasilla side.
6 Memory Lake	RT	Mile 3, Fishhook Road, Wasilla side.

PRINCE WILLIAM SOUND AND COPPER VALLEY

Texans complained when Alaska became the 49th State and Texas became the country's second largest state. One Alaskan retorted, "I think we should split Alaska in two and make Texas the third largest state." The state is over 2.5 times the size of Texas. It has a coastline three times the distance between New York and Melbourne, Australia. Prince William Sound has more coastline than the rest of the United States combined.

The sound's flora, fauna, and weather is similar to Southeast Alaska. Its

Sailboats abound in Prince William Sound.

waterways are lined with thick evergreen forests filled with wildlife. Tidewater glaciers calve off large chunks of millennial-age ice. Large Sitka spruce trees and lush plants thrive on great amounts of rain. Encompassing seemingly endless protected waterways, Prince William Sound is a haven for anglers. It can be accessed by small plane from Anchorage, by boat from Valdez or Cordova, and via the Alaska Railroad at Whittier.

Prince William Sound and the Copper River Valley offer a diversity of sport fishing opportunities. Valdez Arm supports the largest recreational fishery in Prince William Sound and the largest pink salmon fishery in the state. Annual returns of pink and coho salmon to the Valdez fisheries Development Association's Solomon Gulch Hatchery, have created a popular terminal sport fishery for pink and coho salmon.

Valdez claims to be the pink salmon capital of the world, and anglers who fish the sound find out why. Pinks are available to shore fisherman off Rocky Point and Bligh Island. The last week of June will see pinks arrive close to town. By July 4, beaches near Valdez are alive with fish. Wild-stock pinks run strong on even-numbered years everywhere except Valdez. The 1964 earthquake destroyed most of the stock. Hatchery-run fish have replaced the wild run. Each year the hatchery expects over five million returning fish. Most all of them must pass close enough for fishermen to reach them from shore.

Most of the fishing is from shore and everyone catches fish. The best way to fish for Valdez pinks is to walk the shore until you see fish jumping. Usually it indicates there are thirty to fifty fish in the area. Use a 7/8-ounce green or red Pixie. Cast just beyond where you think the fish are headed.

Fishing for pinks in this area is a great way to start a youngster out in the sport. Valdez would be a wonderful spot for the family to spend Independence Day. July 4th is opening day of the Valdez Pink Salmon Derby. This is one derby youngsters have a better-than-even chance of winning.

In another part of the sound, an enhancement project brings several thousand silvers to Shelter Cove, along Chugach Cannery Road each fall. This fishery is within walking distance of downtown Cordova. Saltwater fishing for salmon is popular from shore and boat.

One way to fish the lakes of the sound is to take a hike. Drive the Copper River Highway from Cordova to McKinley Lake trailhead at Mile 21. The trail leads about two miles to McKinley Lake, where anglers may expect to catch cutthroat trout in the lake and its outlet stream, Alagnak Slough. There's an insulated Forest Service cabin on the lake for use by anglers.

An added bonus to this fishing hike is to return by Pipeline Lakes Trail. The trail offers a short, easy hike through wet muskeg to numerous ponds with excellent fishing for rainbow trout. Some public information brochures list grayling in these ponds. Grayling was stocked several years ago but didn't do too well. Anglers may prefer to go in on Pipeline Lakes Trail, fishing along the way and then continuing to McKinley Lake Trail, using the Forest Service cabin at the north end of the lake. Tent camping is near the lake and open country beyond. Fresh fish meals may be supplemented by the profusion of blueberries in the area. The parking area for Pipeline Lakes and McKinley Lakes trailheads are 0.2 mile apart.

Prince William Sound/ Copper River Valley Freshwater

Fish Availability Chart						
Species	**May**	**June**	**July**	**August**	**September**	**October**
King Salmon						
Silver Salmon						
Red Salmon						
Pink Salmon						
Chum Salmon						
Rainbow Trout						
Steelhead						
Lake Trout						
Arctic Char						
Arctic Grayling						
Northern Pike						
Sheefish						
Halibut						

■■■■ = Available ▨▨▨▨ = Peak

Prince William Sound Saltwater

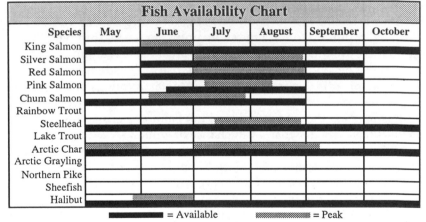

Fish Availability Chart						
Species	**May**	**June**	**July**	**August**	**September**	**October**
King Salmon						
Silver Salmon						
Red Salmon						
Pink Salmon						
Chum Salmon						
Rainbow Trout						
Steelhead						
Lake Trout						
Arctic Char						
Arctic Grayling						
Northern Pike						
Sheefish						
Halibut						

■■■■ = Available ▨▨▨▨ = Peak

In mid-May, thousands of sockeye salmon enter the sound, homeward bound to freshwater streams in Copper River Valley. Copper River empties into Prince William Sound after winding its way across the valley that takes its name from the river. The most used and accessible river in the area besides the Copper is Gulkana. Gulkana receives thousands of red salmon and king salmon each season.

One of my most interesting angling outings to the area didn't see me even getting my outfit out of the motorhome. We drove to Chitna to witness Alaska residents taking red salmon with long-handled dip nets. The Copper River's water near Chitna is filled with glacial silt. Thousands upon thousands of returning red salmon run the river to their natal clear-water stream. Due to the strength of the run, traditional use, and impossibility of sportfishing, the state

Prince William Sound has more coastline than the rest of the United States combined. The waters are full of sea life.

allows residents to subsistence fish using dip nets, with very liberal limits.

Experienced dip-net fishermen develop a technique to capture and preserve their catch. Most purchase a dip net with a ten- or twelve-foot handle. By using hose clamps and duct tape they attach an additional ten-foot extension to the existing handle. To this they add, again with hose clamps and duct tape, a crutch. The crutch gives the user a handle to manipulate the net in deep, swift river water. Most subsistence fishermen wear neoprene chest waders.

Fishing is accomplished by holding on to the crutch handle and throwing the net end of his apparatus upstream and out into the current. By twisting the crutch handle, the user is able to keep the net vertical as it drifts downriver with the water flow. Due to the murky water, the fish can't be seen, and the action is strictly guessing. When the vertically held net drifts as far downriver as possible, its user turns the crutch handle. Turning the handle so the net is horizontal closes the net and traps any netted fish.

We witnessed a family of four generations literally filling their freezer for the winter. They brought a chest-type freezer mounted on a utility trailer and energized by a portable generator. Four family members took turns with two nets. As each fisherman got tired and cold, he would rotate with one of the others. When a red salmon was taken in the net, the fish was given to one of several skilled women or teenagers. They'd quickly and skillfully dispatch the fish, fillet it, and wrap it for the freezer. We arrived in the middle of the afternoon, and their twenty-cubic-foot freezer was nearly full. The young man

I visited, told me they came every year, and one day's fishing supplied their extended family with all the fish it required for a year.

Watching this family work as a team in harvesting one of Alaska's bounties was an interesting experience. Although taking an unseen salmon from muddy water with a net didn't excite either the angler or the spectator like a tail-walking red on a rod, it was fun to observe. I trust their fishing stories over Sunday dinner are not too different from those who subsist with rod and reel.

VALDEZ TO GAKONA VIA RICHARDSON HIGHWAY

Site Number and Name	Fish	Location and Accessibility
1 Valdez	SS, PS, CS, DV, H	Mile 0. Valdez is the gateway to, and the largest sport fishery in, Prince William Sound. Pink salmon fishing from the beach along the road to Alyeska Pipeline Terminal is the best in Alaska. Saltwater silver salmon fishing is superior.
2 Robe River	DV, RS, PS, CS, SS	Mile 2.5. Highway crosses river. Fly-fishing only.
3 Robe Lake	DV, RS, PS, CS, SS	Mile 3.1. Pull-off present.
4 Thompson Lake	GR	Mile 23.3. The lake can be seen from the road. It's east and downhill from the highway.
5 Blueberry Lake	RT	Mile 24.1. Use site.
6 Worthington Lake	RT	Mile 27. Parking area.
7 Tiekel River	DV	Mile 43-50. River parallels highway. Fish are small in size.
8 Little Tonsina River	DV	Mile 74. Use site.
9 Squirrel Creek Pit	GR, RT	Mile 80. Pull-offs and camp sites are present.
10 Klutina River	DV, GR, KS, RS	Mile 100
11 Bear Creek	GR	Mile 127. Pull-off present. Spring and fall fishery.
12 Gulkana River	RT, GR, KS, RS	Mile 128. Fishing trails at mile 129.1, 136.7, 139.6, and 146.5. Use site present at mile 148.

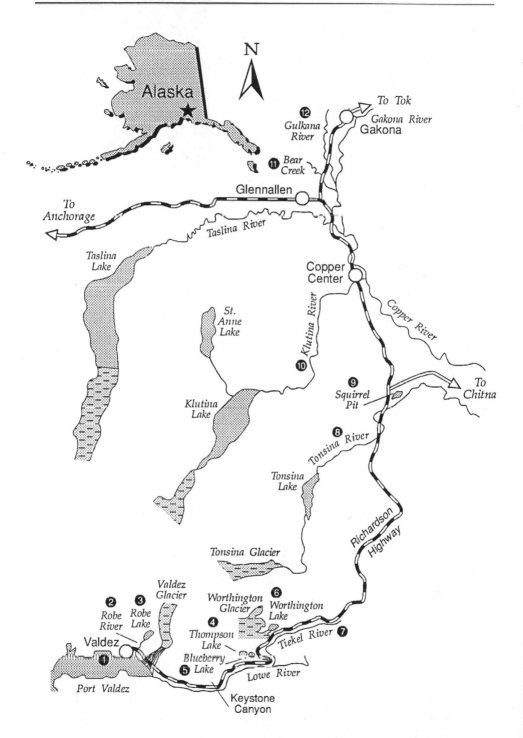

To Tok

Gulkana River

Gakona River

Gakona

Bear Creek

Glennallen

To Anchorage

Taslina River

Taslina Lake

Copper Center

St. Anne Lake

Klutina River

Copper River

To Chitna

Squirrel Pit

Klutina Lake

Tonsina River

Tonsina Lake

Richardson Highway

Tonsina Glacier

Valdez Glacier

Worthington Glacier

Worthington Lake

Robe River

Robe Lake

Thompson Lake

Tiekel River

Valdez

Blueberry Lake

Lowe River

Port Valdez

Keystone Canyon

Alaska

N

RICHARDSON HIGHWAY TO MCCARTHY

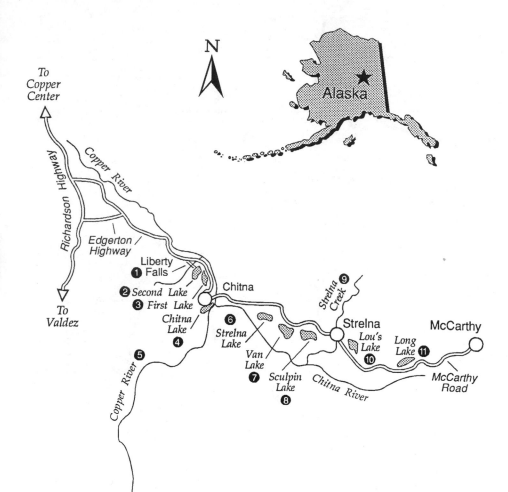

N

To
Copper
Center

Alaska

Richardson Highway

Copper River

Edgerton /
Highway

Liberty
❶ Falls

❷ Second Lake
❸ First Lake

Chitna

Chitna
Lake
❹

To
Valdez

Copper River
❺

❻
Strelna
Lake

Van
Lake

❼

Sculpin
Lake
❽

Strelna Creek
❾

Strelna
Lou's
Lake
❿

Long
Lake ⓫

Chitna River

McCarthy

McCarthy
Road

RICHARDSON HIGHWAY TO MCCARTHY VIA EDGERTON HIGHWAY AND MCARTHY ROAD

Site Number and Name	Fish	Location and Accessibility
1 Liberty Falls	GR	Mile 25, Edgerton Highway. Department of Natural Resources wayside available for parking.
2 Second Lake	RT, GR	Mile 36, Edgerton Highway. Lake is adjacent to road.
3 First Lake	RT, GR	Mile 37, Edgerton Highway. Lake is adjacent to road.
4 Chitna Lake	GR	Mile 39, Edgerton Highway. Lake bordered by the town of Chitna.
5 Copper River	RS, KS	Mile 1.1, McCarthy Road. Campground present.
6 Strelna Lake	RT, SS	Mile 10.6, McCarthy Road. Take trail 0.33 mile north to lake.
7 Van Lake	RT	Mile 11.1, McCarthy Road. Take trail 0.25 mile south to lake.
8 Sculpin Lake	RT	Mile 12.6, McCarthy Road. Take trail 0.25 mile south to lake.
9 Strelna Creek	DV	Mile 15.4, McCarthy Road. Fair fishing.
10 Lou's Lake	SS, GR	Mile 25.7, McCarthy Road. Take trail 0.75 mile north to lake.
11 Long Lake	GR, SS, LT, SS, DV	Mile 45, McCarthy Road.

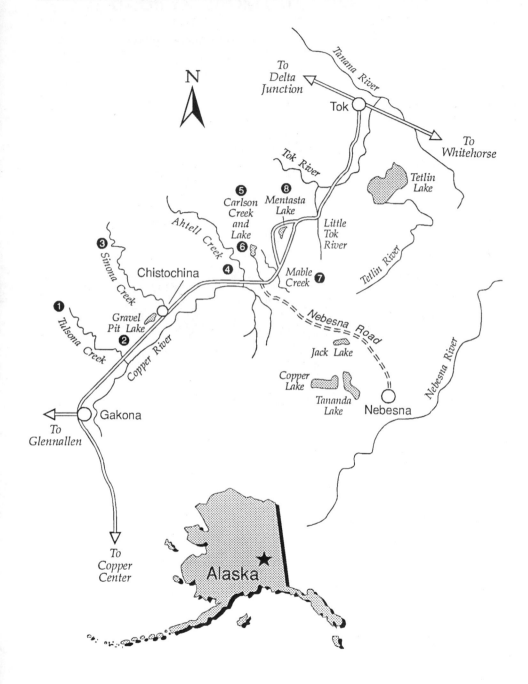

GAKONA TO TOK VIA TOK HIGHWAY

Site Number and Name	Fish	Location and Accessibility
1 Tulsona Creek	GR	Mile 15 to Mile 18, Tok Highway. The creek parallels the highway, with numerous pull-offs.
2 Gravel Pit Lake	GR	Mile 30, Tok Highway. North side of highway.
3 Sinona Creek	GR, DV	Mile 34, Tok Highway.
4 Ahtell Creek	GR	Mile 61, Tok Highway. Use site present.
5 Carlson Creek	GR, DV	Mile 68, Tok Highway.
6 Carlson Lake	GR, DV	Mile 68, Tok Highway. Carlson Lake is 2.5 miles west up Carlson Creek.
7 Mable Creek	GR	Mile 76, Tok Highway.
8 Mentasta Lake	GR	Mile 81.5, Tok Highway. Turn north on the Old Tok Bypass. The inlet and outlet are the best fishing.

GLENN HIGHWAY TO TYONE LAKE VIA LAKE LOUISE ROAD

Site Number and Name	Fish	Location and Accessibility
1 Junction Lake	GR	Mile 0.5. East side of road.
2 Crater Lake	RT	Mile 1.5. West side of road, 200 yards.
3 Little Crater Lake	RT	Mile 1.5. Just below Crater Lake.
4 Old Road Lake	RT	Mile 5.2. Take old road east 0.25 mile. Lake is east of road.
5 Round Lake	RT	Mile 5.2. Take old road east 0.25 mile. Lake is east of road.
6 Tiny Lake	RT	Mile 6.5. Take road west 1.5 miles. Lake is north of road.
7 40-foot Lake	GR	Mile 6.5. Take road west 2 miles. Take trail 0.25 mile north to lake.
8 Peanut Lake	GR	Mile 6.5. West on road 2 miles. Take trail north 0.25 mile to lake.
9 Mendeltna Creek	GR	Mile 6.5. West on road for 5 miles.
10 Forgotten Lake	GR, BB	Mile 7. Pull-off. Lake is east of road.
11 Elbow Lake	GR	Mile 11.5. Lake is east of road.
12 Caribou Lake	GR	Mile 11.5. Lake west of road.
13 Lake Louise	LT, GR, BB, WF	Mile 16.5. Public campground. Accommodations are available.
14 Susitna Lake	LT, GR, BB, WF	By boat across Lake Louise.
15 Tyone Lake	LT, GR, WF	By boat across Lake Louise and Lake Susitna.

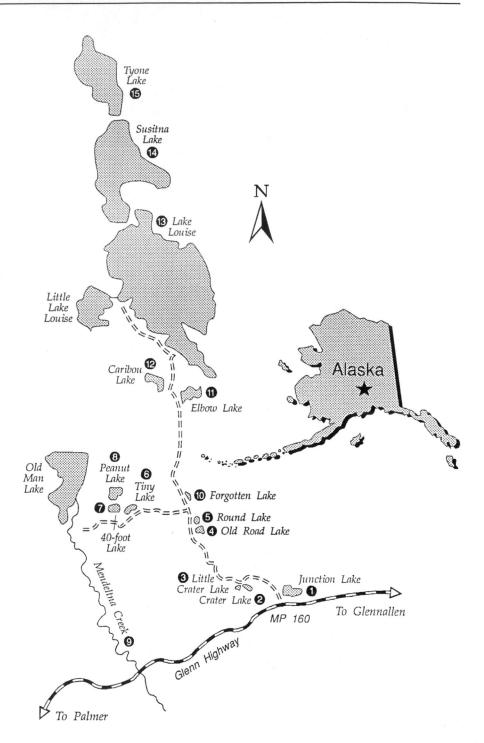

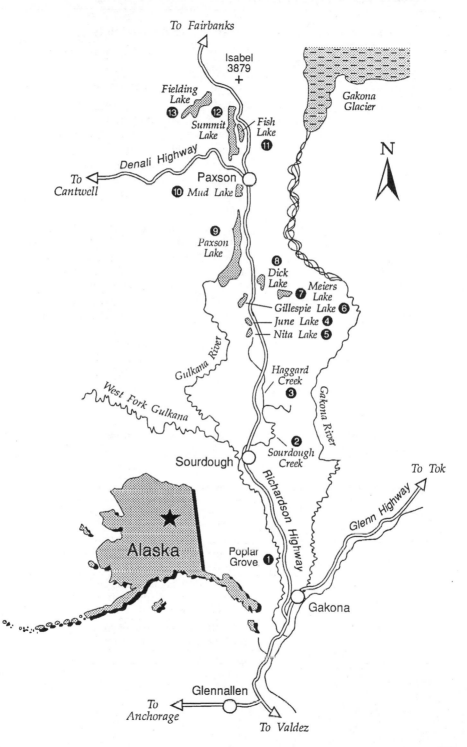

GAKONA TO FIELDING LAKE VIA RICHARDSON HIGHWAY

Site Number and Name	Fish	Location and Accessibility
1 Poplar Grove	GR	Mile 138 Richardson Highway. Spring fishery.
2 Sourdough Creek	GR	Mile 147 Richardson Highway.
3 Haggard Creek	GR	Mile 161 Richardson Highway.
4 June Lake	WF, GR	Mile 166 Richardson Highway. 0.25 mile west.
5 Nita Lake	WF, GR	Mile 166 Richardson Highway. 0.25 mile west.
6 Gillespie Lake	GR	Mile 169.5, Richardson Highway. Walk up Gillespie Creek 0.25 mile.
7 Meiers Lake	GR	Mile 171, Richardson Highway. Pull-offs present Best fishing at inlet.
8 Dick Lake	GR	Mile 173, Richardson Highway. East side of road.
9 Paxson Lake	LT, GR, BB	Mile 181, Richardson Highway. Use sites and numerous accommodations available.
10 Mud Lake	GR	Mile 185.5, Richardson Highway. One mile southwest of Paxson Junction by rough road. Good early season fishing.
11 Fish Lake	GR	Mile 192, Richardson Highway. Pull-off present. Trail parallels creek for 2 miles to lake.
12 Summit Lake	LT, GR, BB	Mile 194, Richardson Highway. Parking areas and accommodations available.
13 Fielding Lake	LT, GR, BB	Mile 200.5, Richardson Highway. Turn south on side road 2 miles. Good fishing.

PAXON TO CANTWELL VIA DENALI HIGHWAY

Site Number and Name	Fish	Location and Accessibility
1 Tangle Lakes	LT, GR, BB	Mile 22.5. The road crosses Tangle River. A use-site is present for camping or picnicking.
2 Landmark Gap Lake	LT, GR	Mile 26. Hike 3 miles due north from highway on a cat trail for good trout fishing. Excellent summer fishing.
3 Glacier Lake	LT, GR	Mile 31. Parking area on north side of highway. Follow the cat trail 2 miles north to lake.
4 Sevenmile Lake	LT	Mile 40. Take the gravel road 0.75 mile to the lake. Excellent summer fishing.
5 Clearwater Creek	GR	Mile 59. Use site present. Fair summer fishery.

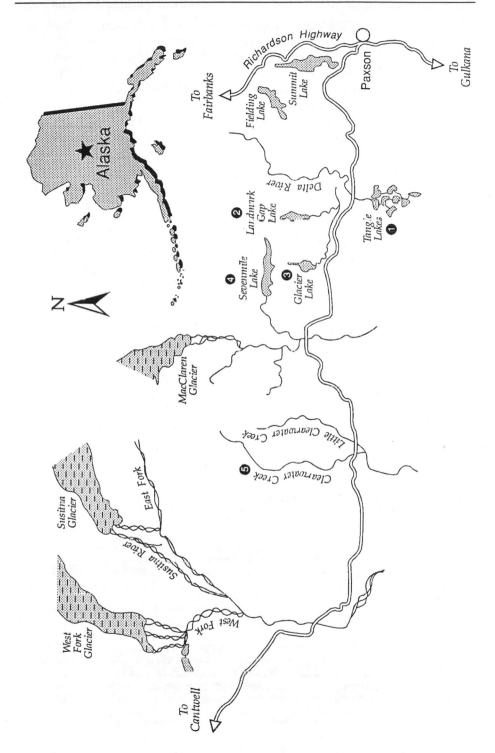

Mt. McKinley's 20,320-foot summit guards the Interior's southern flank, and the Brooks Range stands watch to the north. East is the Yukon border, and the west converges with the Bering Sea. Most of the country is covered with low, rolling hills. Braided rivers cross the country on their way to the sea. The great rivers of the gold rush—Yukon, Tanana, Porcupine, Koyukuk, and others—still serve as much of the Interior's only highways.

The Interior's summer is a paradox—short in number of days, but long in hours of daylight per day. Almost twenty-four hours of light bless anglers who want to fish 'round the clock. This is the place to take off your watch and without thought of time, fish when you want.

While fishing the Interior, anglers may fish until midnight under a brilliant sun. The sun will set slowly and turn pink or red behind northern hills, only to hesitate and begin its upward climb as a stunning sunrise.

What rainbow trout are to Western Alaska, pike, grayling, and sheefish are to the Interior. Northern pike weighing up to thirty pounds may be taken. In season, some area lakes and streams will be choked with migrating grayling. Sheefish haunt the Yukon River and its tributaries, the lower Chena River and Minto Flats streams. Rainbow, not indigenous to the area, have been planted in many lakes along the road system.

Vermont colors pale when compared to an Interior fall. Although short, the period between long, sunny, summer days and freeze-up is an outstanding display of Mother Nature's colors.

While waiting for our ride at the end of an Interior fall outing, we gathered bits and pieces of tundra color. Three of us, during the doldrums of waiting, fashioned an arctic scavenger hunt. We criss-crossed the tundra and retrieved morsels of color to photograph for an outstanding representation of the area's coloring. After an hour of searching, we returned to camp and assembled a

Interior Freshwater

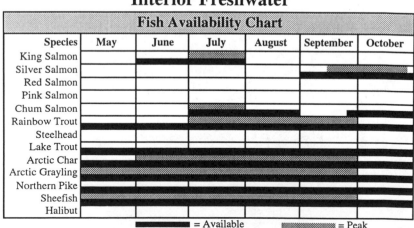

Fish Availability Chart						
Species	May	June	July	August	September	October
King Salmon						
Silver Salmon						
Red Salmon						
Pink Salmon						
Chum Salmon						
Rainbow Trout						
Steelhead						
Lake Trout						
Arctic Char						
Arctic Grayling						
Northern Pike						
Sheefish						
Halibut						

▬▬▬ = Available ▨▨▨ = Peak

Much of the best fishing in the Interior is reached by plane.

composition almost impossible to paint. The resulting photograph is one of my favorites.

Angling the Interior is fishing in a country unpopulated and in waters truly unpolluted. One of my choicest Alaska outings was fishing the Far North with a native Alaskan guide. We were on the Fish River and its tributaries. My guide had learned the river from his grandparents, who had learned from their grandparents; yet his skill with a fly rod and spinning rod were as modern as tomorrow. We were fishing a little "Southeast of Nome," on a river named Fish, in country like Alaska used to be, but will never be again.

Paul, my guide, passed on to me the ancient Eskimo catch-and-release custom he learned from his grandmother who learned it from her grandmother and so on back to the beginning. Ancient Eskimo fishermen returned the first fish they caught, believing it would tell the other fish how well he was treated and the others would come to find out for themselves.

My fishing partner and I decided that if it worked by releasing the first fish, we'd find out what would happen if we released all the fish we caught. The results were so outstanding that we can now write a new chapter in the book on reasons for catch-and-release. Turn back the fish you capture and they'll go and tell the rest how well they were treated, and the others will seek you out.

Paul's grandmother, fishing with primitive instruments, may have known something we, in our age of boron and ball bearings, could learn about our angling pursuits. In Interior Alaska, on the Fish River, a little southeast of Nome, catch-and-release predated Trout Unlimited by centuries.

FIELDING LAKE TO DELTA JUNCTION VIA RICHARDSON HIGHWAYS

Site Number and Name	Fish	Location and Accessibility
1 Rapids Lake	RT	Mile 227, Richardson Highway. Lake is located 0.25 mile south of highway. No facilities.
2 Weasel Lake	RT, AC	Mile 242.8, Richardson Highway. Turn north on dirt road and go 0.75 mile to lake 100 yards east of road. No facilities. There is a primitive camp on Fort Greely Army post. Permit is required, call 873-1111.
3 Donnelly Lake	RT	Mile 244.6, Richardson Highway. Hike 0.5 mile east. No facilities.
4 Ghost Lake	RT, LT	Mile 256, Richardson Highway. Turn south on gravel road and drive 5.1 miles, and turn north and drive 0.2 miles and park. Go west on ATV trail 0.5 miles to lake. No facilities. Fort Greely Army post. Permit is required, call 873-1111.
5 Nickel Lake	GR, RT, LT	Mile 256, Richardson Highway. Turn south on gravel road and drive 5.4 miles to lake. No facilities. Fort Greely Army post. Permit is required, call 873-1111.
6 J Lake	GR	Mile 256, Richardson Highway. Turn south on gravel road and drive 5.4 miles to lake. No facilities. Fort Greely Army post. Permit is required, call 873-1111.
7 Chet Lake	GR, RT, LT	Mile 256, Richardson Highway. Turn south on gravel road and drive 5.6 miles to lake. No facilities. Fort Greely Army post. Permit is required, call 873-1111.

FIELDING LAKE TO DELTA JUNCTION

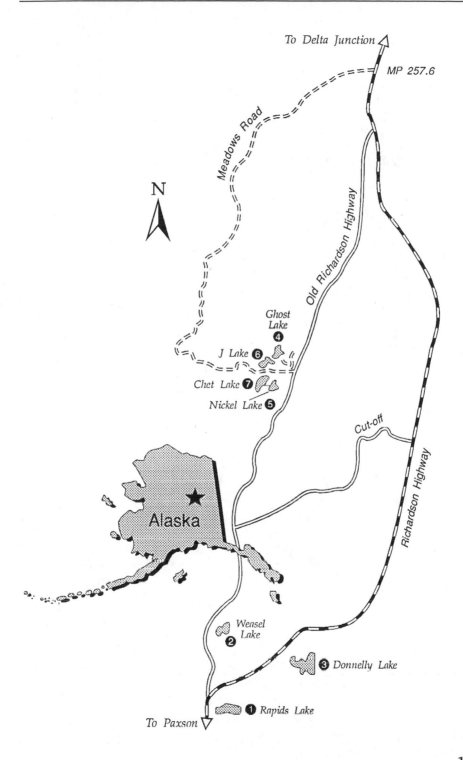

To Delta Junction

MP 257.6

Meadows Road

N

Old Richardson Highway

Ghost Lake ❹

J Lake ❻

Chet Lake ❼

Nickel Lake ❺

Cut-off

Richardson Highway

Alaska

Wensel Lake ❷

❸ Donnelly Lake

❶ Rapids Lake

To Paxson

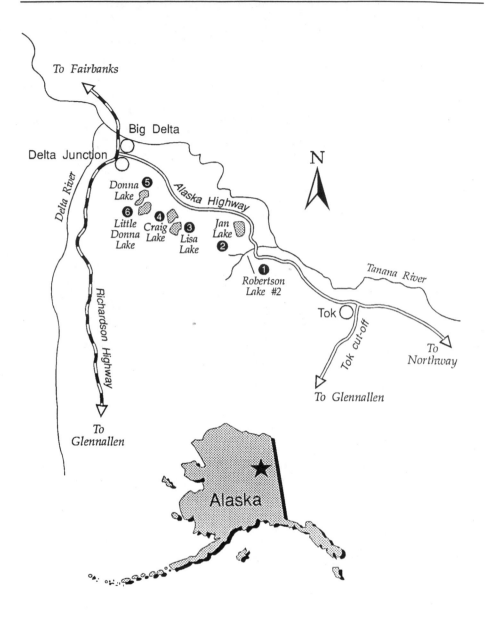

DELTA JUNCTION TO TOK JUNCTION

Site Number and Name	Fish	Location and Accessibility
1 Robertson Lake #2	RT	Mile 1348, Alaska Highway. Go south 0.25 mile on trail from Old Haines Pipeline. No facilities.
2 Jan Lake	RT	Mile 1353.5, Alaska Highway. Take 0.25 mile road to lake. No overnight camping at lake. Day use only.
3 Lisa Lake	RT	Mile 1381, Alaska Highway. Go 0.7 miles south of highway. Winter road only. Trail muddy in summer. No facilities.
4 Craig Lake	RT	Mile 1383.7, Alaska Highway. Turn south on Old Haines Highway bypass and drive 1.1 mile to trail sign. The trail is 0.5 mile long. No facilities and primitive camping.
5 Donna Lake	RT	Mile 1391.8, Alaska Highway. Located 3.5 miles south by trail. No facilities and primitive camp.
6 Little Donna Lake	RT	Mile 1391.8, Alaska Highway. Located 4.5 miles south, 1 mile beyond Donna Lake. No facilities and primitive camping.

DELTA JUNCTION TO FAIRBANKS VIA RICHARDSON HIGHWAY

Site Number and Name	Fish	Location and Accessibility
1 Bluff Cabin Lake	RT	Mile 271.8, Richardson Highway. Drive north on Tanana Loop Road and go 1.3 mile to a junction. Turn right at junction and go 2.3 miles to ATV trailhead. Go north about 4 miles on ATV trail to lake. Map available at Fish and Game office at Fairbanks and Delta Junction. No facilities and primitive camping.
2 Quartz Lake	RT, SS	Mile 277.8, Richardson Highway. Take 2.7 mile gravel road northeast to lake Some facilities, good camping, and public boat launch.
3 Birch Lake	RT, SS	Mile 306, Richardson Highway. Public boat landing, beach pull-offs, and primitive camping.
4 Lost Lake	SS, RT	Mile 306, Richardson Highway. Turn south on dirt access road and drive 0.75 mile to lake. Small parking area at end of access road.
5 Harding Lake	AC, SF, RS, RT	Mile 321.5, Richardson Highway. Turn east at highway sign. Excellent access and complete facilities for picnics, camping, swimming, and fishing. Public boat launch.

Site Number and Name	Fish	Location and Accessibility
6 Little Harding Lake	AC, RT	Mile 321, Richardson Highway. Turn on Salcha Drive to perimeter road located between Harding Lake and Richardson Highway. Access available from Harding Lake perimeter road. No facilities.
7 Johnson Road Lake 1	RT, GR, SS	Mile 330.4, Richardson Highway. Turn north on Johnson Road and go 0.3 miles and turn left. Take immediate right and go 0.4 miles, turn left and go 0.1 miles to lake. No facilities. The lake is man-made from an old gravel pit.
8 Johnson Road Lake 2	GR	Mile 330.4, Richardson Highway. Go past Johnson Road Lake 1 for approximately 0.3 miles. No facilities. The lake is man-made from an old gravel pit.
9 31 Mile Lake	GR, RT	Mile 332, Richardson Highway. Turn north to lake. No facilities. The lake is man-made from an old gravel pit.
10 28 Mile Lake	RT, AC, SS	Mile 335.1, Richardson Highway. Turn north and go 0.1 miles to lake. Picnic tables. On Eielson Air Force Base. Permit is required, call 377-5182.
11 Hidden Lake	RT, GR	Mile 341, Richardson Highway. Turn north and go 0.4 miles, turn right 0.1 miles to lake. Picnic tables. On Eielson Air Force Base. Permit is required, call 377-5182.
12 Grayling Lake	GR	Mile 341, Richardson Highway. Turn north and go 0.4 miles, turn left and go 1.2 miles to lake. Picnic tables. On Eielson Air Force Base. Permit is required, call 377-5182.
13 Bathing Beauty Lake	AC, RT, GR	Mile 343.7, Richardson Highway. Turn south on Eielson Farm Road and drive 50 yards to pond. No facilities.
14 Chena Lake	RT, SS	Mile 346.8, Richardson Highway. Turn at Lawerence Road turnoff. Excellent access, complete facilities for picnics, camping, swimming and fishing. Boating, but no motors allowed.

DELTA JUNCTION TO FAIRBANKS

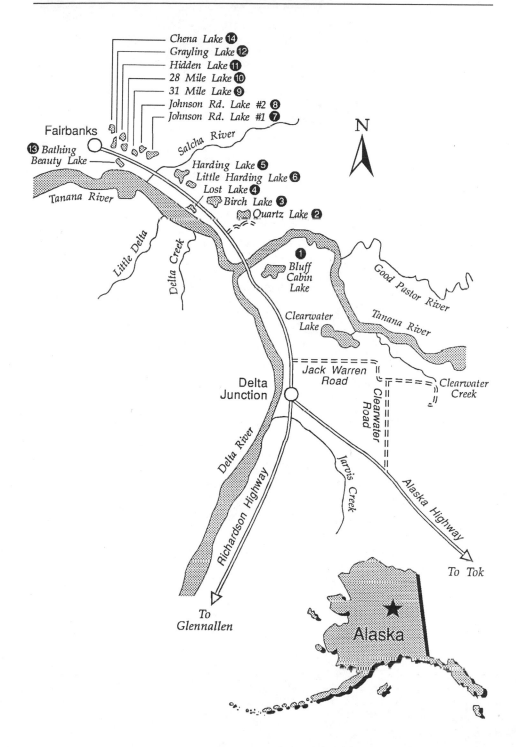

Chena Lake ⑭
Grayling Lake ⑫
Hidden Lake ⑪
28 Mile Lake ⑩
31 Mile Lake ⑨
Johnson Rd. Lake #2 ⑧
Johnson Rd. Lake #1 ⑦

Fairbanks

Salcha River

N

⑬ Bathing
Beauty Lake

Harding Lake ⑤
Little Harding Lake ⑥
Lost Lake ④
Birch Lake ③
Quartz Lake ②

Tanana River

Little Delta

Delta Creek

① Bluff
Cabin
Lake

Good Pastor River

Clearwater
Lake

Tanana River

Jack Warren
Road

Clearwater
Creek

Delta
Junction

Clearwater
Road

Delta River

Richardson Highway

Jarvis Creek

Alaska Highway

To Tok

To
Glennallen

Alaska

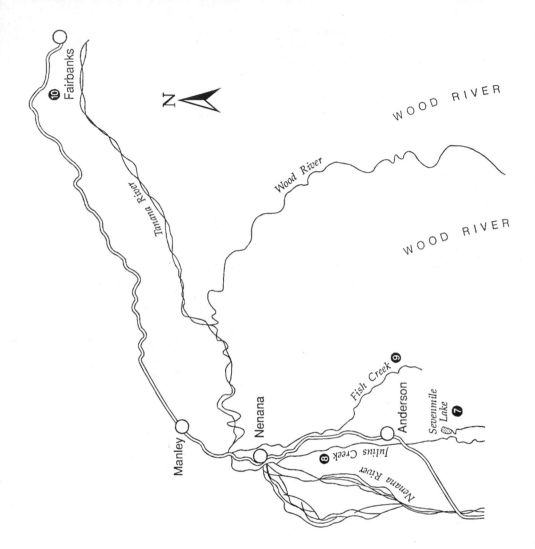

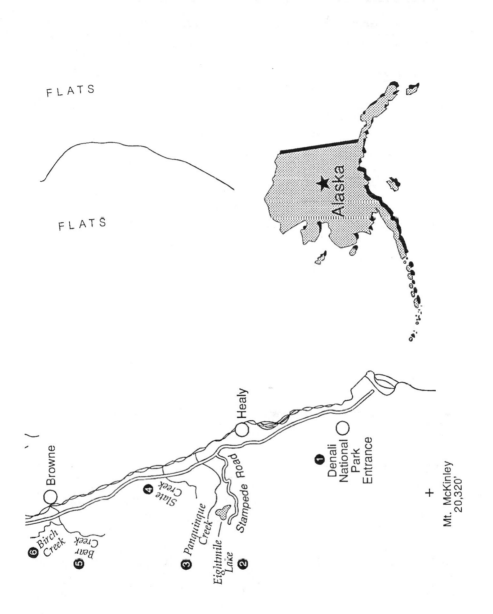

FLATS

FLATS

Alaska

Healy

Browne

Denali
National
Park
Entrance

Stampede Road

Slate Creek

Panguingue Creek

Eightmile Lake

Bear Creek

Birch Creek

Mt. McKinley
20,320'

① ② ③ ④ ⑤ ⑥

DENALI NATIONAL PARK TO FAIRBANKS

Site Number and Name	Fish	Location and Accessibility
1 Denali National Park		There is very little quality fishing accessible by road in the park.
2 Eightmile Lake	GR	Mile 251.2, George Parks Highway. The road to the lake travels 8 miles west on Stampede Road. Lake is 0.25 mile from road.
3 Panquinque Creek	GR	Mile 252.5 ,George Parks Highway.
4 Slate Creek	GR	Mile 257.8, George Parks Highway. Spring fishery if water conditions are right.
5 Bear Creek	GR	Mile 269.4, George Parks Highway. Spring fishery if water conditions are right.
6 Birch Creek	GR	Mile 272.5, George Parks Highway. Spring fishery if water conditions are right.
7 Sevenmile Lake	NP	Mile 280.1, George Parks Highway. The lake is 7 miles east on a winter trail. An undeveloped use site is on the lake.
8 Julius Creek	GR	Mile 285.7, George Parks Highway. Pull-off present.
9 Fish Creek	GR	Mile 296.7, George Parks Highway. Pull-off present.
10 Fairbanks	GR, SS, CS, KS	Mile 358, George Parks Highway. Limited fishing in the Tanana and Chena Rivers. Other area streams and lakes are available to anglers.

FAIRBANKS TO CIRCLE CITY VIA STEESE HIGHWAY

Site Number and Name	Fish	Location and Accessibility
1 29.5-Mile Pond	GR	Mile 29.5, Steese Highway. Turn west to pond. No facilities. Primitive camping.
2 30.6-Mile Pond	GR, AC	Mile 30.6, Steese Highway. Turn west to pond. Limited parking, no facilities, and primitive camping.
3 33-Mile Pond	GR	Mile 33, Steese Highway. Turn east to pond. No facilities and primitive camping.
4 33.5-Mile Pond	GR	Mile 33.5, Steese Highway. Turn west to pond. No facilities and primitive camping.
5 34.6-Mile Pond	GR	Mile 34.6, Steese Highway. Turn south to pond. No facilities and primitive camping.
6 35.8-Mile Pond	GR	Mile 35.8, Steese Highway. Turn south to pond. No facilities and primitive camping.
7 36.6-Mile Pond	GR, AC	Mile 36.6, Steese Highway. Turn north to pond. No facilities and primitive camping.
8 39.3-Mile Pond	RT	Mile 39.3, Steese Highway. Turn south to pond. No facilities and primitive camping.

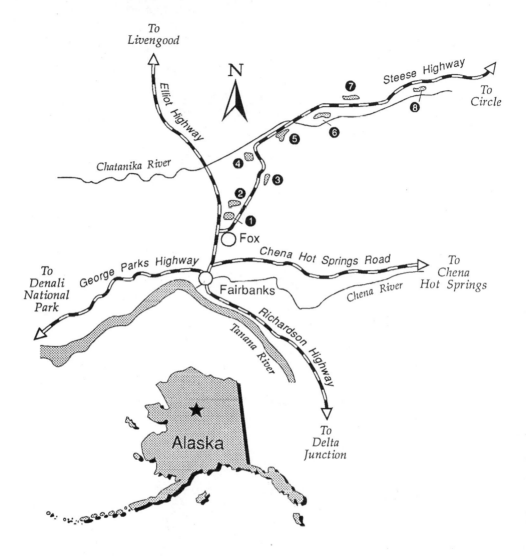

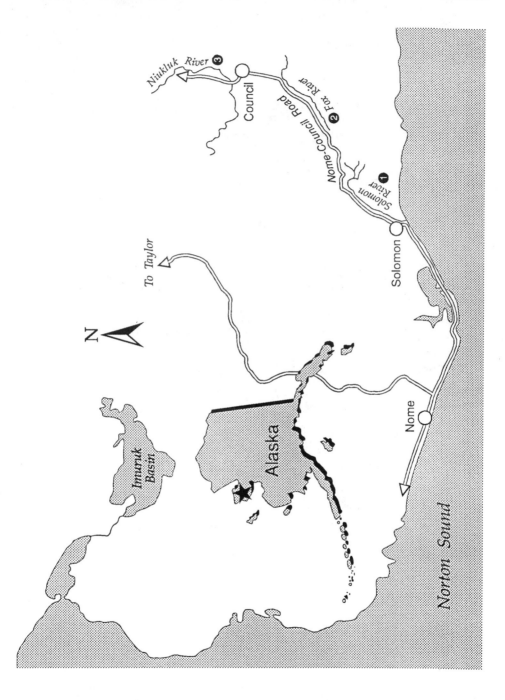

NOME TO COUNCIL VIA NOME-COUNCIL ROAD

Site Number and Name	Fish	Location and Accessibility
1 Solomon River	DV, CS, SS, PS	Mile 40, Nome-Council Road. The road parallels the river between miles 40 and 50.
2 Fox River	AC, CS, PS, SS	After the road crosses Skookum Pass, it follows the river for some distance. The Fox is a small tributary to the Fish River.
3 Niukluk River	DV, KS, AC, NP, CS, PS, SS	The road ends on the south bank of the Niukluk. The river is navigable by jet boat in both directions. The Niukluk provides access to the Fish River.

Nome Area Freshwater

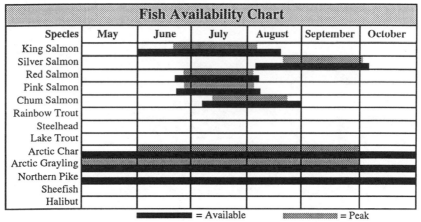

Species	May	June	July	August	September	October
King Salmon						
Silver Salmon						
Red Salmon						
Pink Salmon						
Chum Salmon						
Rainbow Trout						
Steelhead						
Lake Trout						
Arctic Char						
Arctic Grayling						
Northern Pike						
Sheefish						
Halibut						

■■■■ = Available   ▓▓▓▓ = Peak

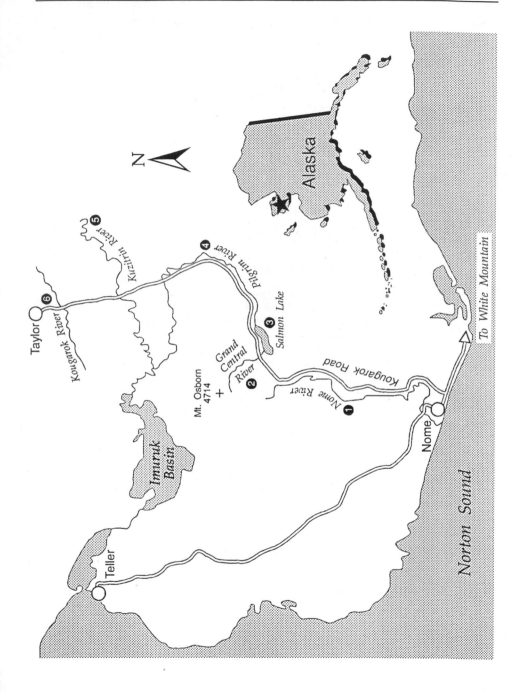

NOME TO TAYLOR VIA KOUGAROK ROAD

Site Number and Name	Fish	Location and Accessibility
1 Nome River	DV, CS, PS, SS KS	Mile 13.2, Kougarok Road. The road crosses the river via a bridge, and the river is accessible by foot. Nome River is the most heavily fished river in the Nome area. The river parallels the road for 20 miles.
2 Grand Central River	GR, DV	Mile 35, Mile Kougarok Road. The Grand Central flows into Salmon Lake. The stream is accessible from a pull-off near the bridge.
3 Salmon Lake	AS, DV RS	Mile 38, Kougarok Road. Salmon Lake is accessed from many different spots along the 8 miles the road parallels the lake. The best access is at the outlet which is the source of Pilgrim River. There's a Bureau of Land Management picnic area and campground.
4 Pilgrim River	CS, SS, RS, DV, KS, NP, GR	Mile 65, Kougarok Road. The road parallels the river for 19 miles, but is usually some distance away. Boats may be launched just downstream from the bridge. The river is navigable from the bridge for 34 miles to Imuruk Basin.
5 Kuzitrin River	CS, SS, GR, DV, KS, NP	Mile 68, Kougarok Road. The river is navigable upstream and downstream from the bridge. Kuzitrin is larger than the Pilgrim River. There are probably more grayling in this river than any river along the Kougarok Road.
6 Kougarok River	DV, GR	Mile 86, Kougarok Road. This is the end of the road, but four-wheel-drive vehicles may travel farther.

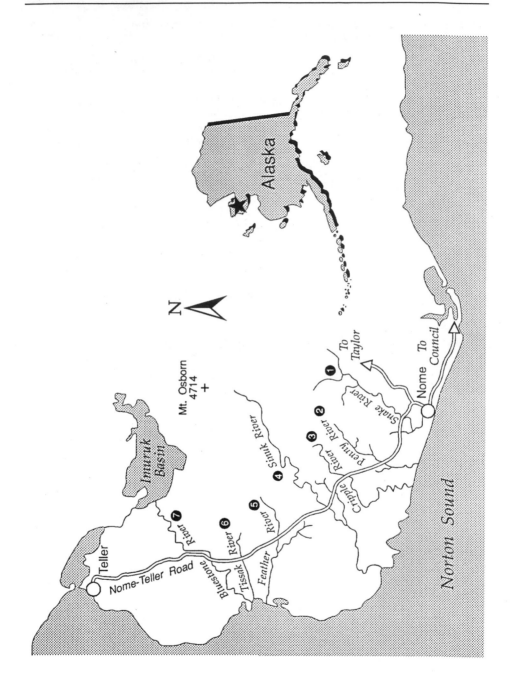

NOME TO TELLER VIA NOME-TELLER ROAD

Site Number and Name	Fish	Location and Accessibility
1 Snake River	CS, PS, SS, GR, DV	Mile 7.9, Nome-Teller Road. The road crosses the river via a bridge, and the river is accessible by foot.
2 Penny River	DV, CS, PS, SS	Mile 13.2, Nome-Teller Road. The road crosses the river via a bridge, and the small river is accessible by foot.
3 Cripple River	DV, CS, PS, SS	Mile 20.3, Nome-Teller Road. The road crosses the river via a bridge, and the river is accessible by foot. Cripple River is somewhat larger than the Penny.
4 Sinuk River	DV, CS, PS, SS, RS, KS, GR	Mile 26.7, Nome-Teller Road. The road crosses the river via a bridge, and the river is accessible by foot. The Sinuk is the largest stream along the road.
5 Feather River	DV, CS, PS, SS, GR	Mile 37.4, Nome-Teller Road. The road crosses the river via a bridge and the river is accessible by foot from a pull-off near the bridge.
6 Tissak River	DV, CS, PS, SS	Mile 48, Nome-Teller Road. The road crosses the river via a bridge, and the river is accessible by foot.
7 Bluestone River	DV, CS, PS, SS, GR	Mile 58.1, Nome-Teller Road. The road crosses the river via a bridge, and the river is accessible by foot. The road also parallels the river for some distance.

KODIAK ISLAND

Kodiak Island, roughly the size of Connecticut, is known as "The island terrific in the North Pacific." The second-largest island in the United States, it is exceeded only by the island of Hawaii. Some have even called it the northernmost island in the Hawaiian chain.

Kodiak Island is about 170 miles long, up to seventy miles wide, contains 3,600 square miles, and due to its deeply indented shoreline, no point in the island is more than fifteen miles from the ocean. The island contains three distinctly different environments. In the northwest corner of Kodiak are scat-

Kodiak represents one of the ultimate vacation destinations. This angler is casting his line in the Buskin River, with the city of Kodiak in the background.

tered pockets at the heads of bays as far west as Uyak Bay, which is rain forest. Lofty Sitka spruce, up to six feet in diameter, tower over carpets of moss, tall ferns, and devil's club thickets. Kodiak's rugged middle section has an alpine environment of glacier-tipped peaks like the highest mountain on Kodiak, 4,470-foot Mount Koniag. The western area is flat, treeless tundra, low, rolling hills, and rounded-off ridges with blueberries, cranberries, and thickets of willow and alder.

Getting to Kodiak is easy. MarkAir has several flights daily from Anchorage to Kodiak. The state ferry, Tustumena, plies the waters between Homer, Seldovia, Seward, and Kodiak. An excellent way to get the whole experience is to fly by MarkAir jet to Kodiak, return to Homer by ferry, and then to Anchorage by air.

The people are friendly to a flaw. The cruise ships have yet to reach Kodiak, and the recreation provider hasn't become jaded by dealing with tourists and professional tourism. The service to the visiting angler is hometown and honest.

Prior to statehood, there were several large canneries on Kodiak. The greedy owners put out so many commercial fishing nets they completely blocked off the rivers during the run. They soon netted themselves out of fish and packed up and left. Since Alaska became a state, the resource has been managed with great care. Today, salmon runs are getting back to the size of earlier times.

The big attraction for fishermen is the hundreds of rivers and small streams where all five species of Pacific salmon run in season. Additionally, steelhead, rainbow, Dolly Varden, arctic char, and grayling may be taken throughout the area. Only six miles from downtown, and within walking distance of the airport, the Buskin River is the most popular fishery on Kodiak. The best known river is the Karluk, which supports runs of salmon in the millions. There is also offshore fishing for halibut. The sheltered waters also offer excellent salmon fishing.

Kodiak Island can be enjoyed during a weekend fling, a week of recreation, or a summer of fishing fun by using the road system. More adventurous anglers may fly out for more remote fishing. Kodiak may be the Alaska you're looking for.

Kodiak, one of nature's treasures, abounds with wildlife, teems with crab and fish, and everywhere magnificent bald eagles soar overhead. Whales, sea lions, sea otters, and sea and shore birds welcome visitors to almost every corner of Kodiak's islands, bays, and beaches.

A whole summer on Kodiak will allow a visiting angler to sample about as much of Kodiak's fishery as Captain Cook discovered when he landed on Point Possession. Kodiak's fishing possibilities await the adventurous angler who wants to find new places and uncover secret holes. A few days or even weeks on Kodiak will still leave the angler with lakes, streams, and ocean depths yet to fish. Wherever in the world you drop anchor or throw a fly line, don't neglect putting Kodiak, the most northern island in the Hawaiian chain, on your list of places to discover.

One Kodiak river I never tire of fishing is the Karluk. It was during the short boat ride from the airport to the lodge that I began receiving my Karluk River education. The guide explained that the fish come in on the tide. It's best to start

Kodiak Freshwater

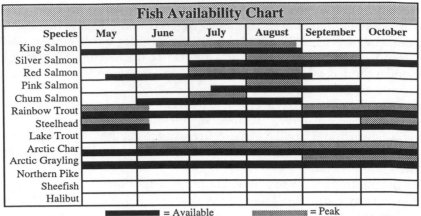

Species	May	June	July	August	September	October
King Salmon						
Silver Salmon						
Red Salmon						
Pink Salmon						
Chum Salmon						
Rainbow Trout						
Steelhead						
Lake Trout						
Arctic Char						
Arctic Grayling						
Northern Pike						
Sheefish						
Halibut						

■■■ = Available   ▨▨▨ = Peak

Kodiak Saltwater

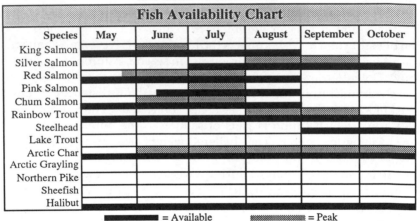

Species	May	June	July	August	September	October
King Salmon						
Silver Salmon						
Red Salmon						
Pink Salmon						
Chum Salmon						
Rainbow Trout						
Steelhead						
Lake Trout						
Arctic Char						
Arctic Grayling						
Northern Pike						
Sheefish						
Halibut						

■■■ = Available   ▨▨▨ = Peak

fishing at the mouth just as the tide starts moving. Follow the fish as they move upriver into the lagoon. Once high water is reached, the fishing will stop. There will be no more fish at the mouth until the next tide. The fish will move upriver into the holes, and it will be hot up there when it's not any good down at the mouth. By the time the fish move through the upper holes and on upriver, it's time to go back and try the mouth again. Somewhere in between there'll be time for three meals and sleep.

My excitement of fishing the Karluk was short lived when I met Paul, one of the lodge's guests. "How's the fishing?" I asked.

"Not too good. It's the same here as at the lodge where I was last year. I had a good time, but the fishing was not what it was cracked up to be. I just don't think Alaska fishing is all that great. My guide thinks I'll do better at the mouth. He says the kings will be coming in on the tide. I hope it's not just another

You can put your car or camper on the state ferry and go to Kodiak Island. There are many places to camp, like this spot along the Olds River.

guide story."

The guide shouted, "Fish on!" as Paul hooked up on his first cast. The fish started upriver and then turned down and headed for the open sea. The guide assumed his role and began to counsel Paul. "Keep the tip up, let the rod do the work."

The fish took line out at about ten yards a second. Paul turned his drag tighter, and the guide told him to leave it alone. "It's set right. Don't tighten the drag, move along the beach with the fish."

As if he didn't hear, Paul planted his feet firmly on shore and tightened the drag. The rod tip dropped until it was pointed directly at the running fish. The line continued to play off the reel as Paul leaned back and held on. The tell-tale rifle shot sound of breaking line signaled the end of the fight as Paul almost fell over backwards when the forward pull quit abruptly.

The guide discovered that Paul's reel was completely worn out. All the gears were gone. "It's a new reel," Paul exclaimed. "It can't be broken already."

The guide tried to explain. "Paul, you're using a very heavy line. The drag is set way too tight. These are big strong fish right from the ocean, and you need to follow them downriver and out of swift water." The guide loaned Paul another outfit he'd brought along for just such an emergency.

Inasmuch as Paul had hooked up on his first cast, he was now the expert and would not listen to the guide. He was wearing chest waders and insisted on standing in water over his waist, even if it meant wading into the hole and casting beyond the fish. As the tide advanced, the guide moved me and two other guests up the lagoon to the rock pile. Paul insisted on fishing where he had earlier hooked fish. We soon limited out and began fishing for sport. Paul continued to ignore the guide and came up empty.

When the tide peaked, the fishing quit. The fish moved on up the lagoon out of reach. We headed for the lodge and dinner. Paul remained to fish the outgoing tide, where he stayed until it got dark. He reported that he didn't even get a bite. He had tenacity, but he didn't have enough sense to listen to the guide.

The next two days were repeats of the first afternoon. Upriver and down everyone caught fish. Sockeyes, kings, Dollies, and rainbows. Everyone except Paul. Finally, in frustration, the guide waded out to where Paul was standing.

"Paul, you've go to listen to me. You're standing right where the fish are moving through. You fish at the wrong time, in the wrong place, use the wrong lure, and the wrong approach. If you want to catch fish, you've go to listen to me."

Paul's response was. "I'll try a few more casts here and then move on up." With that, the guide gave up on Paul.

Guides tell me there are guys like Paul on almost every trip. They think they know more than the guide and keep fishing "a better way." Guides take personal pride in seeing their clients catch fish. When they don't, it's almost a personal affront.

There's competition among guides at every fishing lodge. They add up the score of the day's catch with each other. They don't like it if someone doesn't catch fish. They'll break their backs to make sure their client has the best possible chance to land what he paid money for.

Alaska is a fish-rich state. No one need ever come up empty fishing its waters. Most anglers have enough brains to look around and follow other successful fishermen when they themselves are not doing well. Almost everyone will share bait ideas or techniques with others who are willing to listen.

I hope anyone Paul tells "the fishing in Alaska is not what it's cracked up to be," knows better. Paul, if you read this, come back again. This time listen to your guide and you'll catch fish until you wish you hadn't listened.

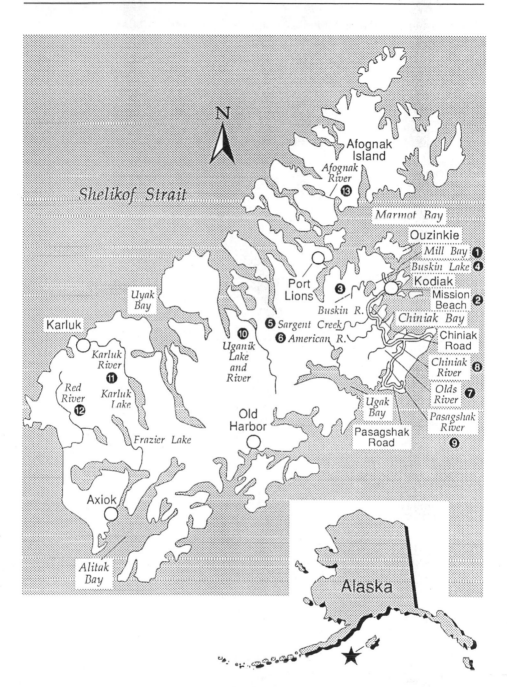

Shelikof Strait

Afognak Island
Afognak River ⑬
Marmot Bay
Ouzinkie
Mill Bay ❶
Buskin Lake ❹
Kodiak
Mission Beach ❷
Chiniak Bay
Chiniak Road
Chiniak River ❽
Olds River ❼
Pasagshak River
❾

N

Port Lions ❸
Buskin R.
Sargent Creek ❺
American R. ❻
Uganik Lake and River ❿

Uyak Bay

Karluk
Karluk River ⓫
Red River ⓬
Karluk Lake
Frazier Lake

Old Harbor

Ugak Bay
Pasagshak Road

Axiok

Alitak Bay

Alaska

KODIAK ISLAND

Site Number and Name	Fish	Location and Accessibility
1 Mill Bay	SS, PS, CS, DV, H	Mill Bay is located on Rezanof Drive East, just before Monashka Bay Road. This is one of the island's most productive beach fishing areas. There's always a crowd, but don't get discouraged. The fishing is so good that a spot will soon open up.
2 Mission Beach	PS, CS, SS, RS, KS	Mission Beach is reached on the east side of Mission Road in downtown Kodiak. All species of salmon run past this beach.
3 Buskin River	RS, SS, PS, CS, DV, SH, RT	Mile 4.0, Chiniak Road. Parking, restrooms, and limited camping.
4 Buskin Lake	RS, SS, PS, CS, DV, SH, RT	Mile 4.7, Chiniak Road. Turn on Larsen Bay Road and travel for about a mile. The road follows the Buskin River.
5 Sargent Creek	SS, RS, PS, CS	Mile 9.6, Chiniak Road. Parking on both sides of the bridge. No camping or restroom.
6 American River	SS, RS, PS, CS	Mile 9.6, Chiniak Road. Parking on both sides of the bridge. No camping or restroom.
7 Olds River	SS, PS, CS, SH	Mile 29.8, Chiniak Road.
8 Chiniak River	SS, PS, RS, CS	Mile 41.5, Chiniak Road. Room to park, but not established camping. The best fishing is between the culverts and the river's mouth.
9 Pasagshak River	KS, RS SS, CS, DV	The Pasagshak River is accessed by turning off Chiniak Road at Mile 30.1 and traveling 9.7 miles.

Kodiak Fly-In Fishing

10 Uganik Lake and River	SS, RS, PS, CS, DV, SH, RT	Available by air charter and mail plane.
11 Karluk River	SS, RS, PS, CS, KS, DV, SH, RT	Available by air charter and mail plane.
12 Red River	SS, RS, PS, CS, KS, DV, SH, RT	Available by air charter and mail plane.
13 Afognak River	SS, RS, PS, CS, RT, DV, SH	Available by air charter and mail plane.

Don Beck prepares to release this fifteen-pound rainbow taken in the Kvichak River.

SOUTHEAST

An angler could spend a lifetime fishing the waters of Southeast Alaska, fish a different place every day, and never fish the same place twice. There are hundreds of fishable small streams, tens of thousands of miles of coastline, and millions of acres of saltwater to explore and fish. Due to its mild climate, Southeast Alaska sport anglers can keep busy all year long. There's fishing for wild trout in remote lakes, salmon in marine areas, stocked trout and salmon in roadside lakes, and even marine species off city docks and floats. In addition, charter boat operators and air taxi companies offer guided fishing trips and drop-off transportation.

The area availability charts in this guide only represent the vast extent of the angling possibilities in Southeast Alaska. Just one island in Southeast Alaska could demand a guide of its own. Prince of Wales Island is the third largest in the United States, exceeded in size by Kodiak and the island of Hawaii. It's host to huge, productive migrating salmon, steelhead, and cutthroat trout runs. The offshore ocean bottom is choked with hungry halibut and other bottom fish. The island is criss-crossed with logging roads, allowing access to remote areas by automobile. Other Southeast Alaskan islands and groups of islands provide similar angling opportunities.

Southeast Alaska's waters are the most fertile in the state. Porpoises, whales, sea lions, and seals ply the saltwaters. All five species of salmon spawn in Southeast Alaskan streams. Dolly Varden, brook trout, rainbow, steelhead, grayling, and cutthroat trout provide excellent fishing for anglers. Outstanding fishing begins in April and extends through September with good fishing the rest of the year.

The Forest Service publishes a guide to many Forest Service cabins in good fishing areas. These cabins may be accessed by floatplane at modest cost, or charter boat transportation may be obtained. Many cabins include an on-site boat for anglers' use.

Other superb remote fishing locations are available for camping. If camping, be prepared with an expedition-quality tent equipped with the best rain fly available. The Southeast's abundance of moisture, creates lush rain forests of Sitka spruce, stately cedars, and hemlock trees growing to enormous size.

Remote areas are profuse with wildlife. Eagles nest near rivers and shorelines. Brown and black bears, Sitka black-tailed deer, and wolves roam the forests, and goats are common on mountain sides. Beaver, mink, marten, wolverine, and river otter often make their presence known.

There are no roads to Southeast Alaska, and even major communities have dead-end roads extending only a few miles out of the town. Locals claim there are two places to go: the end of the road and the other end of the road. In addition to flying by commercial jet, anglers can fish Southeast Alaska by traveling on the State of Alaska Marine Highway ferry boats which serve Southeast Alaskan communities. The ferry allows passengers to bring their own automobiles in order to fish from the road systems of the various communities. Each year a few hardy anglers fish the Inside Passage from private yachts and sailboats. Transient moorage is available at the downtown city floats.

Twice-daily tides average between ten and eleven feet with extremes between fifteen and twenty-three feet. Tides and currents move with speed, due to the many islands, bays, and passages. Small streams entering saltwater through tidal flats, created by low tides, create a difficult but productive fishing area.

When fishing the tidal flats, my suggestion is to stay on the flats if you don't know the area. The undergrowth is rough going and almost impenetrable. An inflatable boat is almost a must if you're on the flats. When fishing the flats don't forget the tide. A fifteen-foot tide change means you will need to know what the tide is doing at all times. An incoming tide can cover the beach you walked in on, and an outgoing tide may make rivers impassable.

Many of the streams entering saltwater contain sea-run Dolly Varden. Many of these little streams will contain pools of fish waiting for more water before going upstream. An angler friend of mine told me of a trip he took to Southeast Alaska. He said of one hole, "As I worked my way downstream, I hooked and released more fish than many dedicated fly-fishermen will encounter in a year, or perhaps a lifetime. I have to admit a fair percentage of these fish released themselves, which isn't surprising since this brush-choked creek resembled an obstacle course more than a fishery. These difficulties only added to the day's challenge." He added, "Many of these tiny, fish-laden streams don't even have names. The fish don't seem to care."

Called the Gateway City, Ketchikan, located on Revillagigedo Island on Tongass Narrows, is the South 48's closest community. Ketchikan is 235 miles south of Juneau and ninety miles north of Prince Rupert, British Columbia. Ketchikan was our location for filming several segments for the Alaska Outdoors television show. The shooting season began in Southcentral Alaska, and ended seven weeks later in George Inlet out of Ketchikan.

George Inlet allows anglers a wide variety of fishing. Our guide took us first to a spot where we caught a good number of fourteen- to eighteen-inch bottom fish. The fishing was tremendous, but contrary to Alaska fishing guides' usual catch-and-release rules, we kept every fish we caught.

When the guide said, "That's enough," we quit fishing and motored up the inlet to a small bay. At a select spot known to our guide, we stopped and baited a couple of crab pots. After tying the pots to a long line connected to an orange buoy, the pots were lowered into ocean depths, and we left for a day of halibut fishing.

During the day, we discussed crab fishing with our guide. He told us the pots were constructed so a marauding crab could enter the pot through an oblong hole in the side. The hole is protected by a trap that allows a crab to slip in but will not let it back out.

Our guide, experienced in crab fishing, told us he was sure the pot would be full. He said the only reason there wouldn't be a full pot is if a passing fishing boat robbed the pot in our absence. When a crab pot is robbed, it's an unwritten rule that the thief replaces the bait and leaves a six-pack for the owner.

Later in the day, we discovered it was easier to lower the pots than to pull them back to the surface. The weight of the pots gave rise to speculation that they would be filled. When the first pot broke the surface, we discovered only a couple of small crab. The bait we had placed there had been replaced with new bait.

"Damn," said our guide. "Our pot has been robbed and the crook didn't even leave a six-pack. Let's see what's in the other pot."

The second pot was harder to pull, and sure enough it was filled with crab. After throwing out the females and small crab, we still had enough of the tasty crustaceans for a mighty meal. Even as we gorged on butter-dipped delicacies, our guide continued to bad mouth the robber of the other pot.

The last two days of our filming saw us catching sea-run silvers while trolling from a comfortable cabin cruiser. The fishing was spectacular, a grand finale to our summer's shooting. As this was the last shoot, and we were heading home, we decided to keep a few fish for the freezer.

I helped the guide put several big silvers in a box. After packing the box full of fish, I sealed it and wrote my name and address on the top. Then I carried the box of fish to the waiting van and placed it in the back with the rest of my gear. We then left for the Ketchikan airport in another vehicle followed by the van of fish and gear.

Ketchikan's airport is on an island accessible by ferry boat. Most passengers, as we did, walk on board. Our gear van drove onto the ferry, and we were all transported to the airport and checked our baggage in, including my box of fish. The south- and north-bound planes arrive and depart about the same time in

Ketchikan. My crew was going south, and I was going north to Anchorage. We said our good-byes and boarded our respective flights.

Back in Anchorage, I told my children I'd brought a surprise for our family. We took the box of fish to our freezer. After cleaning off a shelf, we opened the box. At either end of the box was a George Inlet beach rock packed in newspaper. Sandwiched between the rocks was a six-pack. ·

Knowing I'm a teetotaler, my children looked at me in dismay. They really became confused when I began to laugh. It took a minute before I could stop laughing enough to tell them about the crab-pot-robber-tradition of Southeast Alaska.

I've never admitted the joke to either the guide nor my shooting crew. But some day, some way, I'll get even. I've been planning my revenge, and one day, that old six-pack will end up in somebody's suitcase as a substitute for something I think valuable.

SOUTHERN SOUTHEAST ALASKA

Site Number and Name	Fish	Location and Accessibility
1 Ketchikan	KS, SS, PS, CS, DV, H	A great deal of fishing is done by residents in the channel on the edge of town. Charter boats are available.
2 Mountain Point (Ketchikan Area)	KS, SS, PS, CS, DV, H	Mountain Point, at the end of the road, has a boat ramp, fuel, and water. Charter boats are available.
3 Ward Lakes (Ketchikan Area)	KS, RS, CS, SS, PS, DV, SH, RT, CT	
4 Clover Pass (Ketchikan Area)	KS, SS, PS, CS, DV, H	Clover Pass is at the other end of the road. There's a boat ramp, camping, and fuel.
5 San Alberto Bay (Prince of Wales Island)	KS, SS, PS, CS, DV, H	San Alberto Bay is available by road from Craig. There's a boat ramp, camping, and fuel.
6 Thorne Bay (Prince of Wales Island)	KS, SS, PS, CS, DV, H	Thorne Bay is available by road. There's a boat ramp and fuel.
7 Thorne River	SS, RS, PS, CS, DV, SH, RT, CT	Thorne River is available by road from Klawock.
8 Wrangell Narrows	KS, SS, CS, PS, DV, H	Wrangell Narrows are available by road from Petersburg.

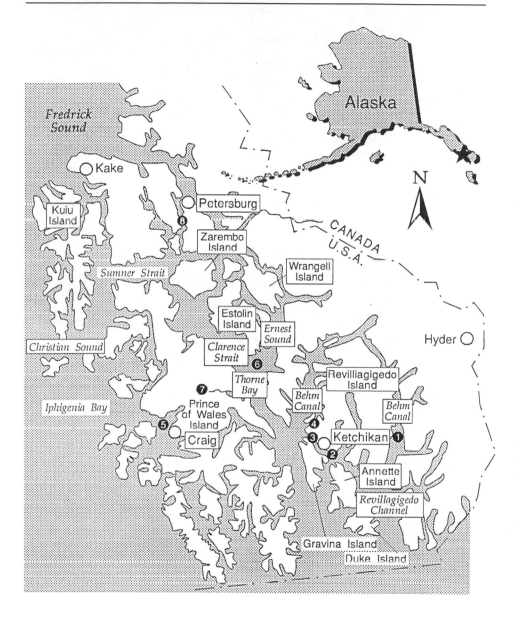

Alaska

N

Fredrick
Sound

Kake

Kuiu
Island

Petersburg

❽

Zarembo
Island

CANADA
U.S.A.

Wrangell
Island

Sumner Strait

Estolin
Island

Ernest
Sound

Hyder

Christian Sound

Clarence
Strait

❻

Revilliagigedo
Island

Iphigenia Bay

❼

Thorne
Bay

Behm
Canal

Behm
Canal

Prince
of Wales
Island

❺

❹

❸

Ketchikan

❶

Craig

❷

Annette
Island

Revillagigedo
Channel

Gravina Island

Duke Island

Southern Southeast Alaska Freshwater

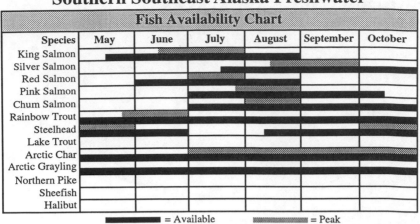

Species	May	June	July	August	September	October
King Salmon						
Silver Salmon						
Red Salmon						
Pink Salmon						
Chum Salmon						
Rainbow Trout						
Steelhead						
Lake Trout						
Arctic Char						
Arctic Grayling						
Northern Pike						
Sheefish						
Halibut						

Fish Availability Chart

■ = Available   ▨ = Peak

Southern Southeast Alaska Saltwater

Fish Availability Chart

Species	May	June	July	August	September	October
King Salmon						
Silver Salmon						
Red Salmon						
Pink Salmon						
Chum Salmon						
Rainbow Trout						
Steelhead						
Lake Trout						
Arctic Char						
Arctic Grayling						
Northern Pike						
Sheefish						
Halibut						

■ = Available   ▨ = Peak

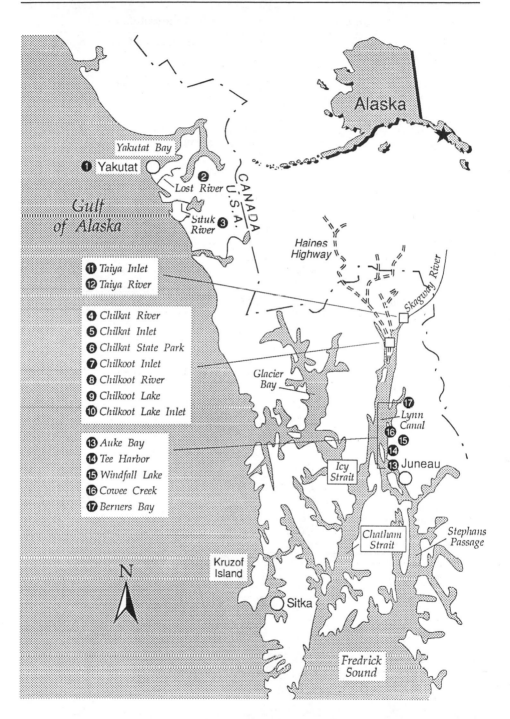

Yakutat Bay

1 Yakutat

2
Lost River

Gulf of Alaska

Situk **3**
River

Alaska

CANADA
U.S.A.

Haines
Highway

Skagway River

11 Taiya Inlet
12 Taiya River

4 Chilkat River
5 Chilkat Inlet
6 Chilkat State Park
7 Chilkoot Inlet
8 Chilkoot River
9 Chilkoot Lake
10 Chilkoot Lake Inlet

13 Auke Bay
14 Tee Harbor
15 Windfall Lake
16 Cowee Creek
17 Berners Bay

Glacier
Bay

17
Lynn
Canal
16
15
14
13 Juneau

Icy
Strait

Chatham
Strait

Stephans
Passage

Kruzof
Island

N

Sitka

Fredrick
Sound

NORTHERN SOUTHEAST ALASKA

Site Number and Name	Fish	Location and Accessibility
1 Yakutat Bay (Yakutat Area)	KS, SS, PS, CS, DV, H	Access from Yakutat small boat harbor.
2 Lost River (Yakutat Area)	RS, SS, PS, CS, DV	Access from Yakutat via Lost River Road.
3 Situk River (Yakutat Area)	RS, SS, PS, CS, DV, KS, SH, RT, BT, CT	Access from Yakutat via Situk River Road. Landing is at end of road.
4 Chilkat River (Haines Area)	SS, RS, CS, KS, DV, CT	Parallels Haines Highway.
5 Chilkat Inlet (Haines Area)	PS, SS, RS, CS, KS, DV, CT, H	Boat and beach access along Mud Bay Road.
6 Chilkat State Park (Haines Area)	PS, SS, RS, CS, KS, DV, CT, RT, H	Mile 6, Mud Bay Road. Boat ramp and campground.
7 Chilkoot Inlet (Haines Area)	PS, SS, RS, CS, KS,DV, CT,H	Boat and beach access from Lutak Road.
8 Chilkoot River (Haines Area)	PS, SS, RS, CS, KS, DV	End Lutak Road.
9 Chilkoot Lake (Haines Area)	PS, SS, RS, CS, DV, CT	End Lutak Road. Boat ramp and campground.
10 Chilkoot Lake Inlet (Haines Area)	PS, SS, RS, CS, DV, CT	End Lutak Road.
11 Taiya Inlet (Skagway Area)	KS, SS, PS, CS, DV, H	Access from Skagway small boat harbor.
12 Taiya River (Skagway Area)	SS, PS, CS,DV	Access along Klondike Highway.
13 Auke Bay (Juneau Area)	KS, SS, PS, DV, CT, RS	Mile 13, Glacier Highway. Boat access from Juneau small boat harbor.
14 Tee Harbor (Juneau Area)	KS, SS, PS, DV, CT, H	Mile 18.5, Glacier Highway. Boat access from Juneau small boat harbor.

Site Number and Name	Fish	Location and Accessibility
15 Windfall Lake (Juneau Area)	SS, PS, RS, DV, CT, RT	Mile 26, Glacier Highway. Trail access from Spur Road, off Glacier Highway.
16 Cowee Creek (Juneau Area)	SS, PS, DV, CT, RT	Mile 39, Glacier Highway.
17 Berners Bay (Juneau Area)	KS, SS, PS, DV, CT, H	End of Glacier Highway.

Northern Southeast Alaska Freshwater

Fish Availability Chart

Species	May	June	July	August	September	October
King Salmon						
Silver Salmon						
Red Salmon						
Pink Salmon						
Chum Salmon						
Rainbow Trout						
Steelhead						
Lake Trout						
Arctic Char						
Arctic Grayling						
Northern Pike						
Sheefish						
Halibut						

■■■■ = Available   ▓▓▓▓ = Peak

Northern Southeast Alaska Saltwater

Fish Availability Chart

Species	May	June	July	August	September	October
King Salmon						
Silver Salmon						
Red Salmon						
Pink Salmon						
Chum Salmon						
Rainbow Trout						
Steelhead						
Lake Trout						
Arctic Char						
Arctic Grayling						
Northern Pike						
Sheefish						
Halibut						

■■■■ = Available   ▓▓▓▓ = Peak

Brett Huber holds an eight-pound rainbow caught in the Iliamna River.

SOUTHWEST

Southwest Alaska includes Bristol Bay, Lower Kuskokwim, and the Alaska Peninsula. The area holds some of the greatest fishing opportunities in North America. Aside from being the world's largest producer of Pacific salmon, Southwest Alaska offers world-class rainbow trout, arctic grayling, and arctic char fishing. No matter what the specific interest or level of skill, there's something to satisfy in Southwest Alaska.

A fishing trip to remote reaches of Southwest Alaska is a dream come true. Limitless fishing opportunities, wildlife viewing, and just the sheer excitement of this region can create exhilaration. The problem with fishing this area is the lack of road access. With the exception of a few miles of maintained road at Dillingham, King Salmon, Iliamna, and Bethel, there are no roads. Access to the area is mainly by light plane from the above-mentioned cities. Other than Brooks Camp in Katmai National Park, there are no established campgrounds.

There are well over 100 professional fishing guides, outfitters, and lodges servicing the area. Most of the logistical problems of fishing this large area is solved by using one of these services. For those on a budget who want a do-it-yourself trip, there are a variety of ways to have a great outing. Usually such an adventure is a float trip down one of the many rivers. Access to the river of choice is generally by floatplane from one of the jumping-off-point communities.

Very little equipment may be obtained beyond Anchorage. Bring your own, or rent it before you leave. Gear should be dependable and of good quality; it's a long way from help.

Timing, like anywhere in Alaska, is crucial. There's no time when all species may be taken. The first two weeks in July are considered best for variety. Large rainbow are most available in late fall, September and the first week in October, before freeze-up are best. This is the time the big 'bows come out of the lakes to feast in the streams on salmon eggs and decaying salmon.

Dolly Varden are found throughout the inland waters of Southwest Alaska. They concentrate in large numbers off river mouths to feed on out-migrating salmon smolts in spring, and off small creek mouths in fall. They can also be caught in summer.

A philosophy of catch-and-release is encouraged by everyone associated with the fishery. Difficulties in preserving fish in wilderness settings discourage most anglers from retaining legal limits. Keep salmon if fish is desired to be taken home, or keep small resident species for shore lunches and camp breakfasts but release the rest.

Although putting the trip together may require a great deal more planning than a trip along the road system, it can be satisfying and within an average vacation budget. Fishing Southwest Alaska is the ultimate.

My first trip to Southwest Alaska was in my old 1948 Stinson Voyager. My daughter, Diane, her friend, and her friend's father completed our party. We flew through scenic Lake Clark Pass and landed at Iliamna. We parked the plane off the edge of the East-West dirt runway and took the forty-five-minute hike to Newhalen River.

The river was choked with red salmon. They were stacked up like cord wood. It was impossible to bring our line in without a fish on. If we had a hook-up and it got off, another took its place. We soon had our limit of six salmon apiece filleted and packed for our hike back to the plane. The balance of the day was spent in fishing off the rocks for resident fish.

I was looking at the photographs of the trip recently and a flood of pleasant memories flowed across my mind. Here's how we made our memory, and any angler can duplicate our experience.

It's a little over a mile to the river. You can either camp off the cross runway or carry your gear to the river. Once you get to the river, you'll see a group of rocks at the end of the river's fast water. You can fish from these rocks. Downriver from these rocks the river opens up into a wide delta. Immediately behind the rocks the fast water meets with still water of the delta and creates a long back eddy directly off the end of the rocks.

The best way I've found to fish here for resident fish is to stand on the rocks and cast as far as I can into the fast water of the main river. I let the current take my lure as far as it will before it swings into the back eddy. When the lure gets into the back eddy I stop my line from going out, move to the left side of the rocks, and begin as slow a retrieve as possible without hooking up on the bottom. Once I get a fish on, I move as far and as quickly as possible to the rocks on the left so I can pull the fish out of the fast water and play him in the slow back water of the eddy. If there is more than one fisherman on the rocks we rotate our casts about one minute apart, keep out of each other's way, and still catch fish without disturbing our partner.

My favorite lure for fishing the rocks is a small Spin-N-Glo. Use a three way, in-line swivel and attach a pencil lead weight about thirty inches above the Spin-N-Glo. Adjust the size of the weight depending on the size line you're using and the amount of current you're fishing in.

An alternate set up is to use a split-shot sinker tied three feet above a single egg or flesh fly. Again, cast out into the current as far as you can and let the fly drift into the back eddy. When the fly swings into the slow water, you'll get a hookup if the fish are there and willing. Try a few casts with the same amount of line out and then shorten your cast four feet and try again. Keep decreasing the length of your cast until you find the fish. Once you get into the hole, it's been my experience that you'll have repeated takers.

Another way to fish the Newhalen is to ship an inflatable boat and motor to Iliamna. Hire one of the locals to transport you and your gear to the village where you can safely launch your boat. Once you get on the river, you can camp in several areas. If you camp on the village side, you may have to pay a small camping fee. Make the same kind of set up as if you were fishing off the rocks only drag the lure behind the boat the same speed as the current. Vary the amount of line you have out until you get the right combination for success.

Fly-in lodges use the Newhalen, and you may find another boat on the river. The guides know how to fish the area. If you see others on the river watch what they're doing and try to duplicate their drift. I've found the guides to be helpful when asked.

When fishing from the rocks, your catch will be a mixed bag of grayling, Dollies, and rainbow. From a boat, you'll catch bigger rainbow, Dollies, and an occasional late-bloomer red. But no matter the species of fish you catch-and-release, you'll always catch and keep a pleasant memory.

Southwest Alaska Freshwater

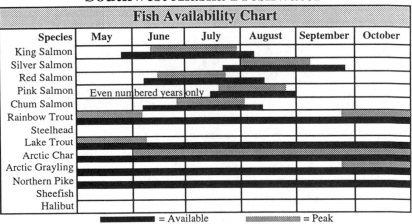

Species	May	June	July	August	September	October
King Salmon						
Silver Salmon						
Red Salmon						
Pink Salmon	Even numbered years only					
Chum Salmon						
Rainbow Trout						
Steelhead						
Lake Trout						
Arctic Char						
Arctic Grayling						
Northern Pike						
Sheefish						
Halibut						

= Available   = Peak

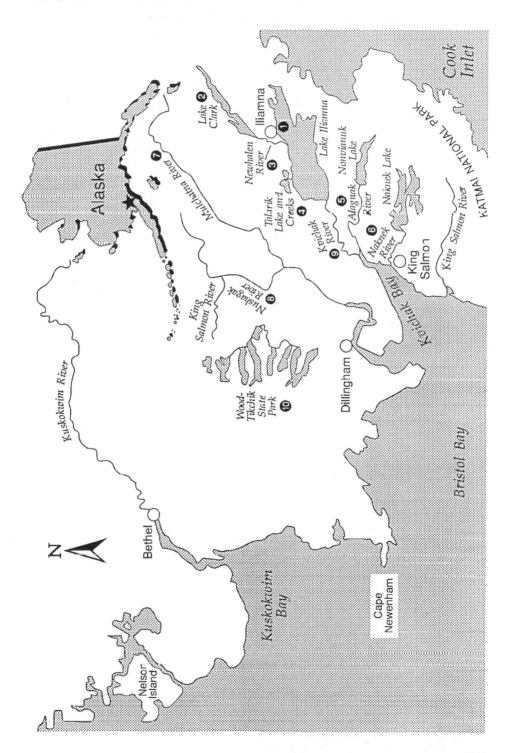

Site Number and Name	Fish	Location and Accessibility
1 Lake Iliamna	RS, DV, RT, LT, NP, GR	Lake Iliamna is accessible via airline and charter. Very little fishing is done in the lake. The lake is used as a jumping off point to the surrounding area. Almost all streams emptying into the lake are productive.
2 Lake Clark	RS, DV, RT, LT, NP, GR	Lake Clark is accessible via airline and charter. Very little fishing is done in the lake. The lake is used as a jumping off point to the surrounding area. Almost all streams emptying into the lake are productive.
3 Newhalen River	RS, RT, DV	Newhalen River is accessible by hiking from the Iliamna Airport.
4 Talarik Creek	DV, RT	Talarik Creek is a popular rainbow fishery. The best time is late fall when the big rainbows come out of Lake Iliamna.
5 Alagnak River	KS, RS, CS, PS, SS, DV, RT, LT, NP, GR	Alagnak River is a popular float trip. It's an easy float for experienced outdoorsmen who are novice boatmen. Fly-in lodges use the lower stretches. The Alagnak Braids are a productive rainbow area.
6 Naknek River	KS, RS, CS, PS, SS, DV, RT, LT, NP, GR	Naknek River is accessed from King Salmon.
7 Mulchatna River	KS, RS, CS, PS, SS, DV, RT, LT, NP, GR	Mulchatna River is accessed from Dillingham. It's a popular float trip. The Mulchatna is a big river and should be given a lot of respect, especially by inexperienced boatmen.
8 Nushagak River	KS, RS, CS, PS, SS, DV, RT, NP, GR	Nushagak River is accessed from Dillingham.
9 Kvichak River	RS, CS, PS, SS, DV, RT, LT, NP, GR	Kvichak River is accessible from both Iliamna and King Salmon. Late fall, just before freeze-up is the best time for big rainbow. Both the river and its outlet at Lake Iliamna produce good catches. It's necessary to use a boat for transportation along the river. A limited amount of fishing can take place at the outlet by flying to Igiugig and walking to the river.

Site Number and Name	Fish	Location and Accessibility
10 Wood -Tikchik State Park	RS, CS, DV, RT, NP, GR, SF	Next to Iliamna, the Wood River/Tikchik Lakes area is the most famous fishery in Alaska. There are numerous safe floats. Bears are prevalent in the area and caution is advised. There have been very few incidents with bears, but that's because most visitors to the area are taken there by guides. Follow the same safety rules the guides use and the chances of trouble are almost eliminated.

A hiking fisherman prepares a fresh lake trout lunch. Most areas of Alaska allow open fires, but it's important that the fire is completely dead before moving on.

50 ALASKA ANGLING TIPS

1. Many guides and informed anglers are switching to single hooks when fishing for king salmon on light tackle. It may be harder to hook a king on a single hook, but it stays solid. A big king can work a treble hook loose.

2. When water levels are low, when fishing in slow water, or if snags are present, attach a float to the line, allowing bait to be fished without hanging up on the bottom. Any buoyant object will work, even a piece of wood. Fish the bait approximately twelve inches off bottom. It works well with children who may have a hard time fishing other ways.

Red salmon, also called sockeyes, can be taken on medium-sized spoons and streamers with short tails.

3. Tie the line to a snap swivel or a split ring before attaching it to the lure. The edges of the eye have sharp edges that can slowly cut through the knot and will result in a frayed line.

4. Attaching a strip of fluorescent-colored tape to the lure will often make the difference in catching fish when fishing in glacier-fed streams. The tape increases the lure's visibility and increases chances for a strike.

5. If it's difficult to get a small lure down to the fish, but a larger, identical lure scares the fish, try sliding on the line a red or green cone-shaped sliding sinker similar to those used in plastic worm fishing.

6. When fishing line gets twisted while trolling, the twist can be eliminated by cutting off the lure and tolling just the line behind the boat.

7. When fishing for burbot, soaking salmon scraps in a jar of fish oil makes for a longer lasting and more effective bait.

8. Many anglers carry two types of monofilament line—clear and fluorescent. They use clear in freshwater and fluorescent in glacial waters.

9. Keep tails short on streamer flies for red salmon. Fish will often hit just the part of the fly extending beyond the hook. Many anglers find it advantages to trim streamers for better results. The same holds true for char and rainbow.

10. Use bait and fish it on the bottom around canneries or fish cleaning tables where scraps are dumped into the ocean or a lake. Halibut, pike, lake trout, and burbot are attracted from great distances to these areas. Try fishing at night.

11. When fishing with bait, use bright, translucent red eggs rather than cloudy or hardened ones.

12. Fish the Homer Spit and Lowell Point near Seward beginning in April. Surf cast for Dolly Varden by using small spoons, spinners, and flies. Fish the incoming tide in two to ten feet of water.

13. Fish for grayling in a lake near the inlet, a spring, or where a snowbank is melting into the lake.

14. Grayling require highly oxygenated water, which may be found in streams and rivers draining or flowing into lakes.

15. In murky water, use a chartreuse lure for kings.

16. The best fishing for lake trout during summer months is at depths of ten to forty feet during early morning and evening hours. Lakers are temperature-conscious fish and will be in or below thermoclines during mid-day.

17. Summer fishing for lakers will be productive if a sonar graph recorder and downrigger is used.

18. An effective method of catching early-season fish is to troll a small lure on four to six-pound-test line about fifty to seventy yards behind a slow-moving boat. Use a zig-zag pattern to cover the water.

19. Use a long rod and a small diving plug to fish for rainbow trout from brushy banks. A long rod gets the lure out from the bank, and the diving plug stays near bottom. Fish under brush and in pockets where large trout like to hold.

20. When fishing for silvers with bait and the fish picks it up then drops it, don't reel in, wait for a few minutes. If the fish comes back, it will be more aggressive next time.

21. Arctic char and Dolly Varden fishing will be easier during August and

September by using large, gaudy patterns.

22. When the stream water level is low, fish the largest, deepest pools and fish them carefully to keep from spooking the fish.

23. Always release large fish with needle-nose pliers to avoid a sudden twist or roll of the fish from burying hooks into fingers, hands, or arms.

24. Fluorescent red and yellow works best when fishing extreme depths.

25. Fishing for salmon with your rod tip down allows a full arc to set the hook.

26. Use a drop or two of herring oil on your lure when fishing for salmon, especially in intertidal areas.

27. Salmon, trout, and Dollies will hold in the freshwater/glacial water breakline. Fish on the bottom where the two currents meet.

28. Always fish the Russian River using polarized sunglasses. Success depends on finding the fish and casting to them.

29. For best results with saltwater pink salmon, retrieve the lure at a forty-five-degree angle to the pink's direction of travel.

30. Fish below salmon schools for char or trout by stripping the fly across the current at the base of riffles. The fish attack thinking it's an escaping salmon egg.

31. For best results always keep pearl-finish spoons polished and buffed to a high luster.

32. Improve chances of catching fish by adding eyes to lures. Paint them on or use colored dots sold in stationary stores. Apply the dots with varnish or shellac.

33. Fish for whitefish with ultralight tackle in shallow water from early evening until dark or on rainy, overcast days.

34. Expose phosphorescent lures to a flashlight beam for a few minutes for maximum glow when fishing glacial waters or fishing at night.

35. Carrying a compact emergency kit containing a pack rod, extra line, reel, and lures will save the trip if rods or reels are broken or dropped overboard.

36. If a hooked, trophy-sized fish is heading for a snag or downriver uncontrolled, quickly open the reel's bail or put the level-wind into free-spool.

37. To enhance the experience take a kid along.

38. Alaska's rainbow trout grow very slowly, and a limited number of areas are accessible to anglers. Release native rainbows carefully and use barbless hooks. A live rainbow trout is beautiful, a dead one is nothing.

39. Silvers will mouth roe so softly the angler can easily miss them if you're not ready. When these strikes register on the rod tip, carefully tighten up the line, hesitating momentarily to see if the hits come in a series of pecks. When this happens, set the hook immediately.

40. An unguided float trip allows anglers to make their own schedule and is a great way to fish the wilderness on a budget.

41. Plunking with salmon roe is a simple technique to catch fish and relax. Select a deep hole, add enough weight to anchor the bait, cast out, reel the line tight, lean the rod against a forked stick, and wait for the salmon.

42. Drifting salmon roe lets the current carry the bait to the fish. Cast slightly upstream, let the bait sink, and then tighten the line. Try to feel every tap as the bait bounces along the bottom. Use enough weight so the bait bumps bottom every 18 inches. Too much weight causes the bait to hang up rather than drift;

Don't let crowds scare you away from popular fishing holes. Most of Alaska enjoys around-the-clock sun during peak fishing seasons, and anglers can fish at two in the morning and miss the crowds.

too little lets the bait float above the bottom and the fish.

43. When using salmon roe as bait, follow this rule: if something feels different, set the hook.

44. If, after catching a few salmon, the hole goes dead, try putting on a different lure. Often a different lure or different color will induce additional strikes.

45. In shallow, clear water, use small lures to keep from spooking fish.

46. Don't let crowds scare you away from popular fishing holes. Most of Alaska enjoys around-the-clock sun during peak fishing season. Anglers can fish at two in the morning and see far fewer anglers than at 2 p.m. Fish early morning hours and nap in the afternoon.

47. Fish for pleasure only by mashing down the hook's barbs or use barbless hooks. It requires greater skill to land a fish and facilitates an easy release with the least amount of handling.

48. Float fishing is particularly effective for kings if other, more conventional, methods fail. Dangle the bait beneath a float with a few splitshot, or other weight, and just enough line to keep it from snagging up. It requires a little practice in judging water depth. Use 4/0 hooks and keep them sharp. Use twelve-pound test line followed by twenty feet of twenty pound test with a double bloodknot. It makes it easy to break off if the rig gets snagged up and gives security when a hook up happens.

49. Most experienced anglers agree that when fishing a chum salmon school, it's important to concentrate on casting to one fish. The more you cast to a single salmon, the more aggravated it becomes, and eventually it'll strike.

50. If you're getting strikes, but no hook-ups, check the point of your hook. If it doesn't stick in your thumbnail under light pressure, it's too dull for fishing. Sharpen the point so that it has three triangular cutting edges, and watch your hookups increase.

ALASKA PUBLIC LANDS: AN ENDURING FRONTIER

Early people called it Alyeshka—The Great Land. Much of The Great Land's 375 million acres will remain a permanent American frontier. Vast areas of special places in Alaska have been dedicated as public lands for the perpetual use by the family of man. Thirteen percent of Alaska, fifty-one million acres, is in public ownership as parks, preserves, wildlife refuges, monuments, and wild and scenic rivers. These lands and waterways comprise the finest parklands in the world, an immense collection of unadulterated wilderness, where people can escape when responding to the call of the wild.

Alaska's parklands are inhabited by great herds of caribou, musk ox, walrus, polar bear, grizzly bear, Dall sheep, moose, wolves, and wolverines. Expansive unblemished landscapes, creation-fresh rivers, legions of fish, numberless lakes, the continent's highest mountains, and the nation's most pristine valleys are Alaska's parkland treasures beyond any hiker's wildest expectations.

The size of land is staggering. The 49th State's land-mass constitutes an area one-fifth the size of the continental United States. If you explored 1,000 acres a day of just Wildlife Refuges, it would take over 1,000 years to see it all.

Alaska'a three million acres of state parkland comprise the largest state park system in the United States. With more than 100 state park units, it holds nearly one third of America's state park acreage.

Alaska has the largest moose, the biggest bears, the tallest spruce, the greatest fishing rivers, scenery without match, hiking trails without number, and enormous nurseries for migratory birds. Alaska reminds us of a time of uncharted frontiers calling to our sense of adventure and hardiness.

All state and federal agencies administering public lands have combined their information services in a central office in Anchorage. The general public may contact them either by telephone or writing. They'll answer specific questions or disseminate generic information. Their service is free, and they'll send requested helpful information at no charge. Hikers may contact the Alaska Public Lands Information Center or the administrative agency direct.

For more information, contact: Alaska Public Lands Information Center, 605 West 4th Avenue, Anchorage, Alaska 99501, (907) 271-2737.

Alaska Peninsula Wildlife Refuge

Alaska Peninsula Wildlife Refuge lies on the Pacific side of the Alaska Peninsula. The refuge's varied landscape includes active volcanoes, lakes, rivers, tundra and rugged coastline. Alaska Peninsula Wildlife Refuge is dominated by the rugged Aleutian Range, part of a chain of volcanoes known as the "Ring of Fire" encircling the Pacific Ocean.

Plants composing the expanses of tundra are slow growing and small. The tundra, together with the influence of volcanos and Arctic seas, provide a showcase of how plants and animals adapt to an Arctic maritime environment.

Large mammals found on the refuge include, moose, caribou, wolves, brown bear, and wolverine. Brown bears are near productive salmon streams. Large populations of sea lions, seals, sea otter, and migratory whales inhabit shores and off-stream waters. Populations of sea otter on the Pacific side of the peninsula numbers at least 30,000. In the 1880's they were nearly extinct. The entire refuge provides habitat for migratory birds: ducks, geese, and shore birds.

The Alaska Peninsula Wildlife Refuge is renowned for big game hunting, especially caribou and brown bear. Fishing is outstanding for king and silver salmon, Arctic char, lake trout, northern pike, and grayling. The world-record grayling was caught on the refuge.

For more information, contact: Refuge Manager, Alaska Peninsula Wildlife Refuge, P.O. Box 277, King Salmon, Alaska 99613, (907) 246-3339.

Aniakchak National Monument and Preserve

The central feature of Aniakchak National Monument and Preserve is the volcanic Aniakchak Caldera created by the collapse of the central part of a volcano. It covers thirty square miles, and is six miles wide. This collapse took place sometime after the last glaciation. Later activity built a cone, Vent Mountain, inside the caldera. Aniakchak last erupted in 1931. The caldera's Surprise Lake, heated by hot springs, cascades through a 1,500-foot rift in the crater wall. Such volcanic features as lava flows, cinder cones, and explosion pits can be seen here, along with hardy pioneer plant communities inching life into a silent moonscape.

Wildlife includes occasional caribou, grizzly bear, and eagles. Sockeye salmon spawn up the Aniakchak River, which originates in Surprise Lake. Fish from this watershed are recognizable by their flavor of soda and iron characteristic of the caldera's mineral-laden outflow.

This is one of the most remote of Alaska's national park areas, and weather on Alaska Peninsula can be severe all seasons. Scheduled air service puts you within charter-flight distance via King Salmon or Port Heiden. Floatplanes can land on Surprise Lake.

For more information, contact: Superintendent, Aniakchak National Monument and Preserve, P.O. Box 7, King Salmon, Alaska 99613, (907) 246-3305.

Arctic National Wildlife Refuge

Arctic National Wildlife Refuge is the most northern of the wildlife refuges. The refuge encompasses one of the world's most spectacular assemblages of Arctic plants, wildlife, and land forms. Designated to embrace the range of the great Porcupine Caribou Herd, Arctic National Wildlife Refuge is also home to free-roaming herds of musk ox, Dall sheep, packs of wolves, and such solitary species as wolverines, polar and grizzly bear.

Winter on the refuge is long and severe; summer is brief and intense. Snow usually covers the ground at least nine months a year. Arctic-adapted plants survive even though permafrost is within eighteen inches of the surface. Annual growth of trees and shrubs is slight. It might take 300 years for a white spruce at tree line to reach a diameter of five inches; small willow shrubs may be fifty to 100 years old.

The Arctic offers a rich pageant of wildlife, including 140 bird species. It protects a large portion of the migration route of the Porcupine Caribou Herd, 180,000 animals, one of the two largest herds in Alaska. Caribou migrate from wintering grounds south of the Brooks Range to calving grounds on the northern coastal plains of the refuge and the Yukon Territory. The migration covers more than 1,000 miles. Arctic recreation use is increasing. Activities include, float trips, hiking, backpacking, hunting, fishing, and wildlife observation.

For more information, contact: Refuge Manager, Arctic National Wildlife Refuge, P.O. Box 20, Fairbanks, Alaska 99701, (907) 456-0250.

Becharof National Wildlife Refuge

Becharof National Wildlife Refuge lies between Katmai National Park and Preserve and Alaska Peninsula National Wildlife Refuge. The refuge is dominated by Becharof Lake, second largest lake in Alaska. The lake covers 1/4 of the refuge and is surrounded by low, rolling hills, tundra wetlands, and volcanic peaks. Salmon spawning streams attract one of the largest concentrations of brown bear in Alaska. Some brown bear of Becharof have a unique habit of making dens on the islands of Becharof Lake. Moose inhabit the refuge in moderate numbers and about 15,000 caribou seasonally migrate through, and winter in the refuge. Other mammals include wolves, wolverine, river otter, red fox, and beaver. In addition, thousands of sea mammals such as sea otters, sea lions, harbor seals, and migratory whales inhabit the seas along the shore.

Becharof Lake and its tributaries contribute over four million salmon annually to the Bristol Bay fishery. Salmon, Arctic char, and grayling flourish on the refuge. Waterfowl are common in the wetlands and coastal estuaries, while nesting eagles, peregrine falcons, and thousands of sea birds inhabit sea cliffs and islands.

Becharof offers outstanding bear and caribou hunting. The refuge receives moderate sport fishing pressure for trophy-size Arctic char, grayling, and salmon. Commercial guide services are available for hunting and fishing.

For more information, contact: Refuge Manager, Becharof National Wildlife Refuge, P.O. Box 277, King Salmon, Alaska 99613, (907) 246-3339.

Bering Land Bridge National Preserve

Bering Land Bridge National Preserve is a remnant of the land bridge connecting Asia with North America more than 13,000 years ago. The land bridge itself is now overlain by the Chukchi Sea and Bering Sea. During the glacial epoch, this was part of a migration route for people, animals, and plants as ocean levels fell enough to expose the land bridge. Scientists find it one of the most likely regions where prehistoric Asian hunters entered the New World.

Today, Eskimos from neighboring villages pursue subsistence lifestyles and manage reindeer herds in and around the preserve, Some 112 migratory bird species may be seen here, along with occasional seals, walrus, and whales. Grizzly bear, fox, wolf, and moose also inhabit the preserve. Other interesting features are rimless volcanos, called Maar craters, Serpentine Hot Springs, and seabird colonies at Sullivan Bluffs.

Air service out of Nome and Kotzebue is the usual means of access to the quiet, isolated preserve's 2.5 million acres.

For more information, contact: Superintendent, Bering Land Bridge National Preserve, P.O. Box 220, Nome, Alaska 99762, (907) 443-2522.

Cape Krusenstern National Monument

The gravel beachscape of Cape Krusenstern National Monument chronologically records 5,000 years of marine mammal hunting by Eskimo peoples. These unrivaled archeological records are locked in 114 lateral beach ridges describing land growth into the Chukchi Sea. The beach ridges were formed by changing sea levels and the action of wind and waves. Artifacts from nearby creek bluffs date back 6,000 years and act as a benchmark for predating the cape's beach ridges.

Eskimos still hunt seals along the cape's outermost beach. With rifles instead of traditional harpoons, they hazard the dangerous spring ice floes to take the oogruk, or bearded seal. In shoreline camps, women trim and render the catch for the hides, meat, and seal oil still vital to their diet. As old sites became land bound by the shoreline's seaward advance, people abandoned their tents and sod houses to establish new camps nearer the sea. This process has continued ever since Eskimos of Arctic Alaska first turned to the sea.

For more information, contact: Superintendent, Cape Krusenstern National Monument, P.O. Box 1029, Kotzebue, Alaska 99752, (907) 442-3890.

Chilkat State Park

Chilkat State Park, south of Haines on the Chilkat Peninsula, offers spec-

Sea Lions in Resurrection Bay.

tacular views of glaciers across Chilkat Inlet. Visitors often spot whales, seals, and other wildlife from the coastline trail. There are campgrounds, picnic areas, and a boat ramp.

For more information, contact: Park Ranger, Chilkat State Park Headquarters, 400 Willoughby, Juneau, Alaska 99801, (907) 465-4563.

Chugach State Park

Development of Anchorage through the 20th century necessitated establishment of Chugach State Park. This area was set aside to assure an open, quality environment available to citizens now facing increasing pressures from urbanization.

Ranging from coastal forests and rushing streams to rugged, high-alpine cirques and glaciers, Chugach State Park provides a variety of recreational possibilities for young and old. The park opens doors to adventuresome experiences, rewards of health, personal satisfaction, and a renewed energy through freedom in the outdoors.

Foot travel is perhaps the best way to explore and experience the park. Hiking carries us at a pace governed by terrain and interests. Today, sections of the Iditarod Trail and a historic settler's route, the old Johnson Trail, give hikers a glimpse into an intriguing era of Alaska history.

For more information, contact: Park Ranger, Chugach State Park Headquarters, HC 52 Box 8999, Indian, Alaska 99540, (907) 345-5014.

Denali National Park and Preserve

Mount McKinley, at 20,320 feet, is North America's highest mountain. The Athabascan Indians called it Denali, "The High One," and in 1980 McKinley National Park's name was changed to Denali.

Mount McKinley is a massive mountain—measured from base to summit, it is the world's highest—the towering centerpiece of the glacier-strewn Alaska Range. Under its shadow in Denali National Park and Preserve are barren-ground caribou, grizzly bear, wolves, moose, Dall sheep, and other wildlife. Meandering, glacier-born rivers laden with silt, or rock flour, create natural dams and periodically change course across their wide flat valleys.

The area is accessible by car, railroad, and scheduled air service. To protect wildlife and to preserve opportunities to see it, private vehicle use is restricted on the park road. Shuttle bus service operates from the entrance to Wonder Lake along the eighty-five mile wilderness road. The shuttle bus will drop you off, or pick you up wherever you like, and at no cost.

For more information, contact: Superintendent, Denali National Park and Preserve, P.O. Box 9, Denali Park, Alaska 99755, (907) 683-2294.

Denali State Park

Denali State Park is an integral part of one of North America's most spectacularly beautiful regions. The park's 324,240 acres, almost half the size of Rhode Island, provide visitors with a great variety of recreational opportunities, ranging from roadside camping to wilderness explorations.

The park is about 100 air miles north of Anchorage and is divided roughly in half by the George Parks Highway, the major link between Anchorage and Fairbanks. Situated between Talkeetna Mountains to the east, and Alaska Range to the west, the landscape varies from meandering lowland streams to alpine tundra. Dominating this diverse terrain are Curry and Kesugi Ridges, a thirty-five-mile-long north-south alpine ridge, the backbone of the eastern half of the park.

Denali State Park's western boundary is shared with its much larger neighbor, Denali National Park and Preserve. The Tanana Indian word "Denali," means "The High One." Denali is the original name for Mount McKinley. At 20,320 feet, McKinley is North America's highest peak. It literally and figuratively towers over south-central Alaska from its base in Denali National Park.

The great mountain, and its companion peaks are accented by spectacular valley-glaciers and steep ice-carved gorges and a year-round mantle of snow and ice above 8,000 feet. Glaciers, such as Ruth, Buckskin, and Eldridge, are from fourteen to thirty-eight miles long and up to four miles wide. They flow from the high peaks and melt into the broad U-shaped Chulitna Valley, giving Chulitna River a milky-colored water and braided channels typical of glacial streams. Though only thirty-five miles from the summit of McKinley, the Chulitna floodplain is but 550 feet in elevation.

Denali State Park has superb vantage points for viewing the breathtaking heart of the Alaska Range. Perhaps the best roadside view anywhere of the Alaska Range is at mile 135.2, Parks Highway. An interpretive bulletin board at this site names the mountains and other terrain features. Other excellent views of Mt. McKinley along the highway are at mile 147.1, 158.1, and 162.3. Day hikers on Kesugi Ridge, or backpackers in the Peter Hills in the western end of the park, have an unencumbered view of the Denali massif that's almost overwhelming in grandeur.

From the alpine tundra of Curry Ridge to the river bottoms of the meandering Tokositna River, the park's varied landscape is home to a diverse exhibit of wildlife. Moose, grizzly, and black bears are found throughout the park. Though seldom seen, wolves frequent much of the park, and caribou occasionally reach the park's northern end. Smaller, elusive residents include lynx, coyote, red fox, snowshoe hare, land otter, and flying and red squirrel. The weasel family is well represented by ermine, marten, mink, and wolverine. Wet areas are habitat for muskrat and beaver, while pika squirrel and marmot may be found in rocky areas above timberline.

Tapestry of habitats in the park yield an especially rich bird community. More than 130 species use the park for breeding or stop during migration. The champion marathoner of the bird world, the Arctic tern, flies 12,000 miles to breed in Denali, repeating the journey to winter in Antarctica. The lesser gold plover nests on alpine tundra after wintering in faraway Polynesia.

For more information, contact: Park Ranger, Denali State Park Headquarters, HC 32 Box 6706, Wasilla, Alaska 99654, (907) 745-3975.

Gates of the Arctic National Park and Preserve

Gates of the Arctic National Park and Preserve lies entirely north of the Arctic Circle. It includes the scenic heartland of the Brooks Range, northernmost extension of the Rocky Mountains. The park and preserve combined are four times the size of Yellowstone National Park. The area's austere beauty and grandeur defy description. This is ultimate wilderness capturing the heart and imagination of Arctic explorer Robert Marshall in the 1930's.

Barren ground caribou and grizzly bear range the area's spacious and fragile tundra, gathering a living from the thin veneer of Arctic soils. The park straddles the crest of the Brooks Ranges; its southern flank sampling of boreal forest in Alaska's interior; and its north slope at the edge of a polar desert with precipitation comparable to the Earth's driest regions. Two distinct cultures are represented here: Athabascan peoples of the spruce-taig forests, and Nunamiut Eskimos, who hunt caribou in the high valleys. Both cultures continue to follow traditional subsistence patterns of life in the park and preserve. Scheduled flights from Fairbanks serve Bettles, Evansville, and Anaktuvuk Pass.

For more information, contact: Superintendent, Gates of the Arctic National Park and Preserve, P.O. Box 74680, Fairbanks, Alaska 99707, (907) 456-0281.

Glacier Bay National Park and Preserve

Glacier Bay National Park and Preserve contains the world's most impressive examples of tidewater glaciers. The bay has experienced at least four major advances and four major retreats of glaciers and thus serves as an outdoor laboratory for contemporary research. Mountains rise in the preserve almost three vertical miles from tidewater. The dramatic variety of plant communities range from terrain just recovering from glacial retreat to lush temperate rain forest. Nowhere is the story of plant succession more richly told than at Glacier Bay.

The park and preserve harbors brown and black bears, whales, seals, eagles, and more than 200 hundred species of birds. Mount Fairweather is the highest peak in Southeast Alaska.

Glacier Bay is accessible by commercial cruise ship, charter boat, aircraft, or by scheduled air and boat service from Juneau and other Southeast Alaska communities.

For more information, contact: Superintendent, Glacier Bay National Park and Preserve, P.O. Box 140, Gustavus, Alaska 99826, (907) 697-2232.

Innoko National Wildlife Refuge

Innoko National Wildlife Refuge is about 300 miles northwest of Anchorage in the central Yukon River Valley. The refuge comprises most of Innoko River Basin and is composed of two separate sections totaling 4.25 million acres. About eighty percent of the refuge is wetlands, providing nesting habitat for at least 250,000 waterfowl. Innoko provides habitat for wolf, black bear, grizzly bear, caribou in winter, and fur bearers. It's renowned for its beaver population. In some years forty percent of all beaver trapped in Alaska originate on the refuge. The annual beaver harvest is about 20,000 pelts. Other fur bearers include muskrat, weasel, wolverine, lynx, marten, and red fox.

The abundant moose on Innoko has meant a food supply for early residents, explorers, trappers, gold seekers, and river boat crews as well as today's residents. The success of the moose population is attributed to flooding along streams enhancing the growth of willows, the major winter food for moose.

A float trip on Innoko River provides an excellent opportunity to view wildlife. Fishing is excellent for northern pike. Sport hunting for moose and black bear is popular.

For more information, contact: Refuge Manager, Innoko National Wildlife Refuge, P.O. Box 69, McGrath, Alaska 99627, (907) 524-3251.

Izembek National Wildlife Refuge

Izembek National Wildlife Refuge faces the Bering Sea on the tip of the Alaska Peninsula. The landscape includes volcanos with glacier caps, valleys, and tundra uplands that slope into lagoons adjoining the Bering Sea. Izembek Lagoon contains a valuable eelgrass bed, one of the largest in the world. The beds are part of a large estuary providing a haven for migratory birds. The world's population of black brant, thousands of Canada and emperor geese, and other waterfowl congregate on the lagoon. They feed on eelgrass before they fly south. Most waterfowl arrive on the refuge in late August or early September. By early November a second wave of northern waterfowl, primarily sea ducks, arrive to winter on Izembek. The colorful Steller's eider, that nests on the Arctic coast of Alaska and Siberia, is the most common wintering duck in the lagoon. In addition, thousands of shore birds feed on invertebrates of the bay at low tide. At high tide they gather in such large flocks that, in flight, they appear as smoke clouds. Other wildlife includes brown bear, caribou, ptarmigan, and fur bearers. Izembek has outstanding waterfowl hunting. Ptarmigan are often hunted in conjunction with waterfowl. Caribou hunting is good. There are some roads and trails to the refuge from Cold Bay, but most of the refuge is accessible only by boat or foot.

For more information, contact: Refuge Manager, Izembek National Wild Life Refuge, P.O. Box 127, Cold Bay, Alaska 99571, (907) 532-2445.

Kachemak Bay State Park

Kachemak Bay State Park is 250,000 acres of ocean, mountains, glaciers, forests, and wildlife. The waters of Kachemak Bay are some of the most productive in the world and are inhabited by whales, sea otters, seals, and many species of fish. The bay's twisted rock formations are evidence of the powerful forces of the movement of the earth's crust and are highlighted by constantly changing weather patterns.

Park visitors will find opportunities for hiking, boating, fishing, and beachcombing. Intertidal zones offer natural settings for marine studies. Many species of birds inhabit the bay, including puffins, gyrfalcons, and bald eagles, making it a popular area for bird watching. Hiking and camping along the shoreline and in the surrounding forests and mountains are excellent, and once above timberline, hikers and climbers will find glaciers and snowfields stretching for miles.

Special attractions in the park include Grewingk Glacier, Poot Peak, China Poot Bay, Halibut Cove Lagoon, Humpy Creek, China Poot Lake, and the Tuka Lagoon Hatchery.

For more information, contact: Park Ranger, Kachemak Bay State Park Headquarters, P.O. Box 1247, Soldotna, Alaska 99669, (907) 262-5581.

Katmai National Park and Preserve

In 1912 a tremendous volcano erupted in the unexplored wilderness that today is Katmai National Park and Preserve. The blast, in which Mount Katmai collapsed, was one of the most violent ever recorded. Afterward, in what would become known as Valley of Ten Thousand Smokes, fumaroles by the thousands issued steam hot enough to melt zinc. Only a few active vents remain today, and the Katmai crater holds a lake.

Katmai's scenery boasts lakes, rivers, glaciers, waterfalls, and a coastline of plunging cliffs and islets. This is the home of huge brown bear—Earth's largest terrestrial carnivore—which in summer fishes the park and preserve's streams to feast on migrating salmon. Scientists regard this area as critical for the brown bear's survival on the Alaska Peninsula. It also boasts some of Southwest Alaska's best trophy sportfishing.

Scheduled jets from Anchorage serve King Salmon on the park's west side. From June through Labor Day, daily commercial flights operate between King Salmon and Brooks Lodge. Air charters from King Salmon or Iliamna are available from May though October.

For more information, contact: Superintendent, Katmai National Park and Preserve, P.O. Box 7, King Salmon, Alaska 99613, (907) 246-3305.

Kanuti National Wildlife Refuge

Kanuti National Wildlife Refuge straddles the Arctic Circle approximately 150 miles northwest of Fairbanks. It is composed of Kanuti Flats, an interior basin characterized by the rolling plains of Kanuti and Koyukuk rivers. The basin is interspersed with lakes, ponds, and marshes. The refuge provides nesting habitat for waterfowl, primarily Canada and white-fronted geese and ducks. Kanuti's contribution to waterfowl increases when the prairies of southcentral Canada and northern midwestern United States lie baked and dry. In times of drought, birds displaced from traditional breeding areas fly northward to stable waters. Additional loss of prairie wetlands from draining and filling will further increase importance of northern wetland such as Kanuti.

The refuge supports sixteen species of fish, including whitefish, northern pike, grayling and salmon. Other wildlife includes moose, black bear, grizzly bear, wolf, and wolverine.

Few people visit Kanuti, and those who do primarily hunt, fish and view wildlife. Fishing for northern pike and grayling is excellent. Because it's remote, the adventurous will find Kanuti Refuge a true wilderness experience.

For more information, contact: Refuge Manager, Kanuti National Wildlife Refuge, 101 12th Ave., Room 112, Fairbanks, Alaska 99701, (907) 456-0329.

Kenai Fjords National Park

Kenai Fjords National Park features the seaward interface for Harding Ice Field, one of four major ice caps in the United States. This may be a remnant of Pleistocene ice masses once covering half of Alaska. Along the coastline are the scenic Kenai Fjords, whose shoreline was carved by glaciers. Sea stacks, islets, and jagged shoreline are remnants of mountains that today inch imperceptibly into the sea under the geological force of the North Pacific tectonic plate. Exit Glacier, the most accessible area of the park, can be reached by car and a short walk.

Moose and large populations of mountain goats inhabit the land. Steller sea lions haul out on rocky islands at the entrance to the fjords. Harbor seals rest on icebergs. Killer whales, porpoises, sea otters, and several whale species also are found here. Thousands of sea birds—horned and tufted puffins, common murres, and black-legged kittiwakes—rear their young on steep cliffs.

Seward, 130 miles south of Anchorage via the Seward Highway, is gateway to Kenai Fjords. Served by scheduled bus and commuter flights, it offers charter boats and aircraft services. The park Visitor Center is next to the Harbor Master's office, in Seward's small boat harbor.

For more information, contact: Superintendent Kenai Fjords National Park, P.O. Box 1727, Seward, Alaska 99664, (907) 224-3175.

Kenai National Wildlife Refuge

The Kenai National Wildlife Refuge consists of the western slopes of the Kenai Mountains and forested lowlands bordering Cook Inlet. The lowlands are composed of spruce and birch forests intermingled with hundreds of lakes. The Kenai Mountains, with their glaciers, rise to more than 6,000 feet, presenting a barrier on the southeastern boundary of the refuge. The refuge is a miniature Alaska, containing examples of all its habitat types: tundra, mountains, wetlands, and forests. Kenai Refuge was established to preserve and maintain a large population of moose on the Kenai Peninsula. In addition, the refuge is host to Dall sheep, mountain goat, caribou, coyote, wolf, grizzly bear, black bear, lynx, wolverine, beaver, small mammals, and birds. Kenai Refuge provides undisturbed spawning for many Cook Inlet salmon.

The refuge is accessible from the Sterling Highway. Travelers are treated to a panoramic view along the 110-mile drive from Anchorage to Kenai's mideastern boundary. Fishing is excellent. There are over 200 miles of established trails and routes, including the Swanson River Canoe route. Visitors can fly to remote lakes, hike or take horse pack trips into roadless areas, or float a whitewater river. Developed facilities are available year-round for day and overnight camping.

For more information, contact: Refuge Manager, Kenai National Wildlife Refuge, P.O. Box 2139, Soldotna, Alaska 99669, (907)262-7021.

Kodiak National Wildlife Refuge

Kodiak National Wildlife Refuge is composed of mountains, forests, bays, inlets, and wetlands. The refuge comprises about two-thirds of Kodiak Island. In addition, the refuge encompasses a portion of Afognak Island, north of Kodiak Island. Kodiak Island has an irregular coastline of bays, inlets, and rugged mountains covered with alpine vegetation. Spruce forests dominate the northern part of Kodiak Island and all of the Afognak Island portion of the refuge.

A killer whale surfaces in Resurrection Bay.

The interior of the refuge is covered with lush, dense vegetation. Southwestern Kodiak is covered with hummocks of grass. No place on the 100 x 40-mile island is more than fifteen miles from the sea. Kodiak was established to protect the habitat of brown bear. Besides brown bear, there are only five other native land mammals on Kodiak: red fox, river otter, short-tailed weasel, little brown bat, and tundra vole.

Black-tailed deer, beaver, and several other species of mammals have been successfully introduced to the island. Bald eagles reside year-round on the refuge, in such numbers they're in view continuously. An estimated two million sea birds inhabit the bays, inlets, and shores. Kodiak is known worldwide for brown bear hunting. Fishing is excellent for all five species of Pacific salmon. Wildlife observation, hiking, photography, rafting, and camping are popular activities. The island is served by commercial flights and the Alaska State Ferry system. A limited number of cabins are available.

For more information, contact: Refuge Manager, Kodiak National Wildlife Refuge, 1390 Buskin River Road, Kodiak, Alaska 99615, (907) 487-2600.

Kodiak State Parks

Kodiak Island has a uniqueness and beauty all its own. The warm Japanese current creates a mild maritime climate and plenty of rain. It's an island of rough, glacier-scarred terrain—mountains rise from the sea, rocky coasts and tide pools beckon the coastal explorer. Forested areas occur infrequently. The majority of the island is blanketed in grasses, willow and alder thickets, and a profusion of wildflowers.

There are four state parks within the Kodiak Archipelago. Except for Shuyak Island State Park, all are accessible on the Kodiak Island road system. These parks welcome visitors with scenery, wildlife, history, and relaxation. Visitors find a variety of opportunities for recreation and education. Over 200 species of birds have been recorded in the Kodiak Archipelago, and bird watching is a main attraction. The parks are laced with trails through lush rain forest in a tranquil setting.

Fort Abercrombie State Historic Park provides a variety of recreational opportunities. Visitors will find quiet forests for tent camping and hiking, tide pools to be explored, and a stunning view from Miller Point. During early summer, gray, humpback, and minke whales can be spotted as they migrate through nearby Whale Passage. August brings ripening salmon berries, which can be picked in any part of the park. Guided and self-guided historical walking tours are available.

Shuyak Island State Park, an 11,000-acre coastal wilderness fifty-four air miles north of Kodiak, contains virgin Sitka spruce forests, rugged coastline, beaches, and protected waterways. The area supports sea birds in infinite numbers as well as sea otters, whales, harbor seals, sea lions, Sitka blacktailed deer, and a small population of Kodiak brown bear. Popular with hunters and anglers, it's also a rewarding spot for bird and wildlife watchers.

For more information, contact: Park Ranger, Kodiak State Parks Headquarters, SR Box 3800, Kodiak, Alaska 99615, (907) 486-6339.

Koyukuk National Wildlife Refuge

Rivers are the heart of Koyukuk country—its living pulse and historic past. Fourteen rivers and hundreds of creeks meander throughout the refuge, providing habitat for salmon, beaver and waterfowl. There are also over 15,000 lakes. The topography is relatively gentle, featuring an extensive floodplain surrounded by hills with boreal forests.

The landscape includes the Nogahabara Dunes, a 10,000-acre active dune field. The field was formed from wind-blown deposits about 10,000 years ago. It's one of two active dune fields in Alaska. Spring flood waters of the Koyukuk River carry away signs of the past season and recharge the lowlands.

The floodplain provides ideal nesting habitat for ducks, geese, and other water-adapted birds. By September, more than four million ducks and geese migrate from the refuge to southern wintering grounds. Black bear are abundant in forests, and grizzly bear inhabit the open tundra. Fur bearers on Koyukuk include otter, lynx, beaver, marten, muskrats, and mink. Wolves and moose are common. Other large mammals on the refuge include caribou from the Western Arctic Herd that often winter on portions of the refuge. Koyukuk has excellent moose hunting and fishing for northern pike and Arctic grayling.

For more information, contact: Refuge Manager, Koyukuk National Wildlife Refuge, P.O. Box 287, Galena, Alaska 99741, (907) 656-1231.

Klondike Gold Rush National Historical Park

When an 1897 issue of the Seattle Post-Intelligence reported a steamer from Alaska putting in at Seattle with a ton of gold aboard, it set off the last great gold rush. At the height of the rush, John Muir called Skagway "a nest of ants taken into a strange country and stirred up by a stick." Klondike Gold Rush National Historical Park preserves historic buildings from this period in Skagway, Alaska, and portions of the Chilkoot and White Pass trails into the Klondike.

The park offers a variety of experiences, from small town to wilderness. A lively nightlife thrives in Skagway, a regular port of call for cruise ships. The Trail of 98 Museum is housed in Alaska's first granite building. Backpacking over the passes has become popular. Access is by ferry, cruise ship, commuter airline, air taxi, or by car.

For more information, contact: Superintendent, Klondike Gold Rush National Historical Park, P.O. Box 517, Skagway, Alaska 99840, (907) 983-2921.

Kobuk Valley National Park

Today's dry, cold climate of the Kobuk Valley still approximates that of late Pleistocene times, supporting a remnant flora once marking the vast Arctic steppe tundra bridging Alaska and Asia. Great herds of caribou still cross the Kobuk River at Onion Portage, and are hunted by today's Eskimo peoples. These herds once fed Woodland Eskimo peoples of 1250 AD. Human occupation at the portage dates back to 12,500 years ago, forming a benchmark by which all other Arctic sites are measured. The valley remains an important area for traditional subsistence harvest of moose, bear, caribou, fish, waterfowl, and many edible and medicinal plants.

The great Kobuk Sand Dunes—twenty-five square miles of shifting dunes where summer temperatures can exceed 100 degrees—is the largest active dune field in Arctic latitudes. Both the Kobuk and Salmon Rivers offer easy canoeing and kayaking.

Daily jet service is available from Anchorage and Fairbanks to Kotzebue. Scheduled air service is available to nearby villages, and local air and boat charter is available by advance arrangement.

For more information, contact: Superintendent, Kobuk Valley National Park, P.O. Box 1029, Kotzebue, Alaska 99752, (907) 442-3890.

Lake Clark National Park and Preserve

Lake Clark National Park and Preserve has been described as the Alaska Alps, for here the Alaska and Aleutian ranges meet. Set in the heart of the Chigmit Mountains along Cook Inlet's western shore, the park boasts great geologic diversity. Its jagged peaks, granite spires, glaciers, two active volcanoes, and fifty-mile-long Lake Clark provide a dazzling array of scenery. The lake, fed by hundreds of waterfalls throughout its rimming mountains, is part of an important red salmon spawning ground. These features combine to create a maze of natural river-running and hiking routes providing spectacular wilderness experiences.

Brown and black bear, caribou, moose, Dall sheep, salmon, and trout inhabit these scenic environs. Within the park and preserve are coastal lowlands of spruce and marshes, alpine meadows, and tundra plains backed by ever-changing mountain scenes.

Air charters are available from Anchorage, Kenai, or Iliamna. Lodging, from primitive to modern, is available from private operators within the park and preserve.

For more information, contact: Superintendent, Lake Clark National Park and Preserve, 4230 University Drive, Suite 311, Anchorage, Alaska 99508, (907) 271-3751.

Maritime National Wildlife Refuge

Alaska Maritime National Wildlife Refuge consists of more than 2,400 islands, headlands, rocks, islets, spires, and reefs off the Alaska coast. The refuge stretches from Cape Lisburne on the Chukchi Sea to the tip of the Aleutians and eastward to Forrester Island on the border of British Columbia. The 4.5 million acre refuge is a spectacular blend of tundra, rain forest, cliffs, volcanos, beaches, lakes, and streams. Most of the refuge's 2.64 million acres is wilderness.

Alaska Maritime Refuge is synonymous with sea birds—millions of them. About seventy-five percent of Alaska's marine birds, 15 to 30 million birds among fifty-five species, use the refuge. They congregate in "bird cities", or colonies, along the coast. Each species has a specialized nesting site—rock, ledge, crevice, boulder, rubble, pinnacle, or borrow—an adaptation allowing many birds to use a small area of land. The refuge has the most diverse wildlife species of all refuges in Alaska, including thousands of sea lions, seals, walrus, and sea otters.

Visitor activities include wildlife observation, backpacking and photography. Bird watching is popular on Attu Island in the Aleutians where Asian birds stop on their migrations. Some islands have restricted access in order to protect wildlife Military clearance is required to visit Adak, Shemya, Amchitka, and Attu Islands of the Aleutian Chain.

For more information, contact: Refuge manager, Alaska Maritime National Wildlife Refuge, 2355 Kachemak Bay Drive, Suite 10, Homer, Alaska 99603, (907) 235-6546.

National Wild and Scenic Rivers

Wild, free-flowing rivers born in cold, mountain lakes or nurtured by runoff from remote highlands provide transportation corridors through some of Alaska's most spectacular geography. Crags and peaks, narrow canyons, rolling tundra-cloaked hills, or forested slopes present themselves in a constantly changing panorama during a float trip.

Congress established the National Wild and Scenic Rivers system to preserve a free-flowing condition for rivers of remarkable scenic, recreational, geologic, fish and wildlife, historic, cultural, or other similar value. All or part of twenty-five such rivers in Alaska are designated wild and scenic. The National Park Service administers thirteen of these, all designated "wild." With one exception, the designated sections lie within the boundaries of parks, monuments, or preserves. Because of their classifications, only minimal development will be allowed along the banks of these rivers. Included are the following rivers: John, Kobuk, Noatak, Alagnak, Alatna, Charley, Koyukuk, Mulchatna, Tilkakila, Tinayguk, Aniakchak, Chilikdrotna, and Salmon North Fork.

For more information, contact: Alaska State Office, Bureau of Land Management, 6881 Abbott Loop Road, Anchorage, Alaska 99507, (907) 267-1203.

Noatak National Preserve

Noatak National Preserve protects the largest untouched river basin in the United States. Above the Arctic Circle, the Noatak River runs from glacial melt atop Mount Igikpak in the Brooks Range out to Kotzebue Sound. Along its 425-mile course, it has carved out the "Grand Canyon" of the Noatak. This striking, scenic canyon serves as a migration route for plants and animals between sub-Arctic and Arctic environment. In recognition of this fine and vast wilderness, UNESCO has made the Noatak River Basin an International Biosphere Reserve.

The Noatak serves as a natural highway not only for plants and animals, but also for wilderness travelers. The preserve is especially popular for canoeing and kayaking, because the river is slow moving and gentle along most of its course. Only in the headwaters is the Noatak rough water. Backpacking in the foothills is an attractive recreational activity. The preserve offers outstanding wildlife watching opportunities. Among its large mammals are grizzly and black bear, caribou, wolves, lynx, and Dall sheep in abundance. Bird life abounds, too, as summer brings migratory birds to Noatak Basin from Asia and the tip of South America. The river itself supports Arctic char, whitefish, grayling and salmon.

Charter flights are available out of Kotzebue and Bettles/Evansville, which are served by air from Fairbanks or Anchorage.

For more information, contact: Superintendent, Noatak National Preserve, P.O. Box 1029, Kotzebue, Alaska 99752, (907) 442-3890.

Nowitna National Wildlife Refuge

Nowitna National Wildlife Refuge is approximately 200 miles west of Fairbanks in the central Yukon Valley. The refuge encompasses forested lowlands, hills, lakes, marshes, ponds, and streams. The dominant feature in Nowitna is the Nowitna River, a nationally designated wild river. This magnificent river provides spawning grounds for northern pike and sheefish. However, the primary reason the refuge was established was to protect waterfowl and their habitat.

Nowitna is one of four refuges, Nowitna, Innoko, Kanuti, and Koyukuk refuges, encompassed by a solar basin. A solar basin is characterized by encircling hills, light winds, low rainfall, severe winters, and short warm summers. The summer sun encircles these refuges without setting. The refuge's mix of habitats supports varied wildlife. Black bear and moose are common throughout Nowitna. Marten, mink, wolverine, beaver, and muskrat are important fur bearers and provide income, food, and recreation for local residents.

The Nowitna River is an outstanding river for floating. Moose and bear hunting are a major activity. Fishing for northern pike and sheefish is excellent.

For more information, contact: Refuge Manager, Nowitna National Wildlife Refuge, P.O. Box 287, Galena, Alaska, 99741, (907) 656-1231.

Point Bridget State Park

Point Bridget State Park, a beautiful 2,850-acre park, is located forty miles north of Juneau. It offers meadows of wildflowers, forested mountains, cliffs, spectacular views, rocky beaches, and the sea. In the winter, the meadows and open forests provide excellent cross-country skiing and snowshoeing opportunities. Long before white men arrived, the Auks, a group of Tlingit Natives, had summer homes here and harvested the area's rich natural resources. Point Bridget was named in 1794 by Captain Vancouver, probably for his mother, Bridget Berners. Cowee Creek was named after the Auk Chief who was credited with guiding Joe Juneau and Dick Harris to the gold in Silver Bow Basin in 1880. This led to the founding of Juneau. Gold was found north of Berners Bay and east of Point Bridget but there's no record of a discovery within the park.

For more information, contact: Park Ranger, Point Bridget State Park Headquarters, 400 Willoughby Avenue, Juneau, Alaska 99801, (907) 465-4563.

Prince William Sound State Marine Parks

Prince William Sound State Marine Parks, about sixty miles east of Anchorage, are undeveloped parks on the shores of Prince William Sound. The sound offers views of tidewater and upland glaciers, forested islands, and fjords surrounded by mountains rising to 13,000 feet. Scenery and wildlife, include brown and black bears, whales, sea otters, eagles, salmon, and many species of marine birds. It's a favorite area for boating, hiking, and photos.

For more information, contact: Park Ranger, Prince William Sound State Marine Parks Headquarters, P.O. Box 1247, Soldotna, Alaska 99669, (907) 262-5581.

Selawik National Wildlife Refuge

Selawik straddles the Arctic Circle in northwestern Alaska about 360 miles northwest of Fairbanks. The refuge is composed of estuaries, lakes, river deltas, and tundra slopes. The most prominent feature is the extensive system of tundra wetlands nestled between Waring Mountains and Selawik Hills. Selawik is located where the Bering Land Bridge once existed. Plants, animals, and humans migrated freely across this land mass connecting Asia and North America many years ago. The refuge retains evidence of these migrations.

Selawik is a breeding and resting area for a multitude of migratory water birds returning from North and South America, Asia, Africa, and Australia. Nesting ducks number in the hundreds of thousands. Thousands of caribou winter on the refuge as they feed on lichen-covered foothills. Other common mammals include moose, grizzly bear, and fur bearers. Sheefish, whitefish, grayling, and northern pike inhabit lakes, ponds, streams, and rivers. Sheefish weighing forty to fifty pounds are not uncommon.

Portions of Selawik River are nationally designated as a Wild River. The river provides good river rafting and sportfishing. A limited commercial guide service is available.

For more information, contact: Refuge Manager, Selawik National Wildlife Refuge, P.O. Box 270, Kotzebue, Alaska 99752 , (907) 442-3799.

Sitka National Historical Park

Sitka is one of Alaska's most scenic and historic cities. Sitka National Historical Park and Preserves is the site of the 1804 battle marking the last major resistance of the Tlingit Indians to Russian colonization. This was Alaska's economic and cultural capital for half a century, serving as the center of Russian-American Company's fur and trading operations. The park displays a collection of totems, and its visitor center explains Pacific Northwest Coast Indian art.

The Tlingit long ago followed salmon streams southward to settle here at Shee Atika, as they called Sitka, on this island-dotted coast. They enjoyed a rich culture, aesthetically and spiritually, in a world of natural abundance. This was interrupted by the Russian-American Company under the determined leadership of Alexander Baranov. The 1804 Battle of Sitka ended when the Tlingit ran out of ammunition and withdrew. Baranov burned their fort and built a new town he named New Archangel.

Sitka is reached by state-operated ferries, commercial cruise ships, and daily jet service.

For more information, contact: Superintendent, Sitka National Historical Park, P.O. Box 738, Sitka, Alaska 99835, (907) 747-6281.

Tetlin National Wildlife Refuge

Tetlin is a showcase of geological and ecological features found throughout Interior Alaska. Here, in a broad valley, the Chisana and Nabesna rivers join near the center of the refuge to form Tanana River. Nearly everywhere the work of wildfires, permafrost, and fluctuating river channels have created a diversity of habitats. For example, extensive stands of birch, aspen, and willow are testimony to positive effects of wildfire.

In these woodlands, moose, black bear, grizzly bear, ptarmigan, grouse, wolf, coyote, and red fox find food and shelter. Thousands of refuge lakes and ponds are interspersed with rolling hills, boreal forests, and snowcapped mountains. Tetlin Refuge supports a high density of nesting waterfowl on its wetlands. Shallow marshes of the refuge thaw early, providing a needed rest stop for birds migrating to nesting grounds throughout the state. The refuge provides habitat for 143 species of nesting birds and seven migrant species. Sandhill cranes move through the refuge each fall and spring in a spectacular event. Other notable birds include Arctic and common loon, osprey, bald eagle, trumpeter swan, and three species of ptarmigan.

Hunting, trapping, hiking, fishing, and photography are common activities. Moose and waterfowl hunting are especially popular. Common fish species include: northern pike, grayling, and burbot (freshwater ling cod).

Tetlin is one of two road-accessible refuges in Alaska. The Alaska Highway borders the refuge for nearly seventy miles. Interpretive information is available along the Alaska Highway and at the Interagency Visitor Center in Tok.

For more information, contact: Refuge Manager, Tetlin National Wildlife Refuge, P.O. Box 799, Tok, Alaska 99780, (907) 883-5312.

Togiak National Wildlife Refuge

Togiak is between Kuskokwim and Bristol bays in southwestern Alaska. Topography includes mountain crags, fast-flowing rivers, deep lakes, marshy lowlands, ponds, estuaries, coastal lagoons, and sea cliffs. The broad glacial valleys of the Ahklun Mountain range cut the tundra uplands and opens onto a coastal plain. Ahklun Mountains encompass eighty percent of the refuge. Togiak is a breeding and resting area for waterfowl and shore birds returning from wintering areas in Russia, Japan, Mexico, South America, New Zealand, and the South Pacific. During summer, numerous sea birds inhabit off-shore waters and cliffs near Capes Newenham and Pierce.

Spotted seals, walrus and seven species of whales use the off-shore waters. The refuge provides more than 1,500 miles of streams and rivers of spawning habitat for salmon. The finest salmon and trout sportfishing waters in Alaska are on Togiak River. Coastal portions of the refuge provide excellent opportunities for photography and wildlife observation. River rafting is popular on several refuge rivers. Commercial guides are available for sportfishing, brown bear hunting, and river rafting.

For more information, contact: Refuge Manager, Togiak National Wildlife Refuge, P.O. Box 270, Dillingham, Alaska 99576, (907) 842-1063.

Tongass National Forest

Over ninety percent of Southeast Alaska is in the largest National Forest in the United States. Tongass covers 16.7 million acres, a land of glaciers, mountains, waterways, and thousands of islands, separated by straits, narrows, and channels. Tongass has over 11,000 miles of coastline, about half that of the entire country. The land is heavily forested with Sitka spruce, hemlock, and cedar. It's home to both black and brown bear, Sitka blacktailed deer, mountain goats, and numerous small animals such as beaver, lynx, wolf, wolverine, red fox, and weasel.

The Forest Service maintains more than 150 recreational cabins at remote lakes, rivers, streams, or on beaches. Cabins are usually placed near good fishing or hunting spots, terrific scenery, hiking areas, or frequently, a combination of all three. The cabins can be reserved at a cost of $15 per night. Most of the cabins are remote and accessible only by boat or aircraft. Getting there can be the main expense.

For more information, contact: Forest Supervisor, Tongass National Forest Headquarters, Federal Building, Ketchikan, Alaska 99901, (907) 225-3101.

Wrangell-St. Elias National Park and Preserve

Wrangell-St. Elias National Park and Preserve abuts Canada's Kluane National Park, across the border in Yukon territory. Together they have been placed on the internationally recognized World Heritage List for outstanding natural areas. This is North America's "Mountain Kingdom." Here the Wrangell-St Elias, and Chugach mountain ranges converge. The park and preserve contains the North American continent's largest assemblage of glaciers, and its greatest collection of peaks over 16,000 feet elevation. One glacier, the Malaspina, is larger than the State of Rhode Island. Mount St. Elias, at 18,008 feet, is the second highest peak in United States.

The park and preserve is characterized by rugged mountains, remote valleys, wild rivers, and exemplary populations of wildlife. It also embraces coastal beaches on the Gulf of Alaska. The area abounds in opportunities for

Floatplanes can get you to some of the most remote areas of Alaska for some of the finest fishing.

wilderness backpacking, lake fishing, car camping, river running, cross country skiing, and mountain climbing. In both stature and numbers, Dall sheep populations of the Wrangells are considered the world's finest.

Access is by road from Chitna to McCarthy, generally passable in summer, by road from Slana on the Tok cutoff to Nabesna, and by air from Glennallen, which is 200 miles by paved highway from Anchorage or Yakutat or Gulkana.

For more information, contact: Superintendent, Wrangell-St. Elias National Park and Preserve, P.O. Box 439, Copper Center, Alaska 99707, (907) 822-5234.

Yukon Delta National Wildlife Refuge

Yukon Delta and Kuskokwim Rivers dominate the landscape of the Yukon Delta National Wildlife Refuge. The rivers form a treeless, wetland plain noted for wildlife variety and abundance. An intricate maze of lakes, ponds, and meandering streams provide nesting and feeding habitat for over 750,000 swans and geese, two million ducks, and 100 million shore and water birds. Moose, caribou, grizzly bear, black bear, and wolves inhabit the northern hills and eastern mountains.

The 1.1 million-acre Nunivak Island portion of the refuge supports an introduced herd of muskox and reindeer. Muskox vanished from Alaska in 1865. The introduced herd of muskox on Nunivak Island has been prolific. The herd is used as breeding stock to establish herds elsewhere in Alaska and the former Soviet Union. The reindeer herd is a major source of food and income for island residents.

Over the centuries, the abundance of wildlife has made the Yukon Delta the heart of Yupik Eskimo culture. The refuge encompasses forty-two Eskimo villages, whose residents depend on the wildlife resources. The legislation establishing Yukon Delta enables rural residents to continue a life style allowing them to live off the land.

Fishing, hunting, and back country recreation may be excellent, although aircraft transportation is needed. The Andreafsky River is a nationally designated wild river. Visitors may view wildlife resources and obtain complete information at the refuge headquarters visitor center.

For more information, contact: Refuge Manager, Yukon Delta National Wildlife Refuge, P.O. Box 346, Bethel, Alaska 99559, (907) 543-3151.

Yukon Flats National Wildlife Refuge

Yukon Flats is about 100 miles north of Fairbanks, the most northerly point reached by the Yukon River. Here the river breaks free from canyon walls and spreads unconfined for 200 miles through a vast floodplain. In spring, millions of migrating birds converge on the flats before ice moves from the river. The migrating birds come from four continents to raise their young. The refuge has one of the highest nesting densities of waterfowl in North America. By August the surfaces of over 40,000 lakes and ponds ripple with scurrying ducklings and molting adults. Yukon Flats contributes more than two million ducks and geese to the flyways of North America.

Birds are not the only migratory wildlife dependent on wetlands of the flats. Salmon from the Bering Sea ascend the Yukon River to spawn in freshwater streams of their birth. Some salmon travel nearly 2,000 miles into Canada. Runs of king, coho, and chum salmon pass through and spawn in the flats each summer—the longest salmon run in United States.

Mammals on the refuge include moose, caribou, wolves, and black and grizzly bears. Most summer use of Yukon Flats is confined to major waterways. Several rivers are floated by canoe, kayak, and rafts. Fishing for northern pike can be excellent.

For more information, contact: Refuge manager, Yukon Flats National Refuge, 101 12th Ave., Room 110, Fairbanks, Alaska 99701, (907) 456-0440.

Yukon-Charley Rivers National Preserve

The Yukon-Charley Rivers National Preserve contains 115 miles of historic Yukon River and the entire eighty-eight-mile Charley River Basin. Old cabins and relics recall the Yukon's importance in the Gold Rush era. Archaeological and paleontological sites in the preserve provide knowledge of both thousands and million of years in the past.

The two rivers are quite different: the broad and swift Yukon flows with glacial silt while the smaller Charley flows crystal clear. Charley is considered one of Alaska's finest recreational streams. The rivers merge between the early-day boom towns of Eagle and Circle. Cliffs and bluffs along the two rivers provide nesting habitat for peregrine and gyrfalcons. Beyond the riverbanks grizzly bear, Dall sheep, and moose may be seen. Floating the Yukon, whether by raft, canoe, or powerboat, is a popular way to see wildlife and scenic resources. The Charley River demands more advanced river skills.

Access is by Taylor Highway to Eagle or Steese Highway from Fairbanks to Circle. Scheduled flights serve both towns from Fairbanks.

For more Information write: Superintendent, Yukon-Charley Rivers National Preserve, P.O. Box 74680, Fairbanks, Alaska 99707, (907) 456-0281.

Wood-Tikchik State Park

Wood-Tikchik State Park, bounded by rugged mountains to the west and open tundra to the east, is Alaska's most remote state park, and the largest state park in the United States. Visitors are attracted by superb fishing, boating, and hiking in Tikchik Lakes and Wood River Lakes areas. Private lodges offer visitor services and sportfishing packages by advance reservations only. The park is 300 air miles west of Anchorage and is accessible by charter flight from Dillingham.

For more information, contact: Park Ranger, Wood-Tikchik State Park Headquarters, P.O. Box 3022, Dillingham, Alaska 99576, (907) 842-2375 Summer, (907) 269-8698 Winter.

INFORMATION CENTERS

Alaska Division of Tourism
P.O. Box E
Juneau, Alaska 99811
(907) 465-2010

Fishing Information:
Department of Fish and Game
Public Communication Section
P.O. Box 3-2000
Juneau, Alaska 99802
(907) 465-4112

Hunting Information:
State of Alaska
Department of Fish and Game
P.O. Box 3-2000
Juneau, Alaska 99802
(907) 465-4190

United States Fish and
  Wildlife Service
Bureau of Sport Fisheries and
  Wildlife
101 E. Tudor Road
Anchorage, Alaska 99503

Information on
Forest Service cabins
is available from:
Forest Service Information Center
Centennial Hall 101 Egan Drive
Juneau, Alaska 99801
(907) 789-3111

Tongass National Forest
Federal Building
Ketchikan, Alaska 99901

Ferry information
is available from:
Alaska Marine Highway
Pouch R
Juneau, Alaska 99811
(800) 642-0066

Topographical Maps
and Travel Guides:
Western Distribution Branch
United States Geological Survey
P.O. Box 25286, Federal Center
Denver, Colorado 80225

State of Alaska Department of Fish and Game Offices

Main Office

Juneau	P.O. Box 25526	99802	465-4180

Field Offices

Anchorage	333 Raspberry Rd.	99518	267-2220
Bethel	P.O. Box 90	99559	543-2919
Cold Bay	P.O. Box 50	99571	532-2419
Cordova	P.O. Box 669	99574	424-3212
Delta Junction	P.O. Box 605	99737	895-4632
Dillingham	P.O. Box 230	99576	842-5227
Fairbanks	1300 College Road	99701	459-7207
Glennallen	P.O. Box 47	99588	822-3309
Homer	3298 Douglas St.	99603	235-8191
Juneau	P.O. Box 3-2000	99802	465-4810
Ketchikan	2030 Sea Level Dr.	99901	225-5195
King Salmon	P.O. Box 37	99613	246-3340
Kodiak	211 Mission Road	99615	486-1880
McGrath	P.O. Box 230	99627	524-3323
Nome	P.O. Box 1148	99726	443-5167
Palmer	1800 Glenn Hwy. #4	99645	745-6300
Petersburg	P.O. Box 667	99833	772-3801
Sandpoint	P.O. Box 129	99661	383-2066
Seward	P.O. Box 285	99664	224-3017
Sitka	304 Lake St. #103	99835	747-5355
Soldotna	34828 Kalifonski	99669	262-9368
Tok	P.O. Box 355	99700	883-2971
Valdez	P.O. Box 812	99686	835-2562
Wrangell	P.O. Box 200	99929	874-3822
Yakutat	P.O. Box 49	99689	784-3222

All phone numbers are in area code 907

Milepost Travel Guide
Bible of North Country Travel
137 East Seventh Avenue
Anchorage, Alaska 99501
(907) 258-2515
(800) 331-3510

Alaska Travel Guide
418 Abel Place
Kelowna, British Columbia
Canada, V1Z 3E1
(604) 769-3073

National Park Service
Alaska Area Office
2525 Gambell Street
Anchorage, Alaska 99503
(907) 257-2699

Alaska Department
  of Natural Resources
Division of Parks
P.O. Box 7007
Anchorage, Alaska 99510
(907) 269-8700

Convention and Visitor Bureaus:

Fairbanks Convention and
  Visitors' Bureau
550 First Avenue
Fairbanks, Alaska 99701
(907) 456-5774

Matanuska-Susitna Convention and
  Visitors' Bureau
191 East Swanson Avenue
Wasilla, Alaska 99687
(907) 746-5000

Anchorage Convention and
  Visitors' Bureau
201 East Third Avenue
Anchorage, Alaska 99501
(907) 276-4118

Valdez Convention and
  Visitors' Bureau
P.O. Box 1603
Valdez, Alaska 99686
(907) 835-2984

Publication:

Alaska Outdoors Magazine
7617 Highlander Dr.
Anchorage, AK 99518
(907) 349-2424
(907) 349-2426 (fax)
alaskaod@alaska.net

ABOUT THE AUTHORS

Evan and Margaret Swensen have been fishing the Great Land for over three decades. Thirty-five years ago their "I'd Rather Be Fishing Alaska" dream came true when they became residents of the Territory of Alaska. Fishing Alaska is their hobby. Sharing their knowledge and experience is their vocation. Alaska is their love. The Swensens have been published in *Fishing and Hunting News, Anchorage Times, Alaska Outdoors, Trailer Life, Chevrolet Outdoors, Sport Fishing,* and *This People* magazines. Evan is the producer of the *Alaska Outdoors* television series airing on the Discovery channel, and host on *The Outdoor Show*, aired locally.

FalconGuides are available for where-to-go hiking, mountain biking, rock climbing, walking, scenic driving, fishing, rockhounding, paddling, birding, wildlife viewing, and camping. We also have FalconGuides on essential outdoor skills and subjects and field identification. The following titles are currently available, but this list grows every year. For a free catalog with a complete list of titles, call The Globe Pequot Press toll-free at 1–800–243–0495.

HIKING GUIDES

Hiking Alaska
Hiking Alberta
Hiking Arizona
Hiking Arizona's Cactus Country
Hiking the Beartooths
Hiking Big Bend National Park
Hiking California
Hiking California's Desert Parks
Hiking Carlsbad Caverns &
   Guadalupe Mtns. National Parks
Hiking Colorado
Hiking the Columbia River Gorge
Hiking Florida
Hiking Georgia
Hiking Glacier & Waterton Lakes National Parks
Hiking Grand Canyon National Park
Hiking Great Basin National Park
Hiking Hot Springs
   in the Pacific Northwest
Hiking Idaho
Hiking Maine
Hiking Michigan
Hiking Minnesota
Hiking Montana
Hiking Nevada
Hiking New Hampshire
Hiking New Mexico
Hiking New York
Hiking North Carolina
Hiking North Cascades

Hiking Northern Arizona
Hiking Olympic National Park
Hiking Oregon
Hiking Oregon's Eagle Cap Wilderness
Hiking Oregon's Three Sisters Country
Hiking Pennsylvania
Hiking South Carolina
Hiking South Dakota's Black Hills Country
Hiking Southern New England
Hiking Tennessee
Hiking Texas
Hiking Utah
Hiking Utah's Summits
Hiking Vermont
Hiking Virginia
Hiking Washington
Hiking Wyoming
Hiking Wyoming's Wind River Range
Hiking Yellowstone National Park
Hiking Zion & Bryce Canyon National Parks
The Trail Guide to Bob Marshall Country

BEST EASY DAY HIKES

Beartooths
Canyonlands & Arches
Best Hikes on the Continental Divide
Glacier & Waterton Lakes
Glen Canyon
Grand Canyon
North Cascades
Yellowstone

- *To order any of these books, check with your local bookseller*
or call The Globe Pequot Press at **1–800–243–0495.**
Visit us on the world wide web at:
www.falcon.com

get
FALCON GUIDED

BIRDING GUIDES
Birding Arizona
Birding Minnesota
Birder's Guide to Montana
Birding Texas

FIELD GUIDES
Bitterroot: Montana State Flower
Canyon Country Wildflowers
Great Lakes Berry Book
New England Berry Book
Plants of Arizona
Rare Plants of Colorado
Rocky Mountain Berry Book
Southern Rocky Mtn. Wildflowers
Tallgrass Prairie Wildflowers
Western Tree
Wildflowers of Southwestern Utah
Willow Bark and Rosehips

FISHING GUIDES
Fishing Alaska
Fishing the Beartooths
Fishing Maine
Fishing Michigan
Fishing Montana
Fishing Yellowstone

WALKING
Walking Colorado Springs
Walking Portland
Walking St. Louis

PADDLING GUIDES
Floater's Guide to Colorado
Paddling Montana
Paddling Oregon

ROCK CLIMBING GUIDES
Rock Climbing Colorado
Rock Climbing Montana
Rock Climbing New Mexico & Texas
Rock Climbing Utah

ROCKHOUNDING GUIDES
Rockhounding Arizona
Rockhound's Guide to California
Rockhound's Guide to Colorado
Rockhounding Montana
Rockhounding Nevada
Rockhound's Guide to New Mexico
Rockhounding Texas
Rockhounding Utah
Rockhounding Wyoming

HOW-TO GUIDES
Bear Aware
Leave No Trace
Mountain Lion Alert
Wilderness First Aid
Wilderness Survival

MOUNTAIN BIKING GUIDES
Mountain Biking Arizona
Mountain Biking Colorado
Mountain Biking New
  Mexico
Mountain Biking New York
Mountain Biking Northern
  New England
Mountain Biking Southern
  New England
Mountain Biking Utah

LOCAL CYCLING SERIES
Fat Trax Bozeman
Fat Trax Colorado Springs
Mountain Biking Bend
Mountain Biking Boise
Mountain Biking
  Chequamegon
Mountain Biking Denver/
  Boulder
Mountain Biking Durango
Mountain Biking Helena
Mountain Biking Moab

FALCON®

• *To order any of these books, check with your local bookseller
or call The Globe Pequot Press at* **1-800-243-0495.**

Visit Falcon on the world wide web at:
www.falcon.com

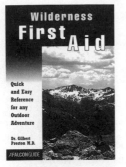

WILDERNESS FIRST AID

By Dr. Gilbert Preston M.D.

Enjoy the outdoors and face the inherent risks with confidence. By reading this easy-to-follow first-aid text, all outdoor enthusiasts can pack a little extra peace of mind on their next adventure. *Wilderness First Aid* offers expert medical advice for dealing with outdoor emergencies beyond the reach of 911. It easily fits in most backcountry first-aid kits.

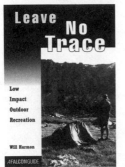

LEAVE NO TRACE

by Will Harmon

The concept of "leave no trace" seems simple, but it actually gets fairly complicated. This handy quick-reference guidebook includes all the newest information on this growing and all-important subject. This book is written to help the outdoor enthusiast make the hundreds of decisions necessary to protect the natural landscape and still have an enjoyable wilderness experience. Part of the proceeds from the sale of this book go to continue leave-no-trace education efforts. The Official Manual of American Hiking Society.

BEAR AWARE

by Bill Schneider

Hiking in bear country can be very safe if hikers follow the guidelines summarized in this small, "packable" book. Extensively reviewed by bear experts, the book contains the latest information on the intriguing science of bear-human interactions. *Bear Aware* can not only make your hike safer, but it can help you avoid the fear of bears that can take the edge off your trip.

MOUNTAIN LION ALERT

By Steve Torres

Recent mountain lion attacks have received national attention. Although infrequent, lion attacks raise concern for public safety. *Mountain Lion Alert* contains helpful advice for mountain bikers, trail runners, horse riders, pet owners, and suburban landowners on how to reduce the chances of mountain lion-human conflicts.

To order these titles or to find out more about this new series of books, call The Globe Pequot Press at 1-800-243-0495.